M000239268

FLASHING STEEL

居合術教範

FLASHING STEEL

Mastering Eishin-Ryū Swordsmanship

Masayuki Shimabukuro

Leonard J. Pellman

Frog, Ltd.
Berkeley, California

Flashing Steel
Mastering Eishin-Ryū Swordsmanship

Copyright © 1995 by M. Shimabukuro & L. J. Pellman. No portion of this book, except for brief review, may be reproduced in any form without written permission of the publisher. For information contact Frog, Ltd.

Published by
Frog, Ltd.

Frog, Ltd. books are distributed by
North Atlantic Books
P.O. Box 12327
Berkeley, California 94712

Cover photograph by Dick Van Patton
Cover and book design by Paula Morrison
Typeset by Catherine Campaigne
Printed in the United States of America by Malloy Lithographing

Library of Congress Cataloging-in-Publication Data

Shimabukuro, Masayuki, 1948–
    Flashing steel : mastering Eishin-ryu swordsmanship / Masayuki
Shimabukuro, Leonard Pellman.
        p. cm.
    ISBN 1-883319-18-8
    1. Iaido. I. Pellman, Leonard. II. Title.
GV1150.2.S55 1995
796.8'6—dc20   93-47690
                                                                CIP

1 2 3 4 5 6 7 8 9 / 98 97 96 95

This book is dedicated to

Hanshi Miura Takeyuki Hirefusa

Grandmaster Miura

The present grandmaster of *Musō Jikiden Eishin-Ryū Iaijutsu*, Miura Takeyuki *Hanshi,* was born January 5, 1922 in Shimane-ken, Japan. At the age of eleven, he entered the Budō Senmon Gakkō, a martial arts training school, where he began his study of *kendō,* the sword-fighting sport based upon *samurai* swordsmanship.

Although it is probable that he studied elements of *iaidō* during his *kendō* training or under other instructors, Miura *Hanshi* began his study of *Musō Jikiden Eishin-Ryū Iaijutsu* in 1959 under Narise Sakahiro, who later became the 19th grandmaster of the style, and also received instruction from the 18th grandmaster, Masaoka Kazumi. Only a year later, Miura *Hanshi* began his training in *Shindō Musō-Ryū Jōdō* under Nakajima Asakichi, who was the most senior disciple of the 25th grandmaster of *jōdō*, Shimizu Takatsugu, under whom he also trained.

Following this, Miura *Hanshi* began studying *Koryū Kakushu Bujutsu* ("Ancient *Samurai* Weapons") in 1965 under the 3rd grandmaster of *Enshin-Ryū*, Kobashi Nikkan. This system includes a variety of traditional *samurai* weapons.

In May, 1970, Miura *Hanshi* undertook the study of *Kukishin-Ryū Bōjutsu* under the instruction of Kanō Takehiko, the 11th grandmaster of *Yanagi-Ryū*.

Culminating more than forty years of martial arts training, including over fifteen years of *iaidō* and other *samurai* weapons, Miura *Hanshi* founded the Nippon Kobudō Jikishin-Kai in May, 1975. He established its *Hombu Dōjō* (Headquarters) on the grounds of Yasaka Jinja, in the Yasaka District of Neya-gawa City in Ōsaka.

Among the rankings currently held by Miura *Hanshi* are 8th *dan* in *Koryū Kakushu Bujutsu* from the Zen Nippon Kobudō Sōgō Renmei (awarded in May, 1975), and 9th *dan Hanshi* in *iaidō* conferred in April, 1992 by the Dai-Nippon Butoku-Kai. Miura *Hanshi* is held in such high esteem that in 1977 he was named 8th *dan* in *Toyama-Ryū Battō-jutsu*, the modern military form of swordsmanship, without having requested such ranking or even joining the organization.

In addition to being its highest ranking living member as 9th *dan,* the Dai-Nippon Butoku-Kai has designated Miura *Hanshi* as *iincho* (Executive Direc-tor) for *Kobudō Shinsa* (rank testing in weapons), *Kobudō Kenshū* (weapons seminars), and *Taikai* (championships). In April, 1985, the *Butoku-Kai* named Miura *Hanshi "Yūshūsho"* ("Most Valuable Member"), and he has served on its Board of Directors since April, 1990.

During his many years of teaching, Miura *Hanshi* has also been recognized for his community contributions with such awards as Honorary Mayor of Kyōtō City in April, 1988 and Honorary Governor of Kyōtō-*Fu* in April, 1993.

Despite these many honors and accomplishments, Miura *Hanshi* demon-strates tremendous humility in his daily life. His humble attitude is probably best characterized by the fact that he is usually the first to bow when greeting someone—even the lowest-ranking of his students—who diligently try to bow before he does. This desire to "out-respect" his students may seem trivial to Westerners, but it makes a powerful impression on his students who know he is entitled to be bowed to first and give little more than a casual nod in return.

If you were to ask Miura *Hanshi* what has been the guiding principle of his life, he likely would answer *"shisei"*—**sincerity.** He has found that sincerity is the secret to success in all areas of life. Sincerity must begin with **attitude,** then it will flow naturally into your words and deeds. As a tribute to the example and leadership of Miura *Hanshi,* we complete his biographical sketch with the word *"shisei"* in his own calligraphy.

Acknowledgments

So many people have contributed to this book in various ways that it would be impossible to thank them all here. We greatly appreciate all of the people who provided assistance to this project who we are unable to mention by name.

We especially acknowledge the following for their essential contributions to this book:

Photography

The photographs for most of the instructional portions of this book were done by Mr. Al Johannesen. A graduate of the University of Washington with a degree in Radio & Television, he served in the U.S. Navy's submarine force, where he taught periscope photography. He has been active in commercial photography for nearly four decades.

Additional photography of instructional material was provided by Mr. Tom Colley.

Models

We wish to thank those who, in addition to the authors, modeled for the instructional portions of this book: Mr. James Williams, Ms. Jennifer Soto, Mr. Eric Shimabukuro, and Ms. Aimee Shimabukuro. We greatly appreciate their patience and dedication.

Special Appreciation

Mr. Alfonso Gomez of the University of California, San Diego, *karate* and *iai-jutsu* clubs has been of tremendous assistance throughout this project, not only in providing the facilities in which the photographs were taken, but also for his encouragement, suggestions, and untiring support and dedication, for which we are extremely grateful.

目次
MOKUJI
Table of Contents

前書
MAEGAKI
Foreword

Although this textbook includes the complete system of *Musō Jikiden Eishin-Ryū Iaijutsu* in terms of technique, in a larger sense it is intended to be merely an introduction to the *true* art of *iaijutsu*, "the art of face-to-face combat." Due to the recent popularity of such movie fiction as the "Ninja Turtles," a great deal of interest has been aroused in *samurai* swordsmanship, but very little genuine information or instruction has been available in Western countries.

One reason for this is that very few legitimate sword masters live outside Japan and, until recently, *iaijutsu* has remained a somewhat esoteric art even there. On top of this scarcity of teachers, people with limited knowledge—and even outright charlatans—have capitalized on the growing interest in *samurai* swordsmanship, promoting instruction which is incomplete at best, and sometimes outright nonsense.

It is also a mixed blessing that there have been many recent television and movie portrayals of *samurai* arts. On the one hand they have increased the awareness of and interest in these arts, but, on the other, they often tend to blur the differences between various martial arts and those who traditionally practiced them. The most obvious example of this is the distinction between *ninja* and *samurai,* which are often made to appear to be merely variations of the same art and philosophy. Even worse, a *ninja* is often portrayed as some type of "super-*samurai*," while nothing could be further from the truth.

The *samurai* were at the pinnacle of the social order in feudal Japan, while *ninja*, considered less than human, were ranked somewhere below the horse. While *samurai* lived by a code of ethics that placed honor above all else, *ninja* would stoop to any means to accomplish their objectives. A *samurai* was typically a master of many arts—not only the arts of combat, but also of poetry, literature, and philosophy. A *samurai* was truly a "renaissance" man. A *ninja* was merely a master of deception, stealth, cunning, and death by artless means. We do not wish to demean those who practice and preserve the craft of *nin-*

jutsu today, since those skills hold a cultural and artistic importance of their own. We are simply relating the historical evidence that the *samurai* and *ninja* were not similar varieties of the same arts and philosophy, but were in fact at opposite ends of the spectrum—both socially and philosophically the antithesis of one another.

Another unfortunate tendency of movie and television swordsmanship is the emphasis on spectacular, acrobatic techniques designed to excite an audience, but which bear little, if any, resemblance to real sword combat. While such portrayals stimulate interest in studying the *samurai* arts, they also create an unrealistic expectation that the arts consist of these flamboyant, whirling, and leaping techniques.

The real beauty of authentic *samurai* swordsmanship is in its utter simplicity and single-minded purposefulness. With his life hanging in the balance, no *samurai* would waste the time or energy needed to perform even the slightest unnecessary movement, let alone grandiose flourishes. Instead, his entire being was intently focused on the sole objective of destroying evil, as personified by his opponent, with maximum efficiency.

Throughout this book we refer to this art as *iaijutsu,* rather than the better known equivalent term, *iaidō.* We have done this deliberately to emphasize a key distinction between *Musō Jikiden Eishin-Ryū Iaijutsu* and other styles of *iaidō.* Arts bearing the suffix *-dō* ("The Way of …") tend to be modernizations of ancient martial arts, and often their training emphasis has shifted from combat effectiveness to the artistic qualities of the techniques. Arts with the suffix *-jutsu* ("The Art of …") more often tend to emphasize the techniques' battlefield effectiveness rather than their aesthetic qualities.

This is precisely the case with *Eishin-Ryū Iaijutsu.* In those aspects in which the techniques differ from those of similar styles, the difference is most often a matter of combat application *(-jutsu)* versus artistry *(-dō).*

Lastly, we also want to remind you that *iaijutsu* simply cannot be learned exclusively from a book. It requires the supervision of a competent instructor to guide the student through the subtleties of this deceptively intricate art. For this reason, our focus is primarily to provide a thorough background in the philosophy and underlying concepts of *iaijutsu* and general description of its techniques. Without observation and correction by a qualified instructor, students would gain little benefit from finely detailed descriptions of *iaijutsu* techniques.

We must also counsel you not to attempt any of the techniques shown in this book without the benefit of supervision by a qualified instructor. Whether you are training with a *bokken* ("wooden sword"), an *iaitō* ("practice sword"), or a *shinken* ("live sword"), you are practicing with a potentially lethal weapon. The authors and publisher therefore accept no responsibility for any injuries or damages you may incur as a result of attempting any of the techniques described or illustrated in this text.

Furthermore, some details were left deliberately vague, since a key purpose of martial arts training is to sharpen the mind as well as train the body. Therefore, this book has been designed to induce the reader to think about the concepts and techniques presented. Any questions we have left unanswered should lead the reader to a closer relationship with a qualified instructor and to a deeper understanding of the art. To mislead a reader into believing that *iaijutsu* could be mastered simply by reading this (or *any*) book, would be a grave disservice.

If instead we can lead you to understand the true nature of authentic *iaijutsu* and interest you enough to seek qualified instruction, then we have achieved our main goal. As you gain experience, this text can also help you sharpen your technique and give you a means of better recalling what you have learned in the *dōjō*. If we achieve these goals, then we will have accomplished all that a book of this type can possibly do.

With this in mind, the authors welcome contact from readers, and we will do our utmost to help you find a source of qualified instruction if it is your sincere desire to train in *iaijutsu*.

Chapter 1

歷史

Rekishi

History

Iaijutsu is the art of swordsmanship in face-to-face combat, as practiced by the *samurai* of feudal Japan. It is impossible to fully understand the history of *iaijutsu* without at least a cursory knowledge of the history of the *samurai* warrior class and their fabled swords.

The earliest forms of what we now call the *samurai* sword seem to have made their appearance around the beginning of the Heian Period, which began in AD 782. Technically, swords of this period were not truly "*samurai*" swords, since the *samurai* caste itself did not actually arise until the twelfth century. These swords were generally much longer and more deeply curved than the type now used in *iaijutsu* practice. Because of their length and shape, these early swords are usually referred to as *tachi* ("large sword").

For the first 250 years of the Heian Period, the Fujiwara clan wielded the true power behind Japan's imperial government, acting as regents to the fig-ure-head emperors. As centuries passed, however, other factions steadily grew in economic and military power, among which the famed Taira and Minamoto families were the most prominent. As the power of the Fujiwara declined in the late Heian Period, disorder quickly arose. By the early eleventh century, it was not uncommon for armed priests and bands of mercenaries to battle in the very streets of Kyōto, Japan's capitol city during this period.

In an attempt to restore order, the imperial family wrested control away from the Fujiwara regents for a brief time. But in 1156, the Taira family defeated its chief rival, the Minamoto, and seized power. Another horrendous battle between the two clans followed in 1160, but the Taira remained in control until they were ultimately defeated by the Minamoto in 1185.

This half-century of continual military conflict between the Taira and Minamoto families and their respective vassals gave rise to the *samurai* as a distinct class in Japanese society. This period also witnessed the development of the warrior's code of conduct which eventually came to be called *Bushidō*, the "Way of the Warrior." Two of Japan's most famous literary epics, the *Genji Monogatari* ("Tale of Genji") and the *Heike Monogatari* ("Tale of Heike") depicted this monumental struggle and the emergence of the *samurai* as the leading social caste. In these and similar works of the period, the heroic deeds of the *samurai* were romanticized and the *samurai* sword itself was elevated to so sacred and mystical a position that it was said to embody the very soul of its owner. It was sometimes even said to possess a soul of its own.

Much of the credit for the excellence of these swords must go to Minamoto Mitsunaka, who not only developed large-scale iron mining on his lands in western Japan, but also cultivated the art of swordsmithing to such a degree that its artisans attained a status akin to priesthood.

No sword created before or since can match the strength and cutting edge of those forged by the master swordsmiths of feudal Japan. Not surprisingly, such weapnons were revered almost as objects of worship by their owners, who perceived their unsurpassed cutting ability as resulting from each sword being imbued with a spirit of its own. The long, deeply curved *tachi* slung edge-down at the left hip remained the tangible symbol of *samurai* spirit and power for the next four centuries.

As the subsequent Ashikaga Period (1338–1500) came to a close, Japan was once again embroiled in widespread warfare. Skirmishes had periodically arisen throughout the country since 1400, culminating in the Ōnin Civil War in 1467. Although the Ōnin War ended after ten years, the Ashikaga Shōgunate was bankrupt. The country continued in turmoil and anarchy for the next three decades leading into the Sengoku ("Warring States") Period. A full century of incessant warfare was obviously a propitious time for the *samurai* caste, and this period gave rise to numerous schools and styles of swordsmanship.

At the height of this tumultuous period, Hayashizaki Jinsuke Minamoto no Shigenobu (usually referred to as Hayashizaki Jinsuke or ocassionally as Hayashizaki Shigenobu) was born in Hayashizaki Village in Okushū Dewa (near modern-day Murayama City, Yamagata Prefecture). He was born in the year 1549 to a *samurai* family under the ruling Minamoto clan. After his father was killed in a duel, young Hayashizaki was determined to avenge his father's death. Knowing he would need a significant advantage to defeat his father's killer, Hayashizaki entered the local *Shintō* shrine, Hayashizaki Jinja. There he spent 100 days in prayer and practice to develop the techniques of drawing and cutting in a single motion that we now call *iaijutsu* or *iaidō*. Hayashizaki prevailed in avenging his father's death, and his style of swordsmanship came to be known as *Hayashizaki-ryū*.

Less than fifty years later, the most significant development in the history of *iaijutsu* occurred. Along with the introduction of firearms into Japan by the Portuguese, the Sengoku Period also witnessed a significant change in sword design. Blades were now made shorter and a little straighter in shape than the *tachi*, and were worn with their cutting edge *upward*. Naturally, with the advent of this newer style of sword, called *katana* or *daitō* (the weapon most commonly known as the "*samurai* sword"), improved techniques of swordsmanship were required to make the best use of this radical change in blade design.

Hasegawa Eishin, the seventh-generation successor to *Hayashizaki-ryū*, widely considered to be nearly equal in skill with the *tachi* to the style's founder, adapted *iaijutsu* techniques to the shorter *katana*. Because of his great skill and his modification of sword techniques for the newer design, the style thereafter became known as *Hasegawa-ryū* or *Eishin-ryū* in his honor. His fame was such that Toyotomi Hideyoshi, the supreme military commander who ruled a recently unified Japan from 1582 to 1598, invited Hasegawa to demonstrate *Eishin-ryū iaijutsu* in Edo (present-day Tōkyō) not long after moving his capitol there in 1590. Toyotomi was so impressed with Hasegawa's skill that he bestowed on him the title *Musō Ken*, "Sword Without Equal."

Eishin's style is considered unmatched and has been passed down through an unbroken succession of grandmasters to the present time. It is now known as *Musō Jikiden Eishin-Ryū Iaijutsu*, or "Unequalled Direct-Lineage Eishin-Style *Iaijutsu*." (A complete listing of the genealogy of *Musō Jikiden Eishin-Ryū Iaijutsu* is presented on pages 9 and 10.) Although each successive grandmaster has left his imprint on the style, this brief history is limited to those whose impact was most significant to the evolution of the style.

With the fall of the Tokugawa Shogunate in 1868, rule again shifted from the military back into the hands of the imperial line. One of the first decrees of the newly enthroned Emperor Meiji was the disarming of the *samurai* caste to prevent their return to power. However, recognizing the historical and cultural importance of the *samurai* to Japan, and perhaps also realizing the future social and economic strength to be gained from the influence of *Bushidō*, Emperor Meiji concurrently established the Dai Nippon Butoku-Den ("Greater Japan Institute of Martial Virtues") as a means to preserve and govern the instruction of traditional Japanese martial arts. In order to teach martial arts, especially in the Japanese school system, it was necessary to be properly accredited by the *Butoku-Den*. Although temporarily disbanded by the American occupation forces at the close of World War II, the organization was re-established at the end of Allied occupation by the Emperor Shōwa (better known as Hirohito in the West) under the name Dai Nippon Butoku-Kai ("Greater Japan Martial Virtues Association"). At the time of this writing, the Butoku-Kai is chaired by Higashifushigi Jigō, the younger brother of Emperor Shōwa's wife, and remains the most prestigious martial arts organization in Japan.

Although the lineage of *Eishin-Ryū* has remained unbroken from the time of Hayashizaki Jinsuke down the present grandmaster, Miura Takeyuki *Hanshi*, the style has not been entirely free of controversy. Through the years, several grandmasters have founded their own styles of *iaidō*, the earliest being Tamiya Heibei, who is considered the second grandmaster of *Eishin-Ryū*, when it was still called *Hayashizaki-Ryū*.

In the late eighteenth century a major schism occurred within the ranks of *Eishin-Ryū*. The 10th grandmaster, Hayashi Yasudayu, and the 11th grandmaster, Ōguro Motoemon, both died shortly after one another in 1776. Following their deaths, two branches of *Eishin-Ryū* arose, each of which considered its grandmaster to be the 12th successor to the *Eishin-Ryū* lineage. One of these branches, *Shimomura-ha*, faded into oblivion earlier this century, while *Tanimura-ha* has survived to the present.

In more recent times, another controversy has arisen. When the 17th grandmaster, Ōe Masamichi, died in 1927, two of his students separately carried on the *Eishin-Ryū* tradition of *Tanimura-ha*. Masaoka Kazumi was widely considered the best swordsman among Ōe's students, and most members of the style gravitated to him as 18th grandmaster after Ōe's death. Another student, who had personally attended to Ōe during his battle with cancer, came into possession of the style's credentials, and many chose to follow him as 18th grandmaster. As a result, two branches now claim to carry on the traditions and lineage of *Musō Jikiden Eishin-Ryū*. A genealogy showing the developments following 11th Grandmaster Ōguro Motoemon is presented on page 11.

However, it was Masaoka Kazumi (of Ōe's and the authors' lineage) who was invited to represent *Musō Jikiden Eishin-Ryū Iaijutsu* when the major *iaidō* styles convened to jointly create the *Seitei Iai Kata* for the *Zen Nippon Kendō Renmei* (All-Japan Kendo Federation). In addition, Masaoka's successor, Narise Sakahiro, was elected to a remarkable three terms of office as president of the *Dai-Nippon Iaidō Yaegaki-Kai*, the most widely recognized *iaidō* organization of its time. Currently, the *Dai-Nippon Butoku-Kai*, Japan's oldest and most prestigious martial arts organization, recognizes Miura Takeyuki *Hanshi*, Narise's successor as 20th grandmaster, as the official representative of the style, and has unanimously awarded him a 9th *dan Hanshi* ranking, the highest of any living member of the *Butoku-Kai*.

In 1975, Miura *Hanshi* coined the name *Nippon Kobudō Jikishin-Kai* for the organization to carry on the traditions and instruction of *Musō Jikiden Eishin-Ryū Iaijutsu*. This name translates literally as "Japanese Ancient Weapons (meaning *samurai* weapons) True Spirit Association," although the term *"jikishin"* also carries such nuances as "Pure Heart" and "Straight Mind." The concepts of true spirit, pure heart, and clear mind certainly embody Miura *Hanshi*'s emphasis on sincerity, but his choice of this name has a much more profound origin.

There is a well-known Zen saying, *"Jikishin kore dōjō nari"*—"A true spirit [pure heart] is a training place [*dōjō*]." His use of this term was intended to convey the multifaceted meanings which lie beneath the surface of this ancient saying.

First, this is an admonition to make your mind **straight**; that is, focused and purposeful, not easily driven off course by the winds of change, nor buffeted by the tides of adversity. Your mind should not be swayed by your environment, but remain unyielding to outside pressures and temptations.

Second, your mind, heart, and spirit must be **pure**. The most obvious attributes of a traditional *dōjō* are that it is clean, uncluttered, and totally functional. Like a *dōjō*, your heart and mind should exude the simple beauty that comes from simplicity and clarity of purpose. Your spirit should shine like a *dōjō* floor that has been polished by the years of the sweat and effort that has gone into your training.

The *dōjō* often seems harsh and punishing, rewarding diligent training only with bruises, aches, and callouses. Yet this apparent harshness disguises the true gentility and compassion of the *dōjō*, which smiles down from its rafters on your toil and disappointment, cherishing the knowledge that you are refining your mind, body, and spirit in the crucible of trial and perseverance. In the same way as the *dōjō*, your mind must be gentle and compassionate toward others, yet with the strength to allow them to endure hardship and pain when it is truly in their best interest.

The open, spacious feeling of a *dōjō* should also reflect the openness of your mind. Your mind should be "open" both in the sense of being uncluttered by unnecessary thoughts and feelings—especially destructive ones like doubt, anger, and fear—and in the sense of being open to learn. In this way, your mind will continue to **expand** as you learn, experience, and grow. This is the true meaning of *ku no kokoro* or *mushin* ("empty mind"). This does not mean that there is nothing there; but that in the spaciousness of your mind, there is ever-increasing room for more.

Finally, the practice of *jikishin* is the very core of good swordsmanship, as best described in another ancient saying, "*Kokoro tadashi karazareba, ken mata tadashi karazu*": "If your heart is true, your sword will also be true."

Miura Hanshi also undertook the construction of the *hombu dōjō* ("headquarters training center") on the grounds of Yasaka Jinja in Ōsaka.

To reach this *dōjō,* you must walk down a narrow path through the grounds of the shrine (Figure 1–1). As you pass through the gardens of the shrine, you feel a tranquil relief from the busy Ōsaka streets that you just left behind. The *dōjō* itself (Figure 1–2), though only about twenty years old, has the appearance and character of its surroundings, which includes buildings hundreds of years old. By the time you ascend its steps, you can almost picture yourself transported into the realm of the *samurai* over four centuries ago.

Once inside, there is a palpable sense of respite from the workaday world only a hundred yards away. Relieved of the pressures of modern daily life, your mind is free to focus on training. As you grow attuned to the traditional surroundings (Figure 1–3), the aroma of wood and *tatami,* and the quiescent sounds of the others training alongside you, it is difficult not to feel a sense of connection to the centuries of masters and disciples who preceded you in the art of *iaijutsu* and have passed down its rich heritage to the present generation, who will in turn pass it on to the generations to come.

Figure 1–1. Dōjō Path

Figure 1–2. Dōjō Front

Figure 1–3. Dōjō Interior

Genealogy of Musō Jikiden Eishin-Ryū Iaijutsu
Calligraphy by Grandmaster Miura

Genealogy of Musō Jikiden Eishin-Ryū Iaijutsu

Ryūsō:	**Hayashizaki Jinsuke Shigenobu**
Ni-dai:	Tamiya Heibei Shigemasa
San-dai:	Nagano Murakusai Kinrō
Yon-dai:	Momo Gumbei Mitsushige
Go-dai:	Arikawa Shōzaemon Munetsugu
Roku-dai:	Manno Danemon no Jō Nobusada
Nana-dai:	**Hasegawa Eishin Shūzei no Suke**
Hachi-dai:	Arai Seitetsu Kiyonobu
Kyū-dai:	**Hayashi Rokudayū Morimasa**
Jū-dai:	Hayashi Yasudayū Seishō
Jūichi-dai:	Ōguro Motoemon Kiyokatsu
Jūni-dai:	Hayashi Masu no Jō Masanari
Jūsan-dai:	Yoda Manzō Yorikatsu
Jūyon-dai:	Hayashi Yadayū Masayori
Jūgo-dai:	**Tanimura Kame no Jō Yorikatsu**
Jūroku-dai:	Gotō Magobei Masasuke
Jūnana-dai:	Ōe Masamichi Shikei
Jūhachi-dai:	Masaoka Kazumi
Jūkyū-dai:	Narise Sakahiro
Nijū-dai:	**Miura Takeyuki Hirefusa**

*Seitō Musō Jikiden Eishin-Ryū Iai Heihō
Sōshi, Miura Hirefusa*

無双直伝英信流の系図

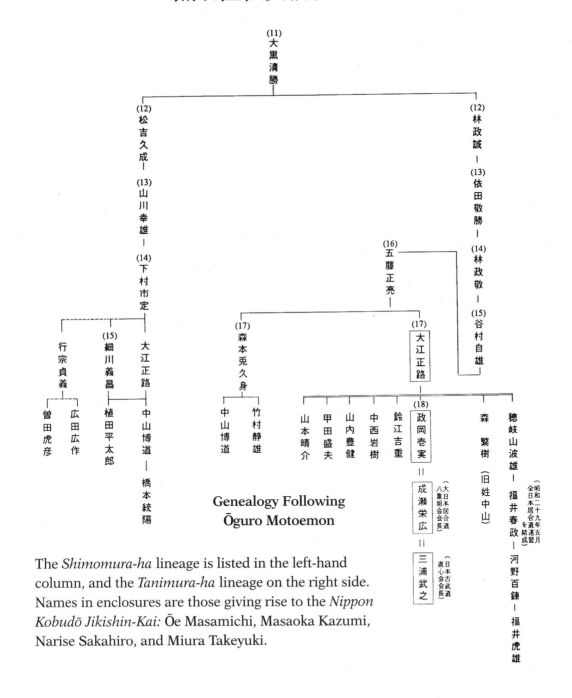

Genealogy Following Ōguro Motoemon

The *Shimomura-ha* lineage is listed in the left-hand column, and the *Tanimura-ha* lineage on the right side. Names in enclosures are those giving rise to the *Nippon Kobudō Jikishin-Kai:* Ōe Masamichi, Masaoka Kazumi, Narise Sakahiro, and Miura Takeyuki.

Chapter 2

人生観

Jinseikan

Iaijutsu Philosophy

It is highly unlikely that you will ever slip into your *hakama*, sling your *katana* at your side, and saunter down the street prepared to use your *iaijutsu* skills to defend yourself or take up the cause of the downtrodden like the *samurai* of old. So what benefit is there in *iaijutsu* training?

The fact that you will probably never engage in a real sword battle may, paradoxically, be the *greatest* benefit of sword training! Those who train in martial arts that have modern practical application, such as *karate-dō* or *jūjutsu*, too often find themselves so involved in developing skill in the physical self-defense applications of their art that they overlook or minimize their mental and spiritual training. Especially in the West, martial arts training often merely gives lip-service to these vital elements of training. This cannot be said of *iaijutsu*.

By its very nature, as a martial art that is highly ritualized, moderately paced, and without obvious "street" application, *iaijutsu* provides an ideal environment in which to refine mental and spiritual discipline. *All* martial arts are supposed to develop these qualities, but few adequately emphasize them in modern practice.

This is not to say that *iaijutsu* is neither practical nor beneficial—far from it! *Iaijutsu* develops qualities which are not only useful for self-defense, if needed, but also improve one's experience of daily life. For this reason, training in this seemingly "impractical" art is far more practical than learning "street-fighting" techniques for anyone but a thug.

BUDŌ NO ARIKATA
Purpose of Martial Arts

To understand the purpose of martial arts training, we need only understand the goal of martial arts: to *win*!

It is that simple.

At the same time, it is far more complex. Obviously, we learn a martial art in order to prevail in an encounter. We certainly don't spend years training in order to be defeated! However, martial arts training involves much more than merely learning how to injure or kill another person in battle.

A Japanese legend relates that centuries ago, there were two *samurai* who were closer than brothers. As they matured and prepared to embark on their *musha shūgyō*—the customary travels to perfect their skills—it was apparent that their paths would separate for many years. So, before departing they met by a quiet stream and vowed to meet again on that very spot twelve years later to share tales of their training and exploits. Just as they had vowed, they returned to the bank of the stream on the very day twelve years later, but found that a recent rain had swollen the gentle stream into a raging torrent, barring their way to the exact spot of their last meeting.

Determined to live up to the letter and spirit of his vow, and to demonstrate the incredible skills he had mastered during their twelve-year separation, one *samurai* dashed to the river and made a spectacular leap that carried him over the deadly current and safely to the other side. The jump far exceeded today's Olympic records, and should have amazed his friend. Instead, the other *samurai* calmly walked a few paces upstream and hired a boatman to row him across for 5 *mon* (about 50 cents).

The skills one man spent a lifetime of sacrifice and dedication to develop could be duplicated effortlessly for a few pennies. Similarly, if our goal is merely to kill people, we can simply purchase a gun, rather than invest years of training. So, the first lesson of *iaijutsu* is to be certain that your training goals are worthwhile.

Next, we must realize that "winning" is not merely defeating an opponent; it is perfecting yourself—your personal character, as well as your skills—to the degree that an opponent cannot prevail against you. Yet, winning is still more than this.

In *iaijutsu,* there is a saying: *"Kachi wa saya no naka ni ari"* ("Victory comes while the sword is [still] in the scabbard"). Physical skills alone, no matter how highly perfected, are simply not enough. There is always someone more skillful, or someone with a dirty trick for which you are unprepared. But *attitude* is more important than *aptitude* in real combat. We have all seen encounters reminiscent of that between David and Goliath, where the underdog defeated a far mightier opponent through sheer determination and faith.

Without the courage or determination to use it, a high degree of skill is useless. It would be like painting a great masterpiece, then storing it away where no one can ever see it. This is not only a waste of time, talent, and effort, but a loss of something valuable to humankind.

So, the higher purpose of *iaijutsu* is to develop the mind and spirit of a warrior, an attitude and strength of character that wins the battle before it begins. This is no simple matter to achieve. It takes years of daily training to cultivate these attributes and to rid oneself of attitudes and reactions, such as anger, fear, selfishness, jealousy, and hate, that are counterproductive or self-destructive.

Furthermore, winning must be accomplished without *trying* to win! Once again, this concept at first seems self-contradictory. After all, how can you be victorious if you don't even try to win? The answer is that the key to winning a battle is a steadfast determination to *not lose.*

This is more than just a semantic difference; it requires a profound shift of focus and commitment. When you are trying to win, you will be inclined to take unnecessary risks in your determination to defeat your opponent. But when you are instead dedicated to not losing the encounter, you have the luxury of waiting for your opponent to make a mistake that you can then exploit to achieve victory.

However, *iaijutsu* training demands a still higher and more noble purpose than merely winning (or not losing) battles. The great Chinese tactician Lao Tsu said that the highest principle in the Art of War is to *win without a battle.* This is the true ideal of *iaijutsu,* as embodied in the Chinese ideograms for "martial art":

BU
"Martial"

JUTSU
"Art"

The symbol on the left, above, which we translate as "martial" (the *"bu"* in *budō*) was formed from the two characters below:

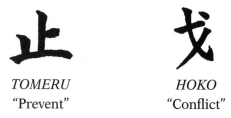

TOMERU
"Prevent"

HOKO
"Conflict"

Thus, the term "martial arts," from the earliest of times, has truly meant "The Art of Conflict Prevention." The way *iaijutsu* training accomplishes this goal can only be discovered by understanding the underlying ideals of the martial arts.

SHŪGYŌ NO MOKUTEKI

Ideals of Martial Arts

Japan's most famous and revered *samurai*, Miyamoto Musashi, once asked his young disciple, Jōtarō, what his goal in life was. Without hesitation, the teenager replied, "To be like *you!*"

"Your goal is too small," Musashi scolded him. He went on to admonish his student to "aspire to be like Mt. Fuji, with such a broad and solid foundation that the strongest earthquake cannot move you, and so tall that the greatest enterprises of common men seem insignificant from your lofty perspective. With your mind as high as Mt. Fuji," he explained, "you can see all things clearly. And you can see all the forces which shape events; not just the things happening near you."

Walking together along a twisting mountain path, Musashi and Jōtarō soon came to a bend at which an enormous overhanging boulder loomed above the path. At first glance, the boulder seemed precariously suspended above them, as if the slightest jar would break it loose and send it crashing down to annihilate them. Yet, a closer look showed it to be so firmly embedded in the mountainside that it would take the forces of nature eons to work it free. Nevertheless, Jōtarō scuttled nervously along the path beneath it, anxious to be out from under it. As Musashi calmly followed, he noticed his disciple's natural reaction to the threatening presence of the massive rock, and used it to reinforce his lesson.

"You should train to become like this boulder," Musashi told Jōtarō, "With most of your strength hidden, and so deeply rooted that you are immovable. Yet, so powerful that what can be seen will make men cringe to walk in your shadow."

This, Musashi felt, was the ultimate goal of training, to be so highly skilled and mentally developed that your mere presence was intimidating and no man would dare challenge you. And, indeed, Musashi reached, even exceeded, this level of personal development during his colorful life. Clearly, someone this highly trained will have to fight few, if any, battles to achieve life's victories.

Later in life, it was this very quality that Musashi looked for in selecting a student to train. After he had retired to refine his character through the arts of painting, sculpting, and calligraphy, Musashi accepted an invitation by the Kumamoto *daimyō* to come to his castle and train an elite corps of *samurai* to become the *daimyō*'s personal retainers. So great was the *daimyō*'s respect for Musashi that he had all of his *samurai*—several hundred of them—form a processional line on both sides of the street, extending from the castle gates to the town. As Musashi strode between the two columns of men, each bowed reverently at his passage. But, as Musashi's keen eye detected, even these elite *samurai* averted their gaze from his bold stare. Only one among them seemed not to be intimated by Musashi's mere countenance.

When Musashi finally reached the *daimyō* and his counselors, the *daimyō* asked if any of his *samurai* had particularly impressed Musashi, perhaps testing to see if Musashi could discern his most skillful swordsmen at just a passing glance. Musashi led the *daimyō* back to the one man who had not cast his eyes down as Musashi passed.

"This man!" Musashi announced.

Ōsaka Castle

"I don't understand," the *daimyō* blustered, "He has little training and only modest rank. In fact, his main duty is stonecutting for the castle."

"This may be so," Musashi answered, "But he is your best trained *samurai*." Turning to the man, Musashi asked him, "Tell me, how do you train that you have no fear of death?"

"I hardly train at all," the *samurai* admitted humbly, "When I go to bed each night, I simply unsheathe my sword and hang it above my face by a slender thread. Then I lie down beneath it and gaze up at its point until I fall asleep."

"This is indeed your best trained *samurai*," Musashi told the *daimyō*, with a knowing smile. "He alone of all your men faces death every day, for he knows that it would take little for that tiny thread to break and end his life. I will train *this* man to be your personal bodyguard."

However, as Musashi continued to mature, he found—to his great dismay—that even such an incredible level of personal development was not enough. Despite the fact that even the bravest *samurai* could not bear to gaze upon Musashi in awe of him, he was still challenged many times and forced to kill more than sixty opponents in sword duels. He found that his reputation and his aura of power and invincibility attracted fame-seekers like moths to a flame. Obviously, anyone who could defeat the legendary Miyamoto Musashi would be instantly famous, able to found his own school of swordsmanship, and command riches, position, and prestige as a high-ranking retainer to any *daimyō*, or perhaps even the *Shōgun*. So, throughout most of his life, Musashi found himself beleaguered by challengers betting their lives against a chance at such fame and fortune.

Several years after his encounter with the Kumamoto *daimyō*, Musashi was once again in the mountains seeking to perfect his character. Together with his life-long friend and mentor, the priest Sōhō Takuan, he was seated beside a gentle stream with a small, tranquil waterfall, engaged in *zazen* meditation. As they meditated, Musashi's keen senses alerted him to another presence nearby. Without disturbing the serenity of his meditation, Musashi allowed his gaze to fall upon a deadly viper slithering into the clearing from some shrubbery near Takuan.

Knowing that the slightest movement might frighten the venomous snake into attacking his friend, Musashi carefully controlled his spirit, watching the serpent in utter stillness. He was surprised to see a faint smile appear on Takuan's lips as he, too, became aware of the snake's approach and calmly watched it crawl across his own thighs. Even more amazing than the priest's complete tranquility in the face of mortal danger was the snake's casual acceptance of Takuan as a natural part of its surroundings.

After slithering across the priest, the lethal serpent continued on its winding course toward Musashi. But, several feet away, the snake sensed Musashi's presence and recoiled, preparing to attack the seated *samurai*. Musashi gave no reaction. Even though his spirit was undisturbed by the ominous, bared fangs of the viper, Musashi's power, skill, and menace were so palpable to the snake that it scurried away into the bushes like a terrified rabbit. Most men would have been proud to possess such an intimidating aura, but Musashi felt only shame as he suddenly understood his own greatest shortcoming.

"What troubles you so?" asked Takuan, sensing his friend's mood.

"All my life," Musashi lamented, "I have trained myself to develop such skill that no man would ever dare attack me. And now that I have reached my goal, all living things instinctively fear me. You saw how the snake fled from me!"

"I saw it," the priest said. "Since it dared not attack you, you defeated it without striking a blow. And because of your great skill, both you *and* the snake are alive now." Although he already knew the answer, Takuan asked, "Why does that sadden you?"

"Because I am so strong that no one can ever grow close to me. I can never have true peace." Musashi pointed a finger at the priest. "Not like you," he said with admiration, "You did not fear the snake, nor did the snake fear you. Your spirit is so calm, so natural, that the snake treated you no differently than the rocks, the trees, or the wind. *People* accept you that way, too."

Takuan only smiled, pleased that his friend had made such an important self-discovery.

Musashi spent the rest of his days training to perfect a spirit like that of his friend Takuan. This mental state, the ideal to which all martial artists aspire, is called *heijōshin*. Literally translated, it means "constant stable spirit," but such a translation hardly does it justice. The nuances of the Japanese language help greatly in understanding the full nature of *heijōshin*, a word comprised of three *kanji* (ideograms):

| *Hei* | *Jō* | *Shin* |

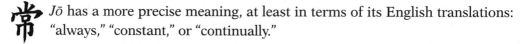

Hei has numerous related meanings in Japanese: "peaceful," "calm," "steady," and so on. The closest English equivalent, however, may be "level" or "even," since these terms can be used in such ways as "level-headed" and "even-handed" in English.

Jō has a more precise meaning, at least in terms of its English translations: "always," "constant," or "continually."

Shin translates both literally and figuratively as "heart," with almost all the same nuances. Thus, to Asians and Westerners alike, *shin* is understood as more than simply the internal organ that pumps blood, but connotes the mind, the spirit, the emotions, the character—the whole inner essence of the individual.

Thus, *heijōshin* is a concept of the whole inner being of a person being continually at peace. For lack of a more effective translation, we will simply call it "peace of mind." However, the fullness of *heijōshin* warrants a more detailed explanation.

HEIJŌ SHIN
Peace of Mind

Heijōshin, true peace of mind, is probably best understood, not as a single attribute but as a combination—or rather the *culmination*—of several character traits. Each of the aspects that together create *heijōshin* may take years of effort, experience, and disappointment to develop, making *heijōshin* the product of a lifetime of patient training. To achieve genuine peace of mind requires a high degree of mental development in three key areas: (1) the intellect, (2) the emotions, and (3) that indefinable element we usually call "character" or "integrity." And these three areas must be developed *in balance*.

Why is *heijōshin* so important?

As we age, our physical prowess, no matter how great, will eventually lessen. This is especially evident in professional sports, where few athletes enjoy a career longer than ten years. But, with diligence, our character and our mental prowess will constantly improve. And we can never be certain that ill health or a serious accident might not leave us with drastically impaired physical ability, while our mental faculties remain strong. The key to lifelong fruitfulness and happiness, then, is not in our physical skills, but in our mental development.

This is why cultivating *heijōshin* is far more important to the martial artist than merely perfecting skill with a sword. Furthermore, *heijōshin* is an unlimited quality. There is always room for more knowledge, greater compassion, stronger love, and a higher level of character development.

How do you obtain *heijōshin*?

Heijōshin is not only difficult to attain, but there is no simple, precise method to develop it. This is a stumbling block to many Westerners, especially in America, where people have become culturally conditioned to a "quick-fix" approach to nearly everything. If something cannot be achieved with a wonder drug, an overnight miracle, or a three-step/five-day program, it seems too difficult and time-consuming to attempt.

So, to begin with, you might as well understand that *heijōshin* demands a lifestyle change: a life of discipline, effort, sacrifice, and commitment. Such a commitment to developing excellence of character sets the martial artist— particularly the *iaijutsu* practitioner—apart from most people in a confused and unhappy society.

Not only is there no easy way to develop *heijōshin,* but for each of us the path will be different, because of our different personality, experiences, and circumstances. To further complicate matters, *heijōshin* is rife with paradoxes. The first of these is the nature of *heijōshin* itself: it is the product of diligent training and continual effort to reshape the mind, yet in the end it must be completely natural and unforced. **So, how do we practice something which must occur spontaneously?**

The tales of Miyamoto Musashi told earlier in this chapter contain some clues that may help answer this question. If you read them again now, you may notice that Musashi did not train himself in the "art" of *heijōshin* itself, but rather in the elements which lead to its development. In effect, in another of its paradoxes, while *heijōshin* is the true goal of martial arts training, it is achieved as a *by-product* of training.

If *heijōshin* was merely a single attribute, it could be practiced and learned, like multiplication tables. But, since it is itself the by-product of a person's complete inner being, it can only be achieved by refining that whole inner essence. And this can only be accomplished if one's intellect, emotions, and character are developed *in balance.*

Why is martial arts training the best method for developing *heijoshin?*

When a person realizes the true nature of martial arts training, and practices accordingly, it leads to a fuller understanding of the nature of life itself. Martial arts are concerned essentially with life and death. This is most apparent, perhaps, in *iaijutsu* training, since the outcome of a sword battle is clearly that one opponent lives and the other dies. This is not the case with *karate-dō* or other "empty-hand" arts, in which the "loser" might merely be rendered incapable of continuing the fight.

So, if the *iaijutsu* student is serious about his or her training, each *kata* (practice pattern) represents far more than simply swinging a sword around. It is a symbolic battle in which your opponent will most certainly die. Will you

Life or Death

end his life without good cause? Will you throw his family into turmoil and perhaps ruin over some triviality? When you have developed true compassion for others, then train in a life-or-death context, you gain a whole new appreciation of life—both your own and the lives of others.

Isn't "life-or-death" training unrealistic in modern society?

The sad fact is that few people, other than the best-trained martial artists, truly understand how tenuous life is. The *samurai* understood this, because he was trained to realize that each new day might bring death. The pioneers of the Old West understood it, because of the tremendous hardships and uncertainties they faced. But, it in age in which hunger, disease, and most of our mortal enemies have been all but vanquished, we seem to have become blinded to the precariousness of our existence. Even when we read of a major celebrity succumbing to AIDS, or a terrible plane crash, or a terrorist bombing, or a drive-by gang shooting, most of us believe that "it can't happen to me."

The life-or-death awareness of *iaijutsu* training allows us to clearly see that death is, quite literally, only one heartbeat away. Part of *heijōshin* is coming to grips with the inevitability of death. That it will eventually claim the "high" and "low" alike—movie stars, drug addicts, sports heroes, bank robbers, politicians, business executives, and even ourselves.

Once we understand how fragile our life is, we have a vital choice to make. We can either live in seclusion, like Howard Hughes in his later years, cowering in paranoid fear of everything from germs to fatal accidents, or we can determine to live each moment we are given to the fullest and die with no regrets.

Yet it is only after deciding to live life to its fullest, that we have the most difficult choices to make. It is then that we must come to grips with what brings true and lasting happiness and fulfillment to life.

If you were given only one week to live, what would you do? Would you live out your final days in a wild, uninhibited bacchanalia of sensual pleasures? Many would. Would you sell all that you had accumulated and spend your last week donating to every worthy cause you could think of? That would be more noble. Would you feverishly attend to every detail of settling your estate, so your loved ones would be provided for after your death? That would demonstrate a high degree of responsibility and integrity. Would you spend every moment possible with your family and closest friends? That would probably give your final hours the greatest comfort. Or would you do nothing different than you had done the previous week, or the week before that? *That* would indicate that your lifestyle has produced *heijōshin*!

This brings us to another paradox: If you have achieved *heijōshin,* you will live every day as if it was your last. But just because you live every day as if it was your last does not mean you have attained *heijōshin*. It is not simply "living like there's no tomorrow" that demonstrates *heijōshin,* but *how* you live your last day that is the barometer of your character. It is the quality and purpose of your life that gives it value.

How should I live my life to have *heijōshin?*

The highest principle of *heijōshin* is to develop your mind (the combination of intellect, emotions, and character) to such an elevated state that you are unaffected by your environment. This is what Musashi was trying to impress upon Jotarō by admonishing him to train himself to be like Mt. Fuji. It means not allowing circumstances to control your emotions, nor emotions to confuse your judgment.

If your happiness and security are based primarily upon your financial status, then you will only be comfortable when things are going well. If you lose your job and begin to have difficulty paying your bills, soon you will find yourself constantly under stress, doubting your own abilities and value, and angered by the loss of the material freedom you once had. In the end, you will likely find yourself taking a job that is not right for you, just to regain your self-esteem and recover your lost financial status. This is an example of your circumstances controlling your emotions, and your emotions in turn confusing your judgment.

But, if your contentment is derived from knowing the type of person that you are *inside,* then you will more readily understand that life has its ups and downs. You will realize that the sun rises upon the evil and the good, and the rain falls upon the righteous and the unrighteous alike. Everyone experiences an occasional windfall, and no one is exempt from times of hardship, so it is foolish to allow these circumstances to dictate your emotions. What is more, the rich and famous are often the unhappiest people in the world, while the so-called "lowly," like Mother Teresa, enjoy a rich and fulfilling life. Once you understand that it is what you *are,* not what you *have,* that is important, you are able to rise above your circumstances.

The second key tenet of *heijōshin* is to understand that you are part of your environment; that what you are and what you do has an effect on other people. Even your emotions affect others. If you are discouraged, you will drop a cloud of gloom on the people with whom you come in contact. If you are joyful, just the sight of you will gladden them. If you behave rudely, you will anger people or hurt their feelings. If you are pleasant and respectful, you will brighten their day. People who look up to you will follow your example, whether it is good or bad.

This presents another of *heijōshin*'s paradoxes: **How can we be unaffected by our environment when we are *part* of our environment?**

Obviously, our environment *will* affect us to some degree. The state of the economy will affect us, our health will affect us, the actions of friends and loved ones will affect us. *Heijōshin* is not a condition in which we insulate ourselves from our surroundings, nor deny that our problems exist, nor deaden our minds and senses to our feelings. *Heijōshin* is not a means of escape, like drugs, which allows you to ignore or be unaware of your emotions. Quite the opposite, to possess *heijōshin* demands that you be deeply in touch with your emotions. It is perfectly natural to *feel* anger, joy, disappointment, love, and the full range of emotions. *Heijōshin,* however, allows us not to be *controlled* by these emotions, so that our actions are not determined by a fleeting impulse, but are the product of a consistent, balanced, and focused mind.

How can I experience my emotions, yet not let them affect my actions?

The answer comes from developing two essential character traits: *understanding* and *compassion.*

First, you must understand yourself; understand *why* you feel the way you do, why certain events or situations evoke certain emotions in you. Then, you must have compassion for yourself. Accept yourself for what you are, and why you are what you are. You cannot change who you are now. You have already become that person. You can only change who you will be in the future. If you condemn yourself for your faults and failures, it is only a waste of your emotional energy and destructive to your self-esteem. But, if you can compassionately accept yourself as you are now, then you have a positive starting point from which to begin developing into the person you want to become.

Second, you must have the same understanding and compassion for others. Once you have thoroughly understood yourself, you can appreciate that other people have become who they are for a reason. There have been influences and circumstances that have shaped them into the people they have become. By compassionately accepting others with both their strengths and weaknesses, you will be able to distinguish between your feelings toward the *person* and your feelings about their *behavior.* This separation is vital to human relationships.

If someone behaves rudely, for example, I can either become offended at the *person* or at the person's *behavior.* If I become offended at the person, my natural reaction will be to avoid that offensive person. If, instead, I look beyond the person and see the behavior as offensive, then my natural reaction will be to try to understand what caused it, because I am now viewing the situation as an offensive action committed by an acceptable person. Rather than shunning the person, I will try to communicate with him or her, and my reaction will be motivated by concern rather than anger or resentment.

Westerners reflect an understanding of this aspect of *heijōshin* in this commonly quoted prayer:

"God grant me the serenity to accept the things I cannot change, the courage to change the things I can, and the wisdom to know the difference."

When should I use *heijōshin*?

Heijōshin is not something you turn on and off like a politician's smile. Once *heijōshin* is rooted in you, it is with you at all times everywhere you go, from the time you wake up to the time you go to bed—even while you are sleeping! It becomes your natural state of mind, not something you summon only when you "need" it.

What are the benefits of *heijōshin*?

Obviously, by developing a constant, peaceful state of mind, you, as an individual, will lead a happier, more serene life, freed from bondage to an emotional roller coaster propelled by forces beyond your control. But, the benefits of *heijōshin* cannot remain exclusively personal. By its nature, *heijōshin* cannot exist in a vacuum, so its benefits will spread from you to society as a whole.

Society is simply a collection of individuals. Social ills, like crime and drug abuse, are merely the reflection of the combined failings of the individuals who comprise society. Laws cannot reform society and cure its ills, they can only punish violators. Society is like our collective shadow. If the shadow is bent and twisted, no amount of effort can straighten it. Only by straightening ourselves does our shadow also straighten, and then it does so effortlessly and automatically. So it is that reform must start with individuals and spread through society. It is a "grass roots" process in which each of us is either part of the disease or part of the cure.

If our behavior is controlled by our circumstances and emotions, rather than by our strength of character and ideals, then we are part of the disease. If, instead, our *heijōshin* lifts us above our circumstances and helps us live with greater purpose and meaning, our example will inspire others to become part of the cure.

Thus, the ultimate objective of *heijōshin* is the same as the ultimate objective of martial arts: **to help each individual reach his or her full potential, and thereby improve society as a whole.**

平 常 心

SHŪGYŌ NO HAJIME

The Journey's Beginning

Having determined to set out on this journey of self-discovery and perfection of character through martial arts training, you need to know where to start. As good as any book or video may be, you cannot learn martial arts from it alone. Martial arts instruction is personal. It is nothing like learning spelling or arithmetic in school.

True martial arts instruction—the development, maturing, and shaping of a good *budōka* (martial artist)—is not a process; it is a *relationship.* For that reason, it requires a good instructor and a good *dōjō* (school). The depth of understanding of both the physical and philosophical aspects of *iaijutsu* can only be passed on through a mentoring relationship. This is why the Japanese place such importance—bordering on reverence—on the close relationship between a student *(seito)* and his *sensei* (teacher), and in the relationship between *sempai* (senior students) and *kōhai* (junior students).

A *sensei* is more than merely a martial arts instructor, he is the model of technical and philosophical excellence to which his students aspire. The *sempai,* or senior student, is a partner in the training process who acts like a nurturing older brother or sister, guiding and encouraging the student on the often difficult and disappointing road toward his or her objectives and ideals.

Dōjō literally means "Place of the Way." It is not just a building in which to practice martial arts; it is a laboratory in which to study, experiment, and refine a complete and fulfilling *way of life.* You should select your *dōjō* with the utmost care, as though your life, or at least the *quality* of your life, depended on it.

The first step, therefore, in reaching your full potential is to find a good *sensei* teaching in a good *dōjō.* Remember that a good player is not always a good coach, so you must look not only at the instructor's technical expertise, but at his ability to lead, instruct, and inspire his students. Some good measures of these abilities are the degree of respect shown by his students, whether the senior students show a nurturing attitude toward their juniors, and whether the students are able to acquire the skills and—more importantly—the *attitudes* the instructor is trying to impart.

The only way to do this is to visit those *dōjō* in your area which have the highest reputation among respected *budōka.* Visit each one in which you are interested several times to observe classes and discuss your training goals with the instructor. You should not only determine if the instructor's teaching style is suited to your personality and the way you best learn, but pay particular attention to his attitude and demeanor. Does he exhibit the highest ideals of martial arts in the way he conducts himself? Does he become disinterested in you if you don't join his *dōjō* right away? Does he show more concern for you as a potential student, or in your ability to pay for the lessons? The "bottom-line" question to ask yourself is: "Is this *sensei* the kind of role model I want to emulate?"

Once you have selected a *dōjō,* it is important for you to seek a close relationship with your *sensei.* After all, *iaijutsu* training is training for everyday life, so in order for it to take root, *your training must be part of your everyday life and your daily life must be part of your training.* The Japanese have a saying, "*Shi-Tei Fu Ni*" ("Master and Disciple are not Two"), meaning that your *sensei* should be like a wise, patient parent to you. Seek the counsel of your *sensei* concerning the opportunities, issues, and problems you are facing, so that he or she can show you how to apply sound martial arts principles to them.

Lastly, *train seriously.* Use your imagination to "feel" your opponent and face death through your training. As you learn to vividly face death while you practice *iaijutsu,* your eyes will be opened to what life is really about!

IKA NI SHINŪKA

How to Die Well

An extremely significant part of a *samurai*'s training was learning to die well. As we have emphasized repeatedly, facing death—either vicariously in the *dōjō,* or literally on the battlefield—was a daily routine for the *samurai.* Part of a *samurai*'s training included instruction in the proprieties of ritualistic suicide *(seppuku),* accomplished by slitting open his own abdomen. A *samurai* was also trained and prepared to act as *kaishaku,* or assistant, in the event one of his peers was called upon to commit *seppuku,* and was well-versed in both the technique and etiquette of this crucial role. Even the women of *samurai* rank were prepared to perform ritual suicide, albeit by a more genteel method, by slitting her throat.

One of the hallmarks of a *samurai* was his avowed purpose: *"Shinu kikai o motomo"* ("Looking for the opportunity to die"). In the West, we often seem to interpret this as an exaggerated sense of fatalism among the *samurai*—a view which reduces them to little more than half-crazed warriors throwing themselves wantonly into battle as if their lives were worthless.

While applying the principle of *shinu kikai o motomo* did free the *samurai* to face his enemy with fearless disregard for his own life, it was not for the reason suggested by this shallow interpretation. Instead, the *samurai* held his life to be of great value. It was therefore to be lost—or even risked—only if the cause was worthy of such a noble and extreme sacrifice!

Thus, in searching for the opportunity to die, the *samurai* really sought the reason to live. As modern *samurai* we should do no less. Facing death in our training helps us to focus on those things that are *truly* important to our lives, such as family, personal relationships, strength of character, and so forth. In this way, *shinu kikai o motomo* leads us to decide what is really worth living for.

When we begin to focus our thoughts, ideals, and desires in this manner, most of the complexities, gray areas, and dilemmas of life are removed from our path. We no longer allow the trivialities and distractions which so complicate most people's lives to be a factor in ours.

By becoming a *complete* martial artist—a person who understands *Budō no Arikata* and *Shugyō no Mokuteki,* who possesses *heijōshin* and has determined their *shinu kikai o motomo*—we will know what truly victorious living is. We will live a life *worth living,* a life with purpose and meaning, filled with rich, intimate relationships. And when we reach the end of our appointed days, we will be able to look back on our lives without regrets.

This is the true purpose of *iaijutsu* training!

Chapter 3

武士の目

Bushi no Me

Eyes of a Samurai

A samurai does not see things in an ordinary way. He has trained his mind and spirit to process the impulses from his optic nerves in a highly refined manner.

Just as in Western culture, *samurai* concepts of "eye" and "sight" include both physical vision (to "see" an object) and mental insight (to "see" someone's point of view). In fact, to the *samurai*, there is probably less distinction between these two concepts than in the West. While, for most people vision seldom rises above the first or second level,because the *samurai* recognizes five distinct levels of eyesight and he tries to "see" at the highest of these levels in a way which *combines* physical sight with deep insight.

NIKUGEN

"Naked Eye"

Nikugen is no more than the plain image received on the retina, devoid of any mental or emotional process. Obviously, it is the lowest of the five levels of vision, and it has three major limitations.

First, *nikugen* is completely superficial. A person using *nikugen* sees nothing beyond the existence of the objects within his or her field of vision. *Nikugen* does not involve any deeper comprehension of these objects, such as how they came to be where they are, how they might interact, or how they might affect the observer or others.

Secondly, *nikugen* is limited by the observer's point of view. Someone using *nikugen* can see only that side of things which is facing his direction. In this sense, *nikugen* is almost two-dimensional. Staring at a circular object, a person using *nikugen* would not know if he sees a true circle, the bottom of a cone, the bottom of a cylinder, or the visible outline of a sphere.

Thirdly, *nikugen* is easily obstructed. By simply placing something in front of the observer's eyes, he would be rendered effectively sightless.

These qualities not only apply to physical sight, but also to the "insight" sense of *nikugen*. A person trying to "see" a problem using only *nikugen*, can see only its superficial aspects. He also sees the problem only from his own point of view, and his vision is easily clouded by his circumstances, preconceived ideas, and/or emotions. For example, using only *nikugen*, a person with no money in his pockets would see himself as penniless. If he wants a sandwich, then he would view purchasing the sandwich as a hopeless impossibility.

With this two-dimensional view, the hungry man is "blind" to other possibilities, such as bartering work for the sandwich, selling another possession to raise money for the sandwich, or seeking food from another source.

TENGEN
"Neutral Perspective"

The next developmental step in vision is *tengen,* translated literally as "heavenly eye." This type of sight is described as heavenly not in an angelic sense, but in terms of the observer's point of view.

With *tengen,* the observer is no longer bound by his own point of view, but has a neutral perspective in which he is able to see objects or a problem as if looking down on them from a great height. Quite literally, *tengen* is being able to "see the forest for the trees." In this way, not only can one clearly see the true nature and shape of objects, as in the first example of *nikugen,* but also all aspects of a problem from a detached and broad perspective. Furthermore, with the less self-centered perspective of *tengen,* the observer's viewpoint is not as susceptible to the distortions of his own preconceived ideas, emotional reactions, or living conditions as he would be with *nikugen. Tengen* cannot be easily obstructed, because clear sight is not dependent upon the observer's point of view.

Using the previous examples, a person with *tengen* is more likely to perceive what the unseen surfaces of the circular object are. By applying knowledge and experience, his or her mind will be able to conclude whether what is seen is just a circle, or an outline of a sphere, or the bottom of a cylinder or cone. Similarly, someone with *tengen* will have the ability to "see" more sides to a problem. Rather than narrowly perceiving a lack of money for a sandwich, a person with *tengen* would view the situation in the broader sense of a need for food, which offers more options for a solution.

However, even with this elevated perspective, the observer's emotions, preconceptions, and life circumstances can interfere to some degree with true understanding, and his or her view is still limited to what the eyes can see.

EGEN
"Interpretive Sight"

Egen (literally "thinking sight") is a higher level, at which the image received by the brain is enhanced by an understanding of the implications of the things being observed. It is important, however, not to confuse *egen* with analytical thought. *Egen* is *not* the product of thinking about what you see; it is an automatic, subconscious process in which the eye and mind work together to interpret the images received by the brain, thus producing a deeper level of vision than mere physical eyesight.

To use a simple example that many of us may have experienced, a person observing two cars approaching a blind intersection at the same time sees an accident about to happen. Most people would not have to stop and think to realize this. By experience, knowing that neither driver can see the other's onrushing vehicle, we automatically and subconsciously know they are about to collide. With only *nikugen* or *tengen,* however, we would only see two cars moving independently of each other, much as a child who had never witnessed an accident might perceive them.

Unfortunately, while most mature adults have *egen* with respect to common physical events, we lack it in other ways. But with true *egen*, we would recognize when a clash of personalities or wills was about to occur just a readily as we can see an accident about to happen. We would see an event not just in its physical form, but in the context of the forces which brought it about and the effects it will later have on other events.

Thus, the main benefit of *egen* is that the observer now naturally and subconsciously perceives and understands the cause-and-effect relationship of the things he or she witnesses. *Egen* is not limited by the observer's point of view, and his or her sight is unclouded by emotions, preconceptions, or life condition. However, *egen* remains impaired in a crucial way.

SHINGEN/HŌGEN
"Compassionate Eye"

For all its benefits, *egen* is still incomplete. Although the observer receives a complete, unobstructed, and untainted view of situations and their causes and effects—even the reasons and motives underlying peoples' actions—this vision is detached and dispassionate.

The next level of vision, *shingen,* adds the most vital ingredient of all: compassion. Compassion is the spark that motivates the *samurai* to take the correct action in a situation. He sees an event not merely from his own perspective and how it may effect him, but how the event will shape the lives of everyone involved. Furthermore, he sees it with understanding and compassion for *all* those affected, so that his action will be not what is best for him, but what will be the best for society as a whole.

The *samurai* does not view the feelings, actions, or desires of others as "right" or "wrong." Therefore, his judgment is not clouded by a need to prove himself right. Nor does the *samurai* have to overcome the natural hesitancy of another person to admit that he or she is wrong. Instead, the *samurai* is only concerned with what has greater *value*. Thus, in a disagreement, the *samurai* sees the views of others only as alternatives, and he is able to use *shingen* to see which of these alternatives has the most value to society, whether it is his own preference or not. With this approach, it is far easier to persuade others to accept the best choice, as well.

A *samurai*'s evaluation also takes into account the immutable laws of nature. He understands the principles of cause and effect, and that even wrongful actions are motivated by these cause-and-effect forces. Because of this, *shingen* is often also referred to as *hōgen*. *Hōgen* translates literally as "Law Sight," but it does not refer to the laws of mankind. Instead, its nuance might be best understood as "Universal Perspective" in the sense of having equal compassion for each person in a world operating under a natural order which never changes, but in which you can choose to intervene. It is from this neutral, compassionate point of view that the *samurai* tries to observe his world and take the most beneficial action.

Thus, as shown in the table below, a *samurai* is trained to "see from the heart." Training in the life-or-death art of *iaijutsu* develops a deep, abiding compassion for people, and the experiences of life teach an understanding of the unchanging forces which shape both people and events. As his training and experience continue, his sight evolves through stages from *nikugen* to *shingen*.

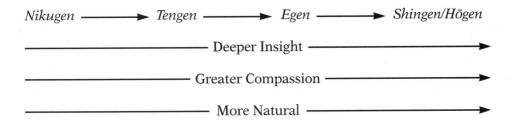

The easiest way to compare the differences—and the effects of those differences—between *nikugen, tengen, egen,* and *shingen,* may be an example from everyday life:

You are running late for a very important business meeting, and when you get onto the freeway the traffic is heavily congested and moving at a crawl.

With *nikugen,* all you can see is that you are going to be extremely late for the meeting and make a terrible impression. As a result, you will probably speed frantically through the traffic, zigging and zagging from lane to lane, trying to gain a few precious minutes.

A person with *tengen*, however, can see that his wild driving might earn him a traffic ticket. He might slow down a little, but more likely he will just be more careful to watch in the mirror for police cars, since he still wants to save as much time as possible getting to the meeting.

The person with *egen*, on the other hand, does not allow his desire to make a good impression cloud his judgment. He realizes that driving recklessly not only could earn him a traffic ticket, but also endangers himself and other people on the road—people who have just as much right to safe use of the highway as he does. Furthermore, he may even realize that his business associates may also be held up by the same traffic jam.

The *samurai* is already at the meeting, waiting for the others to arrive. With the benefit of *hōgen*, he understood that the freeways would be packed, so he got up earlier than usual to be sure traffic would not be a problem. In this way, if traffic was terrible he would be on time; if traffic was not congested, he would arrive early. He also understood that by being early, his associates would feel obligated to "make it up" to him, so he would gain a psychological advantage at the meeting, as well!

A true-life historical example of *shingen* comes from the exploits of one of Japan's greatest military leaders, Takeda Shingen, whose life exemplifies many of the training goals of *iaijutsu*.

In Takeda's time, there was a brilliant tactician and warrior named Yamamoto Kansuke. Yamamoto's prowess, however, was not apparent to the naked eye *(nikugen)*, but his ugliness most certainly was. His battlefield experience left him with only one eye, a maimed leg, and a disfigured finger, in addition to his generally unattractive appearance. One of Takeda's rivals, Imagawa Yoshimoto, took one look at Yamamoto and turned him down flatly for a command position.

Takeda, possessed of *shingen*, quickly saw past the scarred and unpleasant surface appearance of Yamamoto to his strength of character and tactical knowledge. Takeda at once selected Yamamoto as one of his twenty-four *taishō* (generals). Not only did Yamamoto produce numerous victories for Takeda, but as a man who overcame severe physical handicaps, especially for his day, he was a tremendous inspiration to Takeda's other commanders.

BUSHI NO ME NO RENSHŪ

Training to Develop Eye of a Samurai

Understanding *Bushi no Me* is a good start, but developing *Bushi no Me* is quite another task altogether. This is especially true when you are trying to develop the Eye of a Samurai in both its literal and figurative sense.

You should also be aware that *iaijutsu* training does not really change the core of your personality. The essence of your personality was formed by the time you were five years old. Instead, *iaijutsu* training helps you develop your strengths to greater levels and suppress your weaknesses. Since "the eyes are the mirror of the soul," developing *Bushi no Me* allows you to see yourself clearly so you can make the greatest improvement possible in your attitude and character.

To develop *Bushi no Me* in the literal sense, gradually developing eyesight which is all-encompassing and deeply understanding, requires concentrated effort in the *dōjō*. Your objective should be to both *broaden* and *deepen* your sight.

Eye of a Samurai

Broadening your sight means enhancing your use of peripheral vision, and combining sight with your other senses to provide awareness of things and events your eyes alone cannot see. Deepening your sight involves developing an understanding that gets far below the surface. A simplified example is being able to see past the frown on a person's face (surface) to the emotion or problem that put that frown there. Of course, *shingen* is far more subtle, deep, and complex than this simplistic example, but it serves to convey the concept.

Whether you are training literally or figuratively to develop *Bushi no Me*, the first step, obviously, is to *open your eyes*. Of course, this means more than simply looking around—that would merely be *nikugen*. It means to practice being aware, to observe the "big picture" without missing the details, to be cognizant of the causes and effects of the events you witness, to understand other people's point of view and why they hold to it, to notice the subtleties of people's behavior, and to refrain from being judgmental towards them. It equally implies making an effort to "stop and smell the roses," to realize that there are always positive influences in your life—even when you are beset by difficulties—and to give at least equal attention to these.

To train in the figurative sense of *Bushi no Me* and reach a point where you are naturally using *shingen* most of the time is a difficult, life-long process. So it helps to find a good starting point. We recommend *Shin•Ku•I* as a means to begin developing *Bushi no Me*.

SHIN•KU•I
Body•Mouth•Mind

Like most training concepts in *iaijutsu*, *Shin•Ku•I* will seem a bit paradoxical at first. Literally "Body-Mouth-Mind," *Shin•Ku•I* refers to action, speech, and thought. This order is stated in the reverse of causation, but is the proper order of training.

It is practically self-evident that the mind controls speech and action (with the exception, perhaps, of reflexive *re*action), yet martial artists through the centuries have found that in training it is more effective to begin at the surface and work back toward the source.

This approach may also recognize the fact that people readily notice our actions and immediately judge us by them. People also listen to our words, but they usually weigh them against our actions to test for hypocrisy. Our thoughts, of course, remain forever hidden from the public. It doesn't matter to others what our thoughts or intentions are, if our actions are harmful or disrespectful. Similarly, if we speak negatively, our good thoughts and intentions will have no impact.

Therefore, when we train to improve our character, we begin with the *out-*

ward manifestation—our behavior. We act with respect toward ourselves and others. We train with discipline and diligence. As we train with this focus, our actions begin to be reflected in the way we speak. The more we consciously act in a respectful and disciplined manner, the more our language becomes respectful and disciplined, as well. Thus, by learning to exercise control over our actions, we also develop control over our speech.

The ongoing conscious effort to control our actions and speech eventually enables us to exert increasing control over our mind. Once we have developed thoughts and emotions reflective of our improving character, then our words and deeds will continue to demonstrate our increasing maturity. In this way, the process naturally reverses, so that at higher levels of training, the mental discipline brings about change in our actions and speech.

Shin•Ku•I is a vital part of training for a *samurai,* for whom the slightest misstatement or misdeed could result in instantaneous lethal combat. It is therefore essential that a *samurai* exercise discretion in both words and actions. This can only be accomplished if his or her mind is thoroughly in control.

Even in modern Western cultures, *Shin•Ku•I* remains a valuable asset. Read the biographies of highly successful, inspirational people, and you will uniformly find that their lives are guided by principles (the mind), which find their way into every word they utter and every action they take. Those aspiring to any measure of greatness in life must follow this model, and *Shin•Ku•I* is an effective means of developing such a lifestyle.

KEN SHIN ICHI NYŌ

Body and Mind as One

The next stage of training to achieve *Bushi no Me* is known as *Ken Shin Ichi Nyō* ("Body and Mind as One"). In *Shin•Ku•I,* we train our bodies to respond to our minds, so that our actions are the result of our principles and character. *Ken Shin Ichi Nyō* takes that process a step further and makes our mind and body act *in unison.*

Iaijutsu is again an excellent training method to accomplish this unity of body and mind. *Ken Shin Ichi Nyō* is written like this:

This actually has the meaning "Sword and Mind as One," which is a training objective of *samurai* swordsmanship. Rather than the body swinging the sword—wielding it as a tool—which is a beginner's level, the master's sword is merely an extension of his own body. As we train toward mastery, we eventually reach a stage at which rather than the mind instructing our arm to swing the sword, our mind merely instructs the sword to move. In actuality, our mental commands do not bypass our arm; instead, what we have accomplished is to train our mind and body to act as a single unit which in turn controls the sword.

In Japanese poetry, the word *Ken* ("Sword") often serves as an allusion to the body. Perhaps this has come about because diligent *iaijutsu* training causes the literal "Sword and Mind as One," *Ken Shin Ichi Nyō*, to steadily evolve into the more profound "Body and Mind as One."

An interesting paradox to consider while you are progressing through *Shin•Ku•I* to achieve *Ken Shin Ichi Nyō* is the Japanese proverb: *"Kokoro no shito wa narutomo, kokoro o shito sezare."*—"Your Mind can't be your master; you must master your Mind."

How are we to understand this axiom when we are training so that our *mind* controls our speech and action *(Shin•Ku•I),* and our body and mind act as one *(Ken Shin Ichi Nyō)?*

The answer is found in the fact that your mind is a complex mechanism, in which your intellect, emotions, character, ideals, and motivations continually interact to produce your speech and actions. Each of these areas of your mind has both strengths and weaknesses. And each of these elements is also constantly evolving, influenced not only by external forces and circumstances, but by the development of the other parts of your mind as well.

Not only are these elements continuously struggling to control your conduct, but you are relentlessly besieged by outside influences trying to shape your behavior. The most obvious of these are advertising, peer pressure, laws, social forces, financial pressures, and a variety of temptations. As if these were not enough, your own character adds stresses to this complex equation. For example, you might have a tendency toward laziness which is in constant conflict with your desire to succeed, or perhaps it is a sweet tooth at odds with your plans to go on a diet right after you finish the next doughnut ... or the one after that. Each of our internal conflicts are different, both in nature and severity, but they plague every human being.

The point made by the proverb is that the sum total of all these forces will control your mind, *unless* you make a conscious determination that they will *not*. Your mind will either *react* to the inundation of these influences, or you must instead take *proactive* steps to ensure that it will stand against the combined effect of this bombardment.

It is not enough merely to ensure that your mind is in control of your speech and actions, and that your mind and body act as one; you must also ensure that it is *you*—your character and principles and highest aspirations—who is in charge of that mind!

HEN DOKU I YAKU
Change Poison to Medicine

Another way in which *Bushi no Me* helps improve your quality of life is found in the adage, *"Hen doku i yaku"* ("Change poison to medicine"). This is a deeper approach to adversity than simply learning to recognize that "every cloud has a silver lining." It is more akin to the notion that "when life deals you a lemon, make lemonade."

Many of the medicines we use to cure illnesses are quite toxic. They work by killing bacteria or viruses in a small enough dosage that they do not seriously harm us. However, taken in greater quantity, many medicines can be lethal to humans. Recognizing this, the *samurai* have long known that, like certain poisons, adversities can often have a medicinal effect if taken in the right dosage. Once again, the proverb mandates a proactive approach by the *samurai*; not merely looking for the good that might come out of a negative event, but *creating* a positive outcome.

The comparison of difficulties to "medicine" is also quite deliberate in other respects. Most of the time we do not like the taste of medicine, but we take it to cure a malady. Likewise, we seldom enjoy adversity, but we can use it as a means for self-improvement. With insight and effort, we can use life's setbacks to develop such character traits as patience, endurance, determination, winning spirit, moral stamina, and perseverance.

Medicines are used to cure disease. Often, if we reflect honestly on the causes of our adversities, we find that they either resulted from, or were magnified by, our own shortcomings. By making a forthright self-analysis when we encounter a challenge, we can identify the area of our personality or character that requires a dose of "medicine."

Medicines are also frequently preventive. This is also the case with *hen doku i yaku*. If we take our "medicine" every time the symptoms appear, we will find fewer and fewer instances in which it is needed. By maturing in our character and improving our *Bushi no Me,* the frequency and severity of our difficulties will be steadily reduced.

Takeda Shingen knew how to apply the lesson of *hen doku i yaku* in dire circumstances. Itagaki, one of his generals, plunged his troops into a battle that Takeda's other twenty-three generals had strongly advised against and was soundly defeated. Upon Itagaki's return, he was harshly criticized by his peers, and he fully expected Takeda to strip him of all rank and honor.

Takeda could have ordered Itagaki to commit suicide and made an example of him to impress on his other generals the importance of taking sound advice and never losing. Instead, Takeda wisely chose *hen doku i yaku,* so instead of chastising Itagaki, he praised him as a brilliant commander for having minimized his losses under such a crushing defeat, and saying that he doubted any other general could have done so well under the same circumstances.

Instead of being disheartened by his overwhelming defeat, Itagaki's attitude was strengthened with a renewed determination to merit Takeda's praise and faith in him. As a result, he went on to lead several victorious campaigns for Takeda.

YUDAN NASHI

Never Off-Guard

The last—and broadest—aspect of *Bushi no Me* is *Yudan,* being "off-guard." The fighting skills of a *samurai* were so great that the best chance to defeat him was to catch him off-guard. A famous story about Miyamoto Musashi illustrates this point well.

According to the legend, one of Musashi's enemies brought a force of several men to his bathhouse while he was bathing. They heavily stoked the fire under his bathwater, lit the bathhouse on fire, then waited in ambush outside the tiny shed. They intended to leave him only three choices: to be boiled alive, burned to death, or slaughtered by their superior forces. With the benefit of *Bushi no Me,* Musashi had anticipated such an attack, and brought his swords with him to the bathhouse. As the treachery unfolded, Musashi broke out through a weakened side of the burning shed and killed the enemies who were laying in wait for him.

Even when relaxing in his bath, when a sense of fair play would place him off-limits to attack by any but the lowest coward, Musashi never permitted *yudan.* His mind and senses were always alert to danger, almost in the fashion of an animal subject to predation. By virtue of *hōgen,* his eyes were continually evaluating the cause and effect of all they surveyed, so that he could never be caught unaware.

An example of training to avoid *yudan* is the instruction given by the swordmaster Ittō Ittōsai to one of his disciples. Rather than teach his young student the fine points of swordsmanship, as one might expect, Ittō instead spent the first several years of the youth's training merely slapping him on the head at every opportunity. This was, of course, extremely annoying to the young trainee, but month after month—as his perception improved—he received fewer and fewer slaps. As the years past, the great master had to become increasingly treacherous and inventive to catch his disciple off-guard, until at last he was no longer able to do so. After this, with only minimal instruction in the handling of a sword, the disciple quickly developed into a master swordsman, since no opponent was able to find an opening for attack.

If you have *hōgen* and remain constantly vigilant, you will never be caught off-guard. Nothing in life will catch you by surprise. This is not to say that your life will never be beset by adversity or trials, but that you will be prepared to meet these challenges when they arise. Thus, true *Bushi no Me*—the combination of *hōgen* with the complete avoidance of *yudan*—is essential to achieving *heijōshin.*

You should be aware that the most vulnerable time for *yudan* to overtake you is during your happiest times. In ancient days, one of the best times to attack was when the enemy was celebrating a victory. When you are happy, you tend to relax and grow serenely oblivious to the events transpiring around you. It is also a state in which it seems pressing problems can be temporarily ignored. Typically, when you are unusually happy your usual inhibitions are lessened, and it is easier for various pitfalls and temptations to slip unnoticed into your life.

On his deathbed, Takeda Shingen counseled his son to wait three years before leading an attack against any of his enemies. This period of engaging only in defensive battles would allow time for Takeda's army to adjust to his son's leadership, and for Takeda's son to mature and gain experience and credibility as their commander. Ignoring his father's advice, immediately after the mourning period for his father's death had ended, Takeda's son drove his forces into a decisive battle, relying on the legacy of his father's reputation and countless past victories to motivate the troops and intimidate the opponents. Instead, because of the *yudan* of his overconfidence, Takeda's army was crushed. In a single battle-his son lost everything Takeda had spent a lifetime building.

As we have seen throughout this chapter, the *mind* is the focal point of proper training. The mind working in concert with the eyes is *shingen* or *hōgen*. The mind controlling words and actions is *Shin•Ku•I*. The mind working in inseparable harmony with the body is *Ken Shin Ichi Nyō*. The mind never dropping its guard is *yudan nashi*. The constant factor throughout these concepts— the key which makes them all possible—is the mind.

The mind is the key to all of life, so the conclusion to be drawn is: **Make up your mind!**

All other training will be pointless unless you do. You will never achieve *shingen*, you will never progress through *Shin•Ku•I*, you will never find *heijōshin* without first having made up your mind. Once you have set your mind to something, and you believe in yourself strongly enough, nothing can prevent you from accomplishing that goal.

But this is not simply saying to yourself that you will do it. Nor is it merely writing some goals on paper. It means making an unshakable, steadfast determination that nothing short of death will stop you! This is the type of resolve that leads you to train even when you don't feel up to it—when you are bruised and blistered and aching and bone-weary, and you can't bear the thought of going back to the *dōjō*—you go anyway because that is what you made up your mind to do.

The Japanese call this kind of strong spirit *shinnen*. But *shinnen* is more than simply iron-willed determination or merely believing strongly in yourself. It implies a belief that you are part of something greater than just yourself; that you have a moral right and responsibility to do what you are doing. The moral imperative of *shinnen* was a powerful stimulus for self-discipline and noble deeds to the *samurai*, and it is an equally motivating force in our times for those whose character and conduct is righteous.

When you begin to apply this same determination outside the *dōjō*, you find that once you set goals for your life—goals that are worth living and dying for—no power on earth can distract you from achieving them.

Chapter 4

刀の名称

Katana no Meishō

Sword Nomenclature

Throughout this book, as well as in any traditional *dōjō* you might attend, the various parts of the sword are referred to by their Japanese names. The following two illustrations identify the most commonly used parts of the sword. In particular, you should memorize those names printed in **bold** type, as these are the most frequently used terms in *iaijutsu* training.

The sword in its entirety is usually called a *katana*, which is a somewhat generic term. More specifically, the *katana* we generally practice with is a *daitō* ("long sword"), to distinguish it from the *wakizashi* or *shōtō*, the shorter companion-sword often worn by *samurai*. The unsharpened sword used for *iaijutsu* practice is called an *iaitō* ("*iai* sword") You may also occasionally hear reference to *chūtō* ("middle sword"), which in modern times denotes a midlength sword used by children for swordsmanship training. Another generic term for sword is *ken*. This term is most commonly found in such terms as *kendō* (the sport of swordsmanship), *kenjutsu* (the art of sword battle), or in such phrases as *Ken Shin Ichi Nyō,* discussed in Chapter Three.

KOSHIRAE
(Mountings)

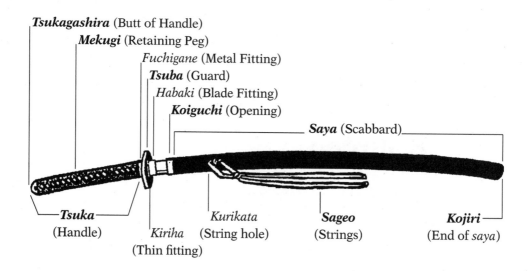

Tsukagashira (Butt of Handle)
Mekugi (Retaining Peg)
Fuchigane (Metal Fitting)
Tsuba (Guard)
Habaki (Blade Fitting)
Koiguchi (Opening)
Saya (Scabbard)

Tsuka
(Handle)

Kiriha
(Thin fitting)

Kurikata
(String hole)

Sageo
(Strings)

Kojiri
(End of *saya*)

TO SHIN
(Bare Blade)

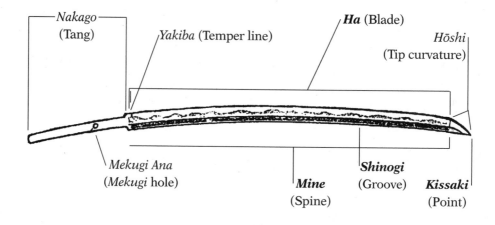

Nakago
(Tang)

Yakiba (Temper line)

Ha (Blade)

Hōshi
(Tip curvature)

Mekugi Ana
(*Mekugi* hole)

Mine
(Spine)

Shinogi
(Groove)

Kissaki
(Point)

Major Parts

The most important parts of the sword for the beginning student to remember are those shown in bold print in the two preceding illustrations:

Japanese Term	*Pronunciation*	*English Term*
1. *Tsuka*	Ts'ᵒᵒ-kah	Handle
2. *Tsukagashira*	Ts'ᵒᵒ-kah-gah-shee-rah	End of the Handle
3. *Mekugi*	Meh-koo-gee	Retaining Peg
4. *Tsuba*	Ts'ᵒᵒ-bah	Guard
5. *Saya*	Sah-yah	Scabbard
6. *Koiguchi*	Coy-goo-ch'ᵉᵉ	Mouth of the *Saya*
7. *Kojiri*	Koe-jee-ree	Butt of the *Saya*
8. *Sageo*	Sah-gay-oh	*Saya* Strings
9. *Ha* or *Shiraha*	Haw (She-rah-haw)	Blade
10. *Mine*	Mee-neh	Spine orBack of the Blade
11. *Kissaki*	Kees-sah-kee	Point
12. *Shinogi*	Shee-no-gee	Groove

These are the parts most frequently discussed throughout the instructional portions of this book, as well as the most often referred to during *dōjō* instruction.

Chapter 5

修行の順序

Shugyō no Junjō

Progression of Training

As you train in *iaijutsu*, you will pass through several stages of development in your progression from beginner to expert to master of the art. You may also reach physical and emotional plateaus, at which your progress may appear to slow or stop—or even decline. Understanding that such plateaus are a normal part of the training process will help you avoid allowing a setback or plateau to discourage you.

KETSUI O SURU

Make Up Your Mind

The first step in your journey is to *make up your mind*. You must decide to make your training a high priority in your life, not merely something you do for entertainment or a diversion whenever you lack something more interesting to do.

Martial arts practice, especially in a serious art like *iaijutsu,* is a lifestyle, not just an extracurricular activity. As you progress, the discipline and dedication of your training will set you apart. You will begin to approach all of life with a martial artist's outlook. Over time, your entire attitude and personality will evolve. But this kind of fundamental improvement of your character cannot occur without a strong determination to train, even when you don't feel like it—*especially* when you don't feel like it.

In Chapter Three we explained extensively the importance of making up your mind and of having *shinnen*—an unwavering determination—as the foundation for all your endeavors. Applying this knowledge now is the first step in your *iaijutsu* training.

KIHON O MANABU
Emphasize the Basics

There is always a great temptation, particularly for beginners, to learn the flashy, fancy, or difficult techniques of any art. It is natural for you to feel this way, especially if you have a desire to excel at *iaijutsu* and truly master it. However, your primary emphasis must be on the fundamentals, which are outlined in Chapter Seven.

It is true with any martial art that a practitioner who has truly mastered the basics will handily defeat one who has trained in advanced techniques after having only a cursory knowledge of the fundamentals. If you understand the nature of basic techniques, it is easy to see why this is universally true.

Basics are no more or less than the *ideal* technique, as it would be performed under ideal circumstances. Fundamentals demonstrate the perfect method of maximizing power, balance, self-protection, and effectiveness of technique. It is only after you have mastered performing under such ideal conditions that you can learn how to best adapt basic techniques to less-than-ideal circumstances.

It is also a mistake to assume that basics are only for beginners. Emphasis on fundamentals must be a lifelong habit. Anyone who has studied the lives of the great martial arts masters has observed that, without exception, they have shared a continuing passion for the improving their basics.

RIRON O SHIRU
Understand the Principles

As you study the fundamentals, it is not sufficient to merely master the body mechanics necessary to perform them with precision and power. To progress beyond the basics, you must understand the underlying principles which make them effective.

With such an understanding, you will then be able to apply the basics to intermediate and advanced techniques and make these techniques as effective and natural as your basics. Furthermore, with a deep understanding of the principles which make techniques effective, you can readily apply *iaijutsu* techniques to a real situation.

KAISŪ O KASANERU
Develop through Repetition

The objective of *iaijutsu* is to make the techniques natural—to make the sword simply another appendage of your body. Nothing becomes this natural without practice, which is another reason for *kihon o manabu*: emphasizing the basics. You must be certain you are developing *good* habits in your training; that you are reinforcing correct technique, not errors or sloppiness, through your countless repetition.

It can truly be said that the only difference between a novice and an expert is *the number of repetitions of technique.* A master is simply a novice who has practiced the techniques literally millions of times! His depth of character and his knowledge of the art came in the same fashion—endless repetition. Repeated practice not only develops the physical skills of the art, but also develops the mental attributes needed for mastery. You simply will not be able to train frequently and regularly for a prolonged period without developing both the physical skills and the mental attitudes—patience, persistence, fighting spirit, *Bushi no Me*, compassion, and *heijōshin*—of a martial arts master.

TAIRYOKU NI ŌJITE OKONAU
Different Strengths—Different People

Different people have different strengths and weaknesses. People learn faster or slower than others, have more or less innate athletic ability, and are in different stages of physical condition. All these things must be taken into account, because they can significantly affect the pace at which one is able to learn new skills.

The only fair and true measure of progress is *your* progress. It is not fair to compare yourself to others, either to yourself or them. Your body structure, learning ability, athletic prowess, age, maturity, and motivation are all vastly different from anyone else's, and your comparative rate of progress in learning *iaijutsu* will likewise be different.

You must also keep in mind how deceptively simple *iaijutsu* appears. Even people with years of training in other martial arts find *iaijutsu* movements difficult to master, because the body mechanics are so different. Paradoxically, while *iaijutsu* stresses the natural posture and movement of the body, it feels extremely unnatural for the first several months of training! It is important to begin your training with realistic expectations, so plan on training at least a year before feeling comfortable with the techniques.

In keeping with such realistic expectations, you should start your training slowly, concentrating on correct movement and easy, natural swinging of the sword, and gradually build up your speed and power. This not only prevents injuries from overtraining and overexertion, but allows your body to assimilate the correct sequence of muscle contractions and extensions before attempting to do them with power.

JISHIN NI TSUITE
Confidence

Just as there will be times during your training that you reach plateaus or encounter disappointments, there will also be times in which your performance really excels or you achieve significant triumphs. And, just as there is danger in allowing disappointment to cloud your perception of your progress, there is equal danger in becoming overconfident when your situation seems favorable.

Confidence is an important strength to possess. A *samurai* had to be confident, not only to face life-or-death battles, but to achieve *saya no naka ni kachi* ("victory while still in the scabbard") in all areas of life. But, confidence must also be realistic, balanced, and tempered with humility.

One of ancient Japan's most famous leaders was Takeda Shingen, who was not only a great general but a great philosopher. He firmly believed that the best fight was *no* fight, and very seldom provoked a conflict. However, between the years 1553 and 1564, one of his most tenacious adversaries, Uesugi Kenshin, engaged his army in no less than five major battles. Takeda's forces were always victorious and could easily have crushed Uesugi's army on several occasions. But Takeda carefully engineered his victories so they appeared to come by only a narrow margin, because he understood the danger of overconfidence.

In Takeda's view, the best victory was by a 60/40 margin—wide enough to allow for unexpected events, yet narrow enough to keep his troops aware of the possibility of defeat and therefore intensely focused. He felt that the closer to an absolute 100/0 victory he achieved, the more likely his warriors would become overconfident, leading to recklessness, lack of discipline, and *yudan*. For his first forty years, Takeda's goal in battle was to win, but as he matured as a commander, his perspective shifted to not losing, as we explained in detail in Chapter Two *(Budō no Arikata)*.

The same reasoning applies to overconfidence at the personal level. If we allow ourselves to become overconfident because of a few triumphs, we are likely to lose our strength of concentration and self-discipline and we will begin to decline rather than progress in our training.

JIGA NI TSUITE
Control Your Ego

It was consistent with Takeda Shingen's philosophy that he selected a wide variety of trees to grow in his garden. He had cherry trees so he could admire their blossoms in the spring, weeping willows to provide spreading shade in the heat of summer, maples to set his garden ablaze with color in the fall, and pines to add bright spots of greenery to the stark winter landscape.

He selected his twenty-four subordinate generals *(taishō)* in a similar manner. These men not only reported to him and controlled his troops in battle, but acted as his trusted advisors. Having risen to such positions of power and prestige, most men would surround themselves with snivelling "yes-men," but Takeda instead chose men of varied backgrounds and ideas, in order to get the very best and most creative advice possible. In addition to their having the courage to speak their minds frankly even if they felt he would not like to hear it, Takeda had five key criteria for selecting each of his generals: (1) they had to be good martial artists, (2) they had to possess deep compassion and understanding for people, (3) they had to exhibit extreme *reigi* (politeness and self-discipline), (4) they had to evidence *heijōshin* in their behavior, and (5) they had to have a resolute sense of loyalty.

In order to receive the best possible advice from this diverse group of leaders, Takeda had to be willing to accept blunt criticism of his own plans and ideas, even of his goals and motives. Furthermore, he was willing to listen to their suggestions because of their wisdom and sincerity, not necessarily because they were his friends or agreed with him. Few of us are truly willing to subject ourselves to this sort of scrutiny, especially when our egos have been enlarged by holding a position of any consequence or power. But to achieve our highest potential we must set our egotism aside and willingly listen to the voice of sincere, constructive criticism, whether it be from our *iaijutsu sensei* in the *dōjō* or our close family members and friends.

In fact, one of the best ways to make significant improvement in areas of personal character is to surround yourself with loving, compassionate friends or family members who are willing to examine your actions and hold you unflaggingly accountable for your personal growth. While this is often a painful ordeal, for most of us it is the only way we can build the resolve needed to tackle the really deep-rooted integrity issues in our lives.

Like Takeda Shingen, you must be extremely careful in your selection of the people who will hold you accountable. They do not all have to be martial artists, but they should all possess the compassion, discipline, *heijōshin,* and loyalty of Takeda's generals. And they must all love you enough to be willing to face you honestly and boldly, but with tenderness, and deal with your worst faults and failings even though to do so will usually be as painful for them as it is for you.

SHIN•KI•RYOKU
Mind•Spirit•Technique

When we presented the concept of *Shin•Ku•I* in Chapter Three, we showed how the mind is the key to self-control. The first topic in this chapter, as well, was making up your mind. There can be no question that the mind is the pivotal aspect of all martial arts training—all human endeavor, in fact. Once again, *Shin•Ki•Ryoku* points to mental focus as the core of *iaijutsu* technique.

Shin•Ki•Ryoku is used to signify that mind, spirit, and technique should be inseparable. But it is an even more refined than the notion of the three simply working together in harmony; it is the concept of technique being the *product* of the mind and spirit working together. For an analogy, think of your left hand as your mind and your right hand as your spirit. When the two hands slap together, the resulting clap is technique.

Thus, a goal of your training should be to so completely unite your mind and spirit that your body's movements are the instinctive and natural response to their combined workings.

DAI•KYŌ•SOKU•KEI
Big•Strong•Fast•Light

Dai•Kyō•Soku•Kei (Big•Strong•Fast•Light) best describes the proper sequence of training emphasis in *iaijutsu*. The progression from one to the next—from "big" to "strong" to "fast" to "light"—must not be forced. Instead, it must be the natural evolution of your skills, passing successively through each stage as you practice and improve.

Big: As a beginner, you should concentrate on the *big* features. This actually occurs in two forms. First, you should initially focus on correctly performing the big movements. Later, as your skill becomes more refined, you can emphasize the smaller details of the movements. This is much like the way a sculptor carves a statue: first shaping the general outline, then gradually refining it and only later delicately adding the tiny details. The second aspect is performing the movements in a "big" manner; that is, almost exaggerating the motions. This allows you to fully understand the mechanics of the techniques you are practicing. As your skill develops, you will strive to make the movements more compact.

Strong: It is difficult to swing powerfully until you first learn to swing correctly. So you should wait until you have developed consistency in performing the larger movements, before you attempt to develop *power* in the techniques. Once you are swinging the sword correctly, it is only a matter of practice until you develop strong technique.

Fast: The next stage is to increase the *speed* of your techniques. Once again, wait until you can perform the techniques properly and with power before trying to develop speed. Otherwise, you are likely to develop fast, sloppy, ineffective techniques instead.

Light: The final stage is to make your techniques *light.* As you reach a point of exercising *Shin•Ki•Ryoku* in which your mind and spirit together produce technique, your movements will become light and subtle. At this phase, you will have more speed and power than ever before—not as a result of body strength, but due to the refinement of your technique—yet you will appear to be moving effortlessly. Again, do not attempt to perform light techniques immediately; they will only be weak. Instead, the lightness must be the product of countless repetitions and diligent training, resulting in speed and power that appear effortless.

Each stage must be taken in order. If you attempt to skip a stage—from "Big" to "Strong," for instance—you will only end up compounding your errors. The technical skills that produce power are learned during the "Big" phase, so if you try to develop power by some other means, you wind up using muscle strength rather than proper technique, and this only compounds your errors.

"Big" and "Strong" are the only levels at which you can practice to improve. You can mentally concentrate on the "Big" movements, correcting the errors you notice, and you can consciously apply correct technique to increase the power of your movements. But "Fast" and "Light"—although they are achieved through practice—cannot be practiced. They are a by-product of repetition: the natural evolution of your training in the "Big" and "Strong."

SHU•HA•RI
Obey • Break • Separate

Shu•Ha•Ri is a term the Japanese use to describe the overall progression of martial arts training, as well as the lifelong relationship the student will enjoy with his or her instructor.

守 SHU

Shu can either mean "to protect" or "to obey." The dual meaning of the term is aptly descriptive of the relationship between a martial arts student and teacher in the student's early stages, which can be likened to the relationship of a parent and child. The student should absorb all the teacher imparts, be eager to learn and willing to accept all correction and constructive criticism. The teacher must guard the student in the sense of watching out for his or her interests and nurturing and encouraging his or her progress, much as a parent guards a child through its growing years. *Shu* stresses basics in an uncompromising fashion so the student has a solid foundation for future learning, and all students perform techniques in identical fashion, even though their personalities, body structure, age, and abilities all differ.

破 HA

Ha is another term with an appropriate double meaning: "to break free" or "to frustrate." Sometime after the student reaches *dan* ("black belt") level, he or she will begin to break free in two ways. In terms of technique, the student will break free of the fundamentals and begin to apply the principles acquired from the practice of basics in new, freer, and more imaginative ways. The student's individuality will begin to emerge in the way he or she performs techniques. At a deeper level, he or she will also break free of the rigid instruction of the teacher and begin to question and discover more through personal experience. This can be a time of frustration for the teacher, as the student's journey of discovery leads to countless questions beginning with "Why . . ." At the *"Ha"* stage, the relationship between student and teacher is similar to that of a parent and an adult child; the teacher is a master of the art, and the student may now be an instructor to others.

離 RI

Ri is the stage at which the student, now a *kōdansha* (high-ranking "black belt"), separates from the instructor having absorbed all that he or she can learn from them. This is not to say that the student and teacher are no longer associated. Actually, quite the opposite should be true; they should now have a stronger bond than ever before, much as a grandparent does with their son or daughter who is now also a parent. Although the student is now fully independent, he treasures the wisdom and patient counsel of the teacher and there is a richness to their relationship that comes through their shared experiences. But the student is now learning and progressing more through self-discovery than by instruction and can give outlet to his or her own creative impulses. The student's techniques will bear the imprint of his or her own personality and character. *Ri*, too, has a dual meaning, the second part of which is "to set free." As much as the student now seeks independence from the teacher, the instructor likewise must set the student free.

Shu•Ha•Ri is not a linear progression. It is more akin to concentric circles, so that there is *Shu* within *Ha* and both *Shu* and *Ha* within *Ri*. Thus, the fundamentals remain constant; only the application of them and the subtleties of their execution change as the student progresses and his or her own personality begins to flavor the techniques performed. Similarly, the student and teacher are always bound together by their close relationship and the knowledge, experience, culture, and tradition shared between them.

Ultimately, *Shu•Ha•Ri* should result in the student surpassing the master, both in knowledge and skill. This is the source of improvement for the art as a whole. If the student never surpasses his master, then the art will stagnate, at best. If the student never achieves the master's ability, the art will deteriorate. But, if the student can assimilate all that the master can impart and then progress to even higher levels of advancement, the art will continually improve and flourish.

SHINGI O OMONZURU
Stand for Righteousness

True martial arts and true martial artists are rooted in a tradition of righteousness. Martial arts are a means of preserving peace and overcoming ill intention. This foundation allows the martial artist to develop *shinnen,* an unflagging strength of conviction which is a powerful motivation.

In battle, however, the martial artist will often find himself pitted against *jadō* (literally, "the Way of Evil") embodied in those who hold to the belief that "all is fair in love and war." You may even encounter instructors whose teaching philosophy would condone such actions as kicking sand into the opponent's eyes to impair his vision while you strike, or similar ploys—no matter how underhanded—to gain an advantage. The true martial artist realizes that *jadō* is more than just unscrupulous fighting techniques. It inevitably degenerates into a perverse approach to life. In effect, this approach applies *Shin•Ku•I* in the negative: misdeeds influence one's speech and ideals, leading to increasingly hostile behavior and an amoral, utterly self-centered attitude.

In addition to its degenerative effects, *jadō* is also inherently weak. There are few people so depraved that their conscience does not bother them when they utilize some underhanded method to gain advantage. This restraining influence, however slight, prevents them from employing *shinnen,* so they cannot put their whole body and soul into their actions. On the other hand, the martial artist who is acting justly can wholeheartedly pursue any endeavor. *Shingi* (righteousness) is therefore an empowering influence, creating a moral imperative that lends not only mental strength, but—through *Ken Shin Ichi Nyō*—physical power as well.

SAIGO MADE EIZOKU SURU
Persist to the End

This chapter began with an exhortation for commitment: a challenge to *make up your mind* to train as a lifestyle. It ends with a similar admonition to *persist until the end.* Commitment and persistence are the beginning and end of all worthwhile human endeavors. Most simply and directly: **DON'T QUIT!**

To understand the importance of persistence, we need only to look at the common struggle to control bulging waistlines. The reason why diets fail and people almost always gain back the weight they lost (usually with a little extra thrown in for good measure), is that a diet—by definition—is only a short-term commitment. Diets are designed to accomplish one of three things: to last a certain amount of time, to lose a certain amount of weight, or to lose a certain amount of weight in a certain amount of time. Once this short-term goal is accomplished, the diet ends—by design.

The only weight-loss programs that ever succeed in the long run are nutritional lifestyle changes. This may sound like merely a semantic distinction, but it is not. A diet is temporary, but a nutritional lifestyle is permanent. Lifestyle changes are not dependent upon reaching a predetermined goal; they are lifelong commitments.

The same holds true for *iaijutsu* training. To succeed, you must make a lifelong commitment. Training is not just for a certain time or until you reach a certain goal. Always remember that *iaijutsu* is a method for perfection of character, not a fitness program.

If an accident or illness, or a drastic change in your life makes a cessation of training necessary or unavoidable, simply resolve that you will resume as soon as you are able. And then do it! Even if you stop training for five years due to some circumstance, you will not have quit if you eventually resume!

Also remember that there is more to *iaijutsu* than just swinging a sword. If an injury leaves you temporarily or even permanently unable to practice your techniques, you can still continue your training by applying *iaijutsu* principles to other areas of your life. You will probably find that you recover faster if you apply *iaijutsu* principles to your recovery process, whether it is recovering from a physical, emotional or even a financial setback.

Iaijutsu is training for life-or-death confrontation. To quit means death. Once you have decided to be an *iaijutsu* practitioner, *you cannot quit!*

Chapter 6

作法と礼法

Sa-Hō to Rei-Hō

Preparation and Etiquette

Preparation *(Sa-hō)* and etiquette *(Rei-hō)* are almost inseparable in the art of *iaijutsu,* since it is nearly impossible to define where one ends and the other begins.

It is likely that the formal etiquette of *iaijutsu* evolved from the incorporation of the *Ōmori-ryū Seiza Waza* into the art by Hayashi Rokudayū in the seventeenth century. The descriptions in this chapter are given in the order in which they would normally be practiced while preparing to perform *iaijutsu waza.*

The formalities of *iaijutsu* begin even before you enter the *dōjō.* Even the process of changing into your *hakama* should not only involve a transformation of your outer appearance but a concurrent transformation of your state of mind. By the time you finish tying the bow on the front of your *hakama,* you should have set aside all the concerns of everyday life in order to concentrate exclusively and intensely on your *iaijutsu* practice. When you pick up your sword, now clothed as a *samurai,* your training has already begun and you perform the first formality of swordsmanship.

TEITŌ

Carrying the Sword

It will seem to the beginner that even the smallest detail of *iaijutsu* is rigidly controlled, starting with something as simple as carrying the sword. But when you consider that an *iaijutsu* battle is won in the blink of an eye, you will realize that such details often meant the difference between life and death to the *samurai*.

Figure 6–1a

Figure 6–1b

When standing or walking prior to, or following, *iaijutsu* practice, the sword is normally held in the left hand at the left hip as shown in Figures 6–1a (front view) and 6–1b (side view).

Note (Figure 6–1a) that the sword is turned slightly outward from vertical (15 to 30 degrees), so the hand is held in a natural position.

As shown in Figure 6–1b, the *tsuka* is slightly higher than the *kojiri* to prevent the sword from falling from the scabbard.

To ensure that the sword remains in the scabbard, especially while moving, it is *extremely* important that the thumb remain hooked over the *tsuba* while holding and carrying the sword.

Posture is discussed in detail in Chapter Five. Generally, however, the body should be held erect but not stiff, with the shoulders relaxed. The head must be straight, but the chin not pulled in.

The left hand, gripping the *saya* just beneath the *tsuba*, should be resting against the body at the left hip with the elbow tucked in close to the body. The right hand is curled into a comfortably loose fist, and should rest along the right thigh.

The cords *(sageo)* are gripped between the index and middle fingers of the *left* hand (gripping the *sageo* in the right hand is done differently—see the "*Tōrei*" section beginning on page 71) to keep them from dangling loosely where they might catch on objects while moving. By gripping them between the index and middle fingers, they can be held securely while holding the *saya*, allowing the thumb to be latched over the *tsuba*.

This is the position in which the sword should be held when entering the *dōjō* to begin *iaijutsu* practice.

HAIREI

Bowing to the Dōjō/Founder

Immediately upon entering the *dōjō*, an *iaijutsu* student must show his respect for his training area and the founder or grandmaster of the style (as represented by his portrait on the wall) by bowing. This initial bow, called *hairei* ("bow of respect"), should be made in the direction of the founder or grandmaster's portrait. If there is no portrait in the *dōjō*, then bow facing an appropriate symbol of the *dōjō* such as its emblem, flag, *dōjō* shrine, or similar focal point.

The *hairei* bow begins from a standing position, with the sword held at the left hip as shown in Figure 6–2a at right.

The sword is transferred from the left hand to the right hand, turning it so the *tsuka* is to the rear of the body, as shown in Figure 6–2b.

Figure 6–2a

During this transfer, care must be taken to handle the *sageo* properly, pinning the cords (still looped) against the *saya* with the palm of the right hand, so they can be readily retrieved by the left hand when the sword is switched back to the left hand after the *hairei* bow is completed.

Notice the direction of the curvature of the *saya* in the photographs. In the proper position for *hairei*, the sharp edge of the sword is held downward, opposite from the correct position for drawing the sword. In addition, the *tsuka* is behind the right forearm, also making it difficult to draw. Since an attack cannot readily be initiated from this position, it is a proper position for demonstrating the deepest sincerity, trust, and respect.

Figure 6–2b

Figure 6–2c

As shown in Figure 6–2c, the bow is made from the hips only. The back, neck, and head remain straight. Do not lift the chin to look forward, but allow the head to tilt at the same angle as the upper body. Similarly, do not "peek" up when bowing, but allow the eyes to sight downward at the same angle as the head.

There is no prescribed duration for the *hairei* bow. The important factor is that the length and character of the bow reflect the sincerity of the student's respect. Even a long bow will be disrespectful if the student's posture and demeanor belie it as hypocritical.

SHIREI

Bowing to the Instructor

At the beginning of class, the students will all assemble facing the instructor in the *seiza* (kneeling/seated) position with their swords placed at their right sides, as shown in Figure 6–3a below.

Once again, posture is erect, with the shoulders and arms relaxed. The head is straight, but the chin is not tucked in. The hands rest naturally on the tops of the thighs.

As seen in Figure 6–3a, the sharp edge of the sword, revealed by the curvature of the *saya,* is facing toward the student. This would make the sword difficult to draw quickly and shows the student's respect and trust for the instructor.

Figure 6–3a

The *sageo* are neatly aligned along the outer curve of the *saya* and folded in half, so the ends rest close to the *kurikata* to which they are tied.

The instructor will give the command, *"Rei,"* and the students bow together toward the instructor *(shirei).*

To bow in the *seiza* position, first place the left hand on the floor with the thumb extended to form an "L" with the index finger. The tips of the thumb and index finger should align in the exact center between the knees. The right hand is placed in "mirror-image" with the left hand with the tips of the thumbs and index fingers touching to form a diamond shape.

The bow is again made from the waist, keeping the back and head straight. Do not allow the hips to rise when bowing in the *seiza* position.

The forehead does not touch the floor, but remains four to six inches above the floor, with the nose centered above the "diamond" formed by the thumbs and index fingers.

The longer the bow is held in this position, the more respect is shown to the instructor. It is always good manners to hold the bow until the instructor has bowed in return, then rise.

To rise, simply reverse the procedure for bowing. Straighten from the waist, being sure to keep the back and head straight. The right hand returns to the right thigh first, then the left hand returns, so you are once again in the posture shown in Figure 6–3a.

TŌREI

Bowing to the Sword

After bowing to the instructor, *iaijutsu* students show respect for their swords by bowing to them as well. The sword was the life of the *samurai*. Without it, he would surely perish in battle, and because of its grace, beauty, and strength the sword seemed to possess a spirit of its own to the *samurai*.

The *samurai*'s respect for his sword goes beyond mere appreciation, however. It more closely resembles the respect the American cowboys of the late nineteenth century had for their horses. At the end of a hard workday, bone-weary and choking on trail dust, the cowboy would unsaddle, curry, feed, and water his horse even before preparing his own well-deserved meal and resting from his labors. *That* was true respect!

There are many parallels between American cowboys and Japanese *samurai*. Without a stout horse, a cowboy might well find himself suffering a lonely, agonizing death by starvation on the vast prairie, so he did well to show his mount proper respect. He usually had a name for his horse, and treated it as a friend and partner. Similarly, a *samurai* depended upon his sword for his life

Figure 6-4a

Figure 6-4b

Figure 6-4c

and livelihood. Many named their swords and treated them as if they had a life of their own.

Perhaps one reason the cowboy and the *samurai* have come to hold such prominence in each of their respective cultures—and both continue to influence their cultures and philosophies to this day—is that both the *samurai* of feudal Japan and the Wild West cowboy developed such a similar appreciation for the fine line between life and death and how to cope with it. Those with an appreciation of western folklore, especially the famed "Code of the West," which had many similarities to the Code of *Bushidō*, may more readily understand the subtleties of *samurai* philosophy.

The *samurai* symbolizes his respect for his sword with the *tōrei* ("Bow to the Sword"). Since the *tōrei* is normally performed immediately after *shirei* at the beginning of a class or just prior to *shirei* at the end of class it will usually begin from the position shown in Figure 6-4a.

To begin the *tōrei* from the position shown in Figure 6-4a, catch up the *sageo* between the middle and ring fingers, using the index finger to hold the *tsuba,* and pick up the sword. Gently place the *kojiri* on the floor to the outside-front of the right knee as shown in Figure 6-4b, with the *saya* tilted back toward you at about a 45-degree angle.

From this point, carefully lay the sword down in front of you, perpendicular to the direction you are facing, as illustrated in Figure 6-4c.

The *tsuba* should be aligned with the outside of the left knee, and the sharpened edge of the sword should be toward you, as evidenced by the curvature of the *saya*.

Next, carefully arrange the *sageo* along the outer edge of the *saya*, so they extend about two-thirds the length of the sword, allowing them to double back from that point and cross the *saya*, as shown in Figure 6-4d.

By draping the ends of the *sageo* over the *saya*, they can more easily be grasped when picking up the sword after the *tōrei* bow is completed.

After arranging the *sageo*, straighten to *seiza* position with erect posture and hands resting on the thighs, looking straight ahead (Figure 6–4e).

Figure 6–4d

The *tōrei* bow is then performed almost exactly as the *shirei* bow. The first exception is that before moving the hands, look at the sword, *then* place the left hand on the floor in front of the sword, followed by the right hand, and bow from the waist, as shown in Figure 6–4f.

Once again, the duration of the bow is a benchmark of the sincerity of your respect for the sword with which you are training, so be certain your demeanor reflects genuine respect from your heart.

As you rise from *tōrei*, your eyes should be gazing straight ahead once again in the manner depicted in Figure 6–4e.

Figure 6–4e. *Seiza* Posture

It is also common to perform *tōrei* from a standing position. This is done, for example, when first picking up the sword to prepare for practice, or when removing the sword after *waza* practice in order to use a *bokken* or *jō* for a portion of class.

A standing *tōrei* begins at "attention," with the feet together and erect posture. The *sageo* should be looped between the middle and ring finger of the right hand and the right index finger should be hooked over the *tsuba* to be sure the sword does not slide from its *saya*. Raise the sword to about shoulder level so it rests on the upturned palms of both hands. As depicted in Figure 6–4g, the left hand should be positioned near the *kojiri* (end of the *saya*), and eyes looking directly at the sword.

Figure 6–4f

From this position, bow from the waist, again keeping the back and neck straight, until your forehead is about level with the sword. This position is shown in

Figure 6–4g. Start of Standing *Tōrei*

Figure 6–4h. End of Standing *Tōrei*

Figure 6–4h at left.

As before, the duration of your bow and your attitude while performing it are an indication of the sincerity of your respect. It is disrespectful to treat this bow as a begrudging duty rather than an opportunity to express heartfelt appreciation.

TAITŌ

Wearing the Sword

In one way of thinking, the completion of *tōrei* and placing the sword in position for practice marks the delineation between *Reihō* (etiquette) and *Sahō* (preparation). However, proper etiquette is a vital part of preparation for training. After all, in *iaijutsu,* as with every true martial art, *"Rei ni hajimari, rei ni owaru"* ("Everything begins and ends with respect"). So, just as respect is an integral part of preparation, proper preparation is part of respect. Although we try to make a distinction between *Sahō* and *Reihō* for instructional purposes, in practice the two are nearly indistinguishable.

Figure 6–5a

Once *tōrei* has been completed from the *seiza* position, use the right hand to grasp the *sageo* between the middle- and ring-fingers (Figure 6–5a) and run the hand along the *saya* to the *tsuba* (Figure 6–5b). Grasp the *saya,* hooking the right index finger over the *tsuba.*

Pick up the sword and stand it straight up in front of you with the *kojiri* resting on the floor, centered between your knees (Figure 6–5c). The curve of the *saya* (denoting the sharp edge of the blade) should be facing toward you.

Figure 6–5b

Once in this position, you should be looking *past* the sword to your training partner, instructor, or any other person who is facing you.

While still looking beyond the sword, reach forward with the left hand, touching the *saya* with your fingertips at a point about one-third the distance from the *kojiri* to the *saya* (Figure 6–5d), then run your left hand down to the *kojiri*.

Lift the *kojiri* slightly off the floor with your left hand, then pull it unhurriedly toward your left hip, as you allow the *tsuka* to tilt forward in your right hand.

Figure 6–5c

Figure 6–5d

Once the *tsuka* has reached your left hip, use your left hand to insert the *kojiri* into your *obi* near your left side (Figure 6–5e). Do not insert the *kojiri* at the hip, but instead at the front left side of your body. The *kojiri* should be inserted only under the first winding of the *obi*, rather than between the *obi* and *iaidō-gi*.

It is also very important not to "stir" the *tsuba* around while inserting it. It is acceptable to move the left hand considerably while inserting the *kojiri*, but the right hand should remain as still as possible.

Figure 6–5e

Once the left hand has manipulated the *kojiri* between the layers of the *obi*, use the right hand to push the sword through, so it emerges at the left hip, while pulling the *saya* with the left hand.

The sword is fully inserted when the *tsuba* is directly in front of the navel, jutting about one foot in front of the body, as shown in Figure 6–5f. Use the left hand to take the *sageo* from the right hand and drape them over the *saya* at the point where it emerges from the *obi* at the left hip.

When the sword is completely in place, lower both hands to the thighs as shown in Figure 6–5f. You are now ready to begin *iaijutsu* practice.

Figure 6–5f

TACHI REI

Standing Bow

Under less formal circumstances, such as when changing partners during practice, a standing bow *(tachi rei)* can be performed for expediency while simply holding the sword at the hip. From a normal standing posture, holding the sword as described under *Teitō* earlier in this chapter, bow forward from the hips, as shown in Figure 6–6a, keeping the back and neck straightly aligned.

It is very important to keep the left thumb hooked over the tsuba during *tachi rei* to prevent the sword from sliding out of the saya while you bow.

Figure 6–6a. *Tachi Rei*

DATTŌ

Removing the Sword

Once you have completed *iaijutsu* practice, you will return to the formal *seiza* position. There are similar formalities at the conclusion of practice to those performed prior to practice, and these are of utmost importance, since they are again a reflection of the respect and dedication of the practitioner.

Removal of the sword at the conclusion of practice is performed in nearly the reverse of the procedure for *taitō,* or wearing the sword.

Beginning from the *seiza* posture, as shown in Figure 6–7a, grasp the *sageo* between the index and middle fingers of the left hand and remove them from behind the *saya.* With a small circular motion of the left hand form a loop with the *sageo* as you pass them to the right hand, gripping them between the middle and ring fingers of the right hand. The right hand then grasps the *saya* near the *tsuba,* with the index finger hooked

Figure 6–7a

over the *tsuba* to secure it in place, and the left hand returns to the left hip.

While the left hand remains at the hip, as though preventing the *obi* from snagging on the *saya* while it is removed, the right hand pulls the *saya* toward the right-front of the body, as shown in Figure 6–7b.

Figure 6–7b

The right hand then tilts the *tsuka* back toward the body, swinging the *kojiri* outward beyond the right knee, where it is carefully placed on the floor, as shown in Figure 6–7c at right.

Gently lay the *saya* on its side in front of you, with the *tsuba* aligned with the outside of your left knee, as shown in Figure 6–7d, and straighten the *sageo* along its outer edge, draping them across the *saya* about two-thirds the distance from the *tsuba* to the *kojiri* (Figure 6–7e).

Figure 6–7c

Straighten, with your eyes looking straight ahead, not at the sword, then perform *tōrei* in the manner described previously (Figure 6–7f).

As always, the duration of your bow is a reflection of the sincerity and depth of your respect for your sword. This fact bears frequent repetition, as it is too often overlooked in martial arts today.

The measure of your respect should not be the value or condition of your sword. Even if your sword is of low quality and minimal commercial value, it is *your* sword. It is the sword with which you train. It is the

Figure 6–7d

sword which you are using to reshape your mind, your values, and your character. For that reason, if no other, it merits your deep and heartfelt respect regardless of its cost or condition!

Figure 6–7e

Figure 6–7f

Figure 6–7g

Figure 6–7h

Figure 6–7i

In a formal class, this *tōrei* would be followed by bowing to the instructor *(shirei)*. In such cases, the instructor will clearly indicate that this is to be the case and it will only be necessary to follow his lead or directions. Refer to the preceding description of *shirei* for a review of this procedure.

Upon rising from *tōrei*, use the right hand to grasp the *sageo* between the middle and ring fingers (as in Figure 6–7e) running the hand along the *saya* to the *tsuba*, then grasp the *saya*, with the index finger hooked over the *tsuba* (see Figure 6–7d), and raise the sword, placing the *kojiri* on the floor, centered between your knees as shown in Figure 6–7g at left.

From this position, take the *sageo* in your left hand, between the index and middle fingers, as you grasp the *saya* with the thumb hooked over the *tsuba*, then hold the sword at your left hip, just as if you were standing upright (see *Teitō* described at the beginning of this chapter).

Rise to your feet by first raising the right foot, then the left foot. If necessary (but avoid this if possible), you may press your right hand against your right knee for assistance in rising. However, *never* use the sword as a crutch to assist you in rising. It is better to fall down than to disgrace your sword in this manner!

As you rise, bring the feet together by drawing the left foot *forward* to the right foot. Although it may seem easier at first, *do not* step back with the right foot, as this can be taken as a sign of timidity unbecoming a *samurai*.

If you have been practicing with a partner, or if an observer or audience has been watching your practice, or if you were not instructed to perform *shirei* to your *sensei* at the close of class, it is customary to perform *hairei* immediately upon standing.

As shown in Figure 6–7h, transfer your sword to your right hand, as described in detail in the earlier section discussing *hairei* in detail, and bow in the manner shown in Figure 6–7i.

Having performed *hairei* to your partner or any observer (unless practicing alone, in which case *hairei* is unnecessary), you are ready to leave the training area.

Turning your back on an observer would be disrespectful, and turning your back on your training partner is not only disrespectful, but could be construed as an insult by implying that your partner's sword skills are not worthy of your concern. For this reason, even if you were training alone, walk backwards to the edge of the training area. Be certain to make your first backward step with your left foot (since a right-foot-forward stance facilitates drawing the sword and makes you less vulnerable to attack).

When you reach the edge of the training area, perform a standing bow with your sword held at the left hip (see Figure 6–7j), then walk to the *dōjō* exit. Before you leave the *dōjō*, turn and again bow in the direction of the *dōjō* emblem, shrine, or other suitable focal point as your final gesture of respect before exiting.

If, for any reason, you did not perform *tōrei* at the conclusion of your practice while in the *seiza* position, you should always give due respect to your sword before changing out of your *hakama* and leaving the *dōjō*.

In such cases, before putting your sword away, raise it in your hands as shown in Figure 6–7k below and perform a standing *tōrei*. (For details on handling and holding the sword for standing *tōrei*, please refer to the description earlier in this chapter.)

The more you perform the formalities of *iaijutsu*, the more profoundly you will understand and appreciate the depth of respect that is inherent to the *sahō* and *reihō* of this art. In addition to the outward expressions of respect performed during *hairei*, *shirei*, and *tōrei*, the very actions of *sahō* themselves—the painstaking handling of the sword during *teitō*, *taitō*, and *dattō*—are suffused with respect. The time and attention we pay to these seemingly insignificant details of ritual, and the degree of sincere devotion we give these actions, are themselves gestures of respect, in much the same way that "quality time" with someone is an expression of our love or respect for them.

Figure 6–7j
Standing Bow

So avoid the temptation to rush through the *sahō* and *reihō* in order to begin the "fun" part of your training. Take the time to appreciate your

Figure 6–7k

sword, your *dōjō*, your teacher, and your fellow students. As you mature in your training, you will discover that it is some of the most enriching time you will spend. By learning the true meaning of respect and practicing it on a daily basis, you will find that the respect you develop for your sword, your *dōjō*, your teacher, and your fellow students will increase the amount of respect you have for yourself.

You will also find that the time you spend cultivating respect through the depth and sincerity of your *reihō* will reap great rewards by improving your personal relationships. As you learn to take the time to demonstrate your respect and appreciation, these attributes will carry over from the *dōjō* into your personal life. There it will manifest itself in your desire and ability to invest time in the people you care about, and help solidify those relationships you hold most dear.

Chapter 7

基本

Kihon

Fundamentals

Kihon, or Fundamentals, are those attributes that underlie all *Eishin-Ryū* techniques. Once you have mastered the fundamentals, it will be far easier to apply them to the performance of *waza*. Generally, these fundamentals are grouped into categories of related items, but since their functions are all interrelated, it is impossible to completely separate them from each other. In this chapter we will first explain the major actions used in *iaijutsu*: *tsuka no nigiri kata* ("gripping the sword"), *nukitsuke* ("drawing cut"), *furikaburi* ("raising"), *kirioroshi* ("downward cut"), *chiburi* ("shaking blood off"), and *nōtō* ("resheathing").

After describing the key elements of these major actions, we will review the general principles that maximize their effectiveness, such as *shisei* (posture), *kamae* (stance), *kokyū* (breathing), *chakugan* (eye contact), *maai* (distance), *kihaku* (focus and power), and *zanshin* (spirit), and relate how these principles affect the physical actions and techniques.

The importance of *kihon* cannot be overemphasized. Without sound fundamentals—all working together flawlessly—you will not be able to perform *iaijutsu techniques* or *waza* with grace and precision. Furthermore, from a practical standpoint, until you have truly mastered the fundamentals, you will not be unable to generate sufficient power, control, and accuracy to actually cut effectively.

Part I—Major Actions

The major actions involved in *iaijutsu* techniques are presented here in the same order in which they would usually be performed.

TSUKA NO NIGIRI KATA
Gripping the Handle

Fundamentals begin with correctly gripping the sword. Without a proper grip, you will be unable to draw or swing the sword correctly, so the grip is the most fundamental aspect of *iaijutsu* basics.

The right hand is placed in front, gripping the *tsuka* just behind the *fuchi-gane* (the fitting directly behind the *tsuba).* This leaves the thumb and index finger about three-quarters-inch away from the *tsuba—not* pressed up against the *tsuba* as many beginners suppose. The groove between the thumb and forefinger rests along the top of the *tsuka* and the middle knuckles of the fingers are aligned on the bottom of the *tsuka.*

Figure 7–1a: Grip, Side View

The left hand is aligned in identical fashion approximately the width of one finger behind the right hand. The correct grip with both hands is shown in Figure 7–1b, below.

As the sword is swung downward to cut, both hands squeeze together, twisting slightly inward toward the center as if wringing out a twisted wet towel. This motion, called *tsuka no nigiri kata* ("wringing the handle"), tightens the grip while the blade is moving and helps ensure that it travels straight downward.

Figure 7–1b: Grip, Top View

NUKITSUKE
Drawing Cut

The dominant characteristic of *iaijutsu,* the element which makes the art unique and distinctive, is that the first movement—drawing the sword from its scabbard—also simultaneously cuts the opponent. This technique, called *nukitsuke,* is referred to as "The Life of *Iaidō*" because, quite literally, life hangs in the balance. If this first cutting stroke is successful, the *samurai* has assured his victory; if not, the advantage will almost certainly shift to his opponent.

With some fifty-two *kata* or, more correctly, *waza* (techniques) in the *Eishin-ryū* system, there are a large number of *nukitsuke* variations. Some are designed to strike level during the draw, others upward or downward, and still others block the opponent's first strike, then counterattack in a single, fluid motion that is all but unstoppable. All of these, however, work on the same basic principles, so only the most basic—the level drawing-cut—will be described in this chapter.

Nukitsuke begins from the preparatory posture, either kneeling seated *(seiza),* semi-seated *(tatehiza)* or standing *(tachi),* depending upon the technique being employed. Since it is the most fundamental posture, *seiza* will be used in this description of *nukitsuke.*

Both hands move simultaneously toward the *tsuka.* In *shoden* (initial level) techniques (Chapter Eight), the left hand encircles the *saya* with the thumb uppermost, near the *koiguchi* slightly before the right hand touches the *tsuka.* Just as the right hand begins to grasp the *tsuka,* the left thumb presses almost imperceptibly forward against the edge of the *tsuba,* pushing it about one half-inch forward. Since the *habaki* usually fits quite snugly into the *koiguchi,* this loosens the sword from the scabbard to ensure a smooth and fast draw. This subtle yet essential movement is called *koiguchi no kiri kata* ("opening the *koiguchi*"). A side view of the hands performing *koiguchi no kiri kata* is shown in Figure 7–2a.

In addition to this basic method of *koiguchi no kiri kata,* there are two variations. One alternative

Figure 7–2a: Begin Draw

is to keep the tip of the thumb hidden behind the *tsuba,* pushing against the flat of the *tsuba,* rather than its outer edge. This hides the movement from the opponent and may delay his reaction a few precious tenths of a second. This stealth variation, called *uchi-giri,* is actually the preferred method in *Eishin-Ryū,* with the more noticeable version *(soto-giri)* being used only in the *Shoden Waza* (Chapter Eight).

The second variation does not use the thumb at all. With the left hand wrapped around the *saya,* very close to the *koiguchi,* the hand is simply squeezed tight, which broadens the hand sufficiently so that the sides of the thumb and index finger press the *tsuba* forward, resulting in *koiguchi no kiri kata.* This variation would normally be employed in a situation in which you were uncertain of your opponent's intentions, but you want an advantage if they are found to be hostile. In this way, the left hand can open the *koiguchi* completely unnoticed, while the right hand remains away from the sword, thus giving no apparent signs of threat. Whenever a *samurai* made an overt *koiguchi no kiri kata,* it signalled hostility to his opponent and nearly always resulted in a preemptive counterattack—an act which this disguised movement would not provoke.

Figure 7–2b
Half Drawn

Just as *koiguchi no kiri kata* is completed, the right hand grasps the *tsuka,* with the middle knuckles aligned along the upturned ridge of the *tsuka.* Initially, the grip is loose, with only the fingers and thumb in contact with the *tsuka* as the drawing motion begins. The right hand pulls the sword from the *saya* while the left hand draws the *saya* back. This dual motion has the effect of nearly doubling the speed of the draw. It is crucial that the right hand guides the *tsuka-gashira* directly toward the opponent's eyes (Figure 7–2b) during the first two-thirds of the drawing motion, preventing the opponent from seeing exactly how much of the sword has been drawn and thus throwing off his timing for a block or counterattack.

Figure 7–2c
Fully Drawn

As the *kissaki* leaves the *saya* both hands twist 90 degrees counterclockwise and the fingers of the right hand tighten into a normal (one-handed) grip, snapping the sword free and causing it to swing forward level to the ground, cutting the opponent (Figure 7–2c).

Your *feeling* while performing *nukitsuke* is extremely important. It should not feel like two separate but linked functions: drawing the sword and cutting the opponent at the end of the movement. Instead, it should have the feeling of one movement, the sole purpose of which is cutting the opponent; drawing the sword is merely a by-product of this cutting motion.

FURIKABURI
Raising the Sword

Figure 7–3b:
Bent Elbow

Once the sword is drawn, and the first cutting motion is complete, the sword is raised overhead in preparation for the powerful, downward finishing cut. This raising of the sword, called *furikaburi,* is performed in a manner which affords the best combination of speed and protection against attack.

With the sword still level from *nukitsuke* (edge toward opponent), the *kissaki* is swung backward by first turning the right wrist. This action should feel as if you are trying to poke yourself in the left ear with the *kissaki.*

As your bent wrist reaches the limit of its range of flexibility, your elbow should then begin to bend, as shown in Figure 7–3b. The motion must remain smooth and uninterrupted until the *tsuba* is directly in front of your nose.

From the position shown in Figure 7–3b, the sword is raised directly overhead. The left hand raises at the same time, so that it grips the sword the instant it has reached the fully raised position shown in Figure 7–3c.

At this point, the sword should be about level with the ground. It is permissible for the *kissaki* to be lower than the *tsuba,* but it should not be higher since this will reduce swinging power and speed.

Figure 7–3c: Side View

Figure 7–3c:
Front View

KIRIOROSHI
Downward Cut

With the sword raised overhead, you are now poised for *kirioroshi*. Although *nukitsuke* is "The Life of *Iaidō*," it does not always inflict a fatal wound but gains the extra few moments a *samurai* needed to execute a killing technique. Also, *nukitsuke* is only effective on the first opponent, so another technique is needed to deal with situations involving multiple opponents. This technique, *kirioroshi* (also called *kirikudashi* in an alternate reading of the same *kanji),* is instantly fatal if performed correctly, since it slices from the top of the skull all the way down to the navel.

Figure 7–4a
Furikaburi

While this may conjure brutal images, it is not only necessary for self-defense, but—equally important to the *samurai*—it was an act of respect and compassion for his enemy. The safest way to win a sword battle is to cut the adversary's arm. Wounded, the opponent cannot wield his sword and will either bleed to death or succumb later to infection. However, to allow a foe to die in such an ignominious manner would be highly disrespectful. A *samurai*, after all, lived for *giri* (duty and honor). To lose his ability to serve his master or to die pitifully ravaged by gangrene would be the ultimate shame to himself and his family. On the other hand, to die at the hands of a master swordsman, serving his lord proudly and making the supreme sacrifice, would bring only honor to his memory. Thus, the *samurai*'s goal in a sword battle was to dispatch his enemy as quickly and painlessly as possible, both as a matter of self-preservation and out of respect for an honorable foe. The surest way of accomplishing this is *kirioroshi*.

Kirioroshi begins with the sword raised at the completion of *furikaburi* (see Figure 7–4a).

Figure 7–4b
Half Swing

As the sword is swung forward and down, the arms and wrists straighten and reach full extension at a point just above the target, as shown in Figure 7–4b.

At the point of impact (Figure 7–4b), the blade is turned upward at about a 45-degree angle. From this point, it completes the cut by following the natural downward arc of your hands as they drop to waist level (Figure 7–4c).

Figure 7–4c
Front View

Figure 7–4c
Side View

The sword completes *kirioroshi* when the hands reach waist height. At this point, the sword is almost level, with the *kissaki* only slightly lower than the base of the *tsuba*. When *kirioroshi* is performed kneeling (as shown in Figure 7–4c), the *tsuba* is aligned with the front of the knee, and the *tsuka* is at thigh level. When standing, *kirioroshi* is completed at precisely the same point, but the knee and thigh are not available as handy reference points. Instead, the *tsuka* will be at or just below belly-button level and the *tsukagashira* will be about six inches in front of the body.

No muscle strength is involved in making the sword cut; it is purely a matter of technique. In Japanese, all of the technical aspects of cutting are collectively referred to as *te no uchi* ("inside the hands").

TE NO UCHI
Cutting Technique

The objective of *kirioroshi,* and all other cutting techniques, is to make the blade *slice*—not hit—the target, so the blade must travel straight and cut completely through the target. A *samurai* cannot afford to get his sword wedged in an opponent's body. The time it takes to work it free might easily cost him his life!

The first way to ensure a straight cut is to be certain the blade does not wiggle as it swings downward. This is called *hasuji o tōsu.* Proper *tsuka no nigiri*

Figure 7–5a
Half Swing

Figure 7–5b
Kirioroshi

kata is one important way to keep the sword traveling straight. A correct grip, as previously described, with the hands close together and tightening inward as the sword swings downward, reduces the degree to which the blade can waggle from side to side. To completely eliminate shimmy in the sword, be certain both hands swing in exactly the same line.

In addition to a proper grip and straight alignment of the hands while swinging the sword, the key to cutting technique is *enshin-ryoku,* or centripetal force. The Japanese *katana* is, without question, the finest sword ever produced by human hands. It was painstakingly designed to slice perfectly if swung correctly, so it is only necessary to guide the sword to the target and let it do the job for which it was designed!

By snapping the arms and wrists forward so they reach full extension just above the target, the cutting section *(mono-uchi)* of the sword reaches a high velocity just before impact (Figure 7–5a). From there, the weight of the sword and its natural path of follow-through will cause it to slice effortlessly downward.

A simple exercise for practicing correct cutting technique is to swing the sword in a half-cut, stopping at the point shown in Figure 7–5a, then raise the sword overhead again and make a full cut, finishing as shown in Figure 7–5b.

By repeating this half-swing/full-swing, you will develop a habit of reaching full extension just above the target and allowing your arms to fall naturally to the finishing position. If your sword has a *shinogi* (blood groove), you will hear a loud and very satisfying *swoosh* when you swing the blade correctly.

CHIBURI

Blood Removal

At the completion of each *iaijutsu* technique, a movement is performed which is designed to remove the opponent's blood from the blade before it is resheathed. This movement is called *chiburi,* and there are three basic types: "wet umbrella," "flicking," and "dripping."

The type of *chiburi* most beginners will encounter first is the "wet umbrella" method *(kasa no shizuku o harao),* which gets its name from its resemblance to flinging the water from a wet umbrella. This style of *chiburi* is found in most of the *seiza waza,* the first techniques usually taught to beginners.

After completing *kirioroshi* (Figure 7–6a), the left hand releases the *tsuka* and the sword is drawn slowly to the right side, keeping the arm relatively straight and rotating the blade one-quarter turn clockwise so the edge is forward by the time the *kissaki* is pointing directly out from the right side, as shown in Figure 7–6b. The left hand simultaneously returns to the left hip, cradling the *koiguchi* in the web between the thumb and forefinger.

In a continuous motion, the sword is raised toward the head until the *tsuka* is directly in front of the forehead (see Figure 7–6c). The fingers grip the *tsuka* loosely, allowing the sword to tilt down and away from the body at about a 45-degree angle.

From this point, the blade is swung counterclockwise, using the sudden tightening of the right hand to snap it sharply downward, completing the motion as shown in Figure 7–6d. The *kissaki* should finish about in line with the outside of the right foot. The right hand should be about a foot ahead of the body and no more than a foot to the right of the right hip.

Figure 7–6a
Kirioroshi

Figure 7–6b
Pointing Right

Figure 7–6c
Held High

Figure 7–6d
Blade Down

Figure 7–6e
Kirioroshi

Figure 7–6f
"Flick"

Figure 7–6g
Kirioroshi

Figure 7–6h
Tilted Blade

The most common type of *chiburi* is the "flicking" method *(katana o kaesu)*. This method is used in most of the *tatehiza* and *tachiwaza*, which are normally taught to intermediate and advanced students. It is also frequently referred to as *Eishin-Ryū chiburi,* since it was originated by Hasegawa Eishin when he adapted *iaijutsu* to the shorter swords of modern design.

At the completion of *kirioroshi,* the fingers of the left hand are loosened, with the exception of the little finger which remains hooked tightly around the *tsuka* (Figure 7–6e).

With a snap of the wrist, the right hand twists the blade one-quarter turn counterclockwise on its longitudinal axis, while the hooked little finger of the left hand tugs in the opposite direction as the left hand pulls away.

At the completion of this motion (Figure 7–6f), the right hand has snapped outward a few inches and is still level with its starting point, and the *kissaki* has not moved appreciably from its original spot. The left hand has darted back to the left hip and cradles the *koiguchi* in the web between the thumb and forefinger.

The "dripping" method of *chiburi, chi no shizuku o otosu,* is used occasionally in both *seiza* and *tachiwaza,* and it is most likely to be the third type encountered by most students. In this method, after the completion of the final cut (Figure 7–6g), the blade is tilted at about a 45-degree angle and rested against the right outer thigh as shown in Figure 7–6h.

NŌTŌ

Resheathing

Nōtō is the act of returning the sword to its *saya* at the completion of a technique. Since *iaijutsu* always begins with the sword in its scabbard, no *waza* is truly completed until the sword has been resheathed so that another technique can be begun.

Nōtō begins at the point at which *chiburi*—regardless of which style is used—ends. The method of *nōtō* described in this chapter is that which is performed in connection with the *Shōden Waza*. Since the basic motion is the same for *Chūden* and *Okuden Waza*, the variations in *nōtō* will be pointed out in the chapters describing those *waza*.

Figure 7–7a
Blade Down

Regardless of whether the *waza* concludes with a "wet umbrella" (as in Figure 7–7a) or "flicking" (as in Figure 7–7b) *chiburi, nōtō* is essentially the same in either case.

While the sword is still positioned as shown in either Figure 7–7a or 7b, the left hand envelopes the *koiguchi* so that the *koiguchi* itself is one-quarter to one-half inch inside the hand. Thus, the aperture between the thumb and forefinger form an extension of the *koiguchi*. This opening should be made as narrow as possible to ensure that the *kissaki* drops directly into the *koiguchi* during *nōtō*.

Once the left hand has grasped the *koiguchi* in this fashion, the blade is swung to the left side—in a broad motion, almost exaggerated in *Shōden Waza*—and positioned edge-upward along the left forearm, from the crook of the elbow to the web between the thumb and index finger, as shown in Figure 7–7c.

The sword is then drawn forward with the *mine* sliding across the crease between the thumb and forefinger, as the left hand pulls simultaneously back. This motion should be timed so that just as the *saya* is

Figure 7–7b
Flick

Figure 7–7c
Blade Resting

Figure 7–7d
Kissaki Dropping

Figure 7–7e
Finished

Figure 7–7f
Hand at *Kashira*

Figure 7–7g
Dripping

Figure 7–7h
Palm Down

tilted nearly vertical by the rearward motion of the left hand, the *kissaki* passes the web between the thumb and forefinger and drops into the *koiguchi* (see Figure 7–7d).

At this point the motion of the two hands is reversed, so the left hand pushes the *saya* forward while the right hand pushes the sword inside. This dual motion should be timed so that the *tsuba* meets the left hand directly in front of the navel about a foot away from the body, as shown in Figure 7–7e.

Once the *habaki* has been fully inserted into the *saya*, the left thumb hooks over the *tsuba* to secure it in place and the right hand slides along the *tsuka* to the *tsuka-gashira* (Figure 7–7f), where it remains until the very end of the *waza*.

The single notable variation of *nōtō* is used in connection with the "drip" method of *chiburi*. This variation of *nōtō* begins after holding the position depicted in Figure 7–7g for several seconds to represent most of the blood having dribbled from the blade.

The right hand is then inverted, so that it holds the *tsuka* palm-down, as shown in Figure 7–7h.

The sword is then swung to the left side—again in an almost exaggerated motion—and positioned edge-upward along the left forearm from the crook of the elbow to the web between the thumb and index finger, this time with the right hand in reverse position (see Figure 7–7i).

This time, as the sword is drawn forward, with the *mine* sliding across the

Figure 7–7i	Figure 7–7j	Figure 7–7k	Figure 7–7l
Blade Resting	*Kissaki* Dropping	Finished	Hand at *Kashira*

crease between the thumb and forefinger and the left hand pulling simultaneously back, the body turns about 45 degrees to the right. This motion should be timed so that just as the *saya* is tilted nearly vertical by the rearward motion of the left hand and the *kissaki* drops into the *koiguchi,* the body is again facing directly forward, as shown in Figure 7–7j.

Again, the motion of the two hands is reversed at this point, although the right hand remains in an inverted position while the left hand pushes the *saya* forward and the right hand pushes the sword inside. This motion should also be timed so that the *tsuba* meets the left hand directly in front of the navel about a foot away from the body, as shown in Figure 7–7k.

After the *habaki* has been fully inserted into the *saya,* the left thumb hooks over the *tsuba* to secure it in place and the right hand slides along the *tsuka* to the *tsuka-gashira* just as before, remaining there (Figure 7–7l) until the very end of the *waza.*

Part II—General Principles

Like any art, *iaijutsu* is experiential by nature. Many elements of it simply cannot be understood except through practice and actually *feeling* and *experiencing* what is meant. Therefore, most attempts at explanation often sound at first like a *koan,* one of those annoying, self-contradictory parables for which Zen monks became famous. If you find any of these explanations frustrating in that way, we suggest that you simply *try* what is stated and keep the paradox in mind while you practice. With time, we are certain that you will come to experience and understand what we mean.

It is impossible to present the general principles outlined in this section in order of importance, since they are all of equal importance in terms of their contribution to effective *iaijutsu* technique. Nor can they be explained in order of use, since they all occur simultaneously during the performance of *iaijutsu waza*. Instead, we have tried to present them in the order in which they might naturally become apparent to the beginning *iaijutsu* student.

SHISEI
Posture

Since each *iaijutsu* technique is begun by assuming a sitting, crouching, or standing posture, this subject is a logical starting point to review the general principles of *iaijutsu* technique.

The basic rule of posture is to remain erect and natural. For most of us, this is already a contradiction in terms, since slouching or slumping has become "natural" to us. The body must be held erect and alert, but this carriage must not be forced or artificial. The neck and back of the head should be in a straight line with the spinal column, but with the chin not tucked in. This is definitely a paradox, since the back of the head cannot be truly straight unless the chin is, in fact, tucked in. Again, what is meant by this admonition is that a happy medium must be found, so that the head is held high with the neck and back straightly aligned, yet the chin is not tucked so far in as to cause a double or triple chin.

In the simplest terms it means to sit straight when sitting, and stand tall when standing. If you can do this and still remain relaxed, then you are on the right track. It is especially important for beginners to avoid muscle tension in the shoulders. In the awkwardness of trying to perform *iaijutsu* techniques the first several times, it is quite common to tense and raise the shoulders in an effort to maintain better control over the sword, which often seems to have developed a mind of its own. This tension will usually throw off the balance and cause the arms to swing unnaturally, robbing the body of power and causing the sword to waggle while moving.

Until the basic movements of *iaijutsu* begin to feel natural and comfortable, it often helps to make a conscious effort at the beginning of every technique to relax and lower the shoulders.

This upright yet relaxed bearing is maintained in every aspect of *iaijutsu*, from the time you assume a preparatory position for performing a technique until you rest after completing the technique. Figure 7–8a depicts correct posture while seated in the *seiza* position, and Figure 7–8b shows proper standing posture.

Figure 7–8a
Seiza Shisei

Shisei is of greatest importance while you are moving during *iaijutsu waza*. Much of your power and correct swinging technique rely upon proper posture. Your balance also stems predominantly from correct posture.

An essential element in maintaining posture and balance while moving is *iaigoshi*, or *iai*-hips. *Iaigoshi* involves keeping the hips—and thus, the body's center of gravity—low while moving; not allowing the body to bob up and down as you step forward or back. At first, this will require conscious effort, and it will feel like you are trying to balance a glass of water on your head while you are moving.

It is important to maintain this upright alignment of back, neck, and head regardless of your stance. Whether you are seated, kneeling, crouching, standing upright, or lunging in to attack, both *iaigoshi* and straight spinal alignment must be maintained for optimum balance, speed, and power.

Figure 7–8b
Standing *Shisei*

Try to avoid training in *shisei* only while performing *iaijutsu* techniques. Instead, if practiced from the moment you enter the *dōjō* to the moment you leave, proper posture will soon become habitual. With sufficient time and training, it will simply become your natural state, no longer requiring any conscious effort. You will have correct posture whether you are practicing *iaijutsu*, driving your car, or relaxing at home.

CHAKUGAN
Eye Contact

The next element you will probably become aware of is eye contact, called either *chakugan* or *metsuke* in Japanese. As soon as you try to draw a sword for the first time, you will find yourself wondering where to look: Should you watch your sword? Should you stare at your target? When you are looking at your opponent, should you look at his eyes? His hands? His feet?

As you might imagine, *chakugan* is crucial to *iaijutsu*. If a *samurai* failed to notice an opponent's attack, he met a sudden and premature end. If he was fooled by a feint, the result was the same.

There are as many theories about eye contact as there are schools of swordsmanship, and each theory has much merit. Some say to watch the opponent's eyes, but the eyes can often be used to deceive with a fake glance. Others advocate watching the opponent's hands, because the hands cannot lie. But a swordsman's hands can move so swiftly that by the time you notice them moving, it may be too late for a parry! Another idea is to watch the opponent's hips, since he cannot move without betraying it in his hips. Still others believe the opponent's elbows should be the focal point for the same reason. How can we possibly know which theory is right?

Eishin-Ryū is not concerned with which of these theories is right, because it uses *enzan no metsuke* ("distant mountain sight"). By viewing the opponent with the same slightly out-of-focus eyesight we use when viewing a panorama of distant scenery, with the eyes directed at about the level of the adversary's solar plexus, our vision encompasses the entire person. In this way, we can watch our adversary's eyes, hands, elbows, hips, and feet all at the same time. This method also prevents us from being duped by an eye-fake or a distracting hand movement, because the positions of the hips, elbows, and feet will betray any deception attempted by the rest of the body. The *Eishin-Ryū* swordsman only reacts when the opponent's whole body reveals his true intentions.

When practicing without a partner, *enzan no metsuke* is performed by directing the line of sight toward a spot on the ground about fifteen to twenty feet away. This angle approximates the correct direction and focal length that would be used with an opponent.

KOKYŪ

Breath Control

The commencement of every *iaijutsu* technique is keyed to breathing, so *kokyū*, or breath control, will be another factor of immediate interest to anyone practicing the art.

At the beginning of each *waza*, after assuming the initial posture, take three breaths before moving. These three breaths should be natural but deep. The feeling should be as though the air is being drawn in through the nostrils up around the crown of the head, then down the spinal column to the *tanden*—the lower abdomen. Exhaling is done normally. Of course, the air cannot actually follow this path. When inhaling, it goes straight down into the lungs as always. But by breathing with this circular feeling, the diaphragm draws air more deeply into the lungs, so breathing is more efficient. This type of breathing is called *fukushiki kokyū*.

As the third breath is drawn in, the initial movement of the *waza* is begun. If possible, the third breath should be held throughout the *waza*. However, in longer *waza* this is not always possible, especially for beginners. The objective in those cases is to breathe in such a way that the opponent cannot detect your breathing and exploit it. This involves breathing soundlessly, and letting the breath fill the *tanden*, so there will not be any noticeable swelling of the chest cavity to alert an enemy to your breathing.

Although breath control is crucial for maximizing balance, power, and stamina while fighting, the most important aspect of breath control is mental, rather than physical. Physically, the act of breathing brings fresh, oxygen-rich air into the body as we inhale, and expels impure, carbon dioxide-laden air as we exhale. In a very real sense, breathing serves to purify our bodies. Our goal in *iaijutsu* is to use our breathing to purify our minds at the same time.

As a beginner this is done by consciously "drinking in" positive thoughts and emotions while inhaling, and releasing negative thoughts and emotions while exhaling. Negative thoughts and emotions, such as fear, worry, doubt, selfishness, jealousy, and hatred, are self-destructive and burdensome. Science has shown that excesses of these emotions are actually toxic to the body, leading to ulcers, higher incidence of cancer, and susceptibility to disease. So it is quite beneficial—even necessary—to regularly cleanse the body and mind of these influences. But our minds cannot contain a vacuum. There is always something filling our thoughts. To truly drive out the destructive influences, we must replace them with positive thoughts. So, while we fill our lungs with fresh air, at the same time we fill our minds with refreshing feelings like confidence, faith, compassion, love, respect, and courage.

After a time of consciously practicing this mental cleansing, called *jaki o dasu*, it will become a habit. Once it has become habitual in *iaijutsu* practice, it will become part of our normal lifestyle, so that we are constantly refreshing and cleansing our mind and body as we go about our daily lives.

KAMAE

Stance

There are no "stances" in *iaijutsu*!

Despite this fact, *kamae,* or stance, is vital to correct technique. It is another of *iaijutsu's* infinite paradoxes that great emphasis is placed on correct stance, or *kamae,* while at the same time it is also stressed that *iaijutsu* stances are all *natural* and therefore *kamae* is essentially nonexistent.

The most literal translation of *kamae* is "structure," although it is commonly rendered as "posture" or "stance." For purposes of *iaijutsu* practice, "body structure" may be the best way to conceptualize *kamae,* since it encompasses more than just the foot positions of "stance" or the bearing of "posture."

Although the *seiza* and *tatehiza* positions are not considered "stances" as such, we have included descriptions of them here, since they are the beginning positions for some thirty-five of the *waza* you will practice in *Eishin-Ryū*.

SEIZA

Seiza (see Figure 7–9a) is the formal kneeling/seated position used during audiences with those of high rank, in tea ceremony, and in other similarly ritualistic or formal occasions.

To assume the *seiza* position, first bend slightly at the waist and knees and use your right hand to slap the "skirts" of your *hakama* outward behind your knees (left, then right) to prevent them from binding underneath you, as shown in Figure 7–9b.

Keeping your upper body erect, lower your left knee to the floor, then your right knee, leaving a space of five to ten inches between them. Lean slightly forward, taking the weight off the balls of your feet and flatten them outward behind you, then settle down onto your heels.

Figure 7–9a
Seiza Front View

Figure 7–9b
Slapping *Hakama*

Shisei must be erect while seated in *seiza,* as shown in Figure 7–9c. The line from your buttocks to your head should be almost as straight as if you were resting against a wall. Your big toes should be just touching each other beneath you.

Figure 7–9c
Seiza Side View

TATEHIZA

Unlike *seiza, tatehiza* did not originate as a formal sitting position, but was the posture taken by *samurai* while relaxing. When you first experience the discomfort of *tatehiza,* you will find it difficult to imagine it as a way of resting. It is likely, however, that *tatehiza* was one of the few comfortable positions a *samurai* could assume while dressed in *yoroi,* the pleated bamboo battle armor, which may account for its common usage.

To get into *tatehiza* position, first bend slightly at the waist and knees and

Figure 7–10a
Tatehiza Front View

Figure 7–10b
Slapping *Hakama*

use your right hand to slap the left side "skirt" of your *hakama* outward behind your knee, as shown in Figure 7–10b.

Keeping your upper body erect, lower your left knee to the floor and curl it beneath you, so that you sit atop your foot with your ankle bone situated between the cheeks of your behind. Next swat the right side of your *hakama* free behind your right knee and draw it in, so that your right foot is tucked just inside your left knee with your right shin tilted outward at about a 45-degree angle. Only the toes of your right foot should extend forward of your left knee. With your hands closed into loose fists, rest them atop your knees.

Shisei must also be erect while seated in *tatehiza*, as shown in Figure 7–10c. For most Westerners, there is a tendency to lean forward to alleviate some of the weight from the left ankle to ease the discomfort of *tatehiza*, so be sure to keep the line from your buttocks to your head as straight as possible. At first you may also feel as if your balance is precarious in *tatehiza* and be tempted to tense your upper body to remain erect, so you must make a conscious effort to keep your shoulders and upper body relaxed.

Figure 7–10c
Tatehiza Side View

STANDING POSTURES

Another reason we can say that *iaijutsu* has no stances is that the standing postures used in *iaijutsu* are all identical to those used in the related art of *kenjutsu,* so we utilize the same descriptive terms for them.

Probably the most basic and universal of these stances is *chūdan no kamae* ("mid-level stance"). Throughout this text, we will more often use the term *seigan no kamae* for this posture, since it accurately describes pointing the *kissaki* directly at the opponent's eyes. Another term occasionally used is *hito no kamae* ("person stance").

In *seigan no kamae,* the feet are kept shoulder-width apart in a long stride, with the front knee bent so the shin is vertical. The foot position would be identical to a *karate-dō zenkutsu dachi* ("front stance"), except that in *kenjutsu* and *iaijutsu* the heel of the back foot is slightly raised and the back knee is slightly bent. When using *seigan no kamae,* the right foot is almost always kept in front. (See Figure 7–11a).

In *seigan no kamae,* the hands grip the *tsuka* at the natural level about navel-high, with the blade angled upward so the *kissaki* points at the opponent's eyes (or where the opponent's eyes would be, if he were standing at neutral distance). *Seigan no kamae* is a neutral stance which can be used with equal effectiveness for either attack or defense. Of the various defensive postures, *seigan* is the safest, since from it can be initiated a defense against any kind of attack.

Jōdan no kamae ("high-level stance") is an attacking stance. It is sometimes called *ten no kamae* ("heaven stance"), because the sword is held overhead. It is also referred to as *hi no kamae* ("fire stance"), because your fighting spirit must be so strong

Figure 7–11a
Seigan no Kamae

Kamae

Figure 7–11b
Jōdan no Kamae

Figure 7–11c
Gedan no Kamae

and evident that it nearly "burns" the opponent, oppressing his spirit and resolve. Without such strong spirit behind it, *jōdan no kamae* is merely a weak and dangerously exposed posture.

The foot position for *jōdan no kamae* is a little taller than that for *seigan*, and the left foot is usually kept forward. The position of the feet is more akin to the *kōkutsu dachi* of *karate-dō* or *hanmi dachi* of *aikidō* or *kendō*, with the rear foot pointed outward, both knees comfortably flexed, and the feet spread about the distance of a normal walking step. In *iaijutsu*, we usually refer to this posture as *shizentai* ("natural stance").

The sword is held directly overhead with the blade either level or the *kissaki* a little higher than the *tsuba*. The top of the left (front) hand should be in line with the plane of the face, and the elbows spread to a natural width, just wide enough to allow unobstructed forward vision. In *samurai* movies, you may see the elbows pulled quite wide, but this is done for dramatic effect only, and should not be practiced in the *dōjō*. Figure 7–11b shows *jōdan no kamae*.

Gedan no kamae ("low-level stance") is considered a defensive stance, and for this reason it is sometimes called *shubi no kamae* ("defense stance") or *chi no kamae* ("earth stance") because the sword is pointed toward the ground (Figure 7–11c). However, *gedan* is far from the neutral, guarded posture that is *seigan*. Instead, by deliberately exposing the head and upper body, *gedan* is actually an invitation to attack, especially when the opponent is standing in *jōdan*. If a *kiriageru* (upward cut) is initiated from *gedan*, it is impossible for an opponent in *jōdan* to block it in time. Yet if the opponent responds to this threat with an attack, it *can* be effectively be blocked or counterattacked from *gedan*.

The overall posture of *gedan no kamae* is the same *shizentai* as that for *jōdan*, except that the sword is pointed downward with the cutting edge turned toward the opponent.

Another stance using *shizentai* is *hassō no kamae* ("eight-phase stance"), sometimes called *kanshi no kamae* ("watching stance"), which is essentially a neutral stance although it bears the appearance of an attacking posture. *Hassō* is a versatile posture, from which you can easily shift to *jōdan* or *chūdan,* as well as directly attack or defend. Another name for *hassō* is *in no kamae, in* being the Japanese word for the better-known Chinese concept of *yin* — the passive, yielding component of *yin* and *yang.*

Hassō no kamae again uses the same *shizentai* as that for *jōdan* and *gedan,* except that the sword is held high at the side of the body and pointed upward. The natural gripping position of the hands should cause the blade to be angled back about 45 degrees. The elbows should be held naturally, as if the sword was suspended in air and your arms hanging from it. The *tsuba* should be about the level of your jaw, about four to six inches from your cheek.

Figure 7–11d
Hassō no Kamae

Waki no kamae is also sometimes called *kanshi no kamae,* because it is also a neutral or "watching" stance. It is sometimes referred to as *yō no kamae,* the *yō* being the *yang* to *hassō's yin,* since it is more overtly aggressive in nature and appearance. In *waki no kamae,* the feet are spread wide — twice shoulder width — and the knees bent severely to make the stance low and stable. The sword is held parallel to the ground at the rear hip with the edge facing outward. This is not a defensive posture, since the sword is not in a position to readily guard. Instead, the position of the sword is hidden from the opponent's view, making it harder for him to judge its reach. This uncertainty, if coupled with strong fighting spirit as in *jōdan no kamae,* puts tremendous pressure on the opponent.

Figure 7–11e
Waki no Kamae

MAAI

Distance

As soon as you begin to draw your sword for the first time, you will become aware of the concept of distance. Obviously, controlling the distance between yourself and your opponent is of life-or-death importance in *iaijutsu.*

Generally, your starting position should be the distance from which you can correctly strike the opponent by taking one full step forward. This places you out of the adversary's reach unless he takes such a step. If you are too close, you are obviously in danger, and if you are too far away, your opponent will see and deflect your attack too easily. Due to differences in body size, arm length, and speed of motion, correct *maai* varies for everyone.

To determine this safe starting distance, you must work backward from the correct striking distance; and to determine the correct striking distance, you must first understand how to strike with the sword. The striking area of the blade is not the middle, as many novices suppose, and it is certainly not the portion closest to the *tsuba*. The striking area, called the *monouchi*, is the one-third of the blade (approximately ten inches) closest to the *kissaki* (Figure 7–12a).

monouchi

Figure 7–12a

If you remember that the cutting ability of the blade comes from *enshin ryoku* (centripetal force) rather than muscle strength, this is easier to understand. The closer to the *kissaki,* the faster the blade is moving at the time of impact, so the more striking power it has. Since the blade must slice—not hit—the target, enough blade must be employed to cut deeply. The balance of speed and slicing depth predicates the ideal location of the *monouchi* as the one-third of the blade nearest the *kissaki.* In actuality, the *monouchi* is not the entire last one-third of the blade, since the last three or four inches is susceptible to breaking, but the area indicated in Figure 7–12a which does not include those last few inches.

Thus, *kirima*—the correct distance from which to effectively cut—is the distance at which, when swung naturally and correctly, the *monouchi* will strike the target at the precise instant immediately after the arms reach their full extension. The correct starting distance is determined by taking one large or lunging step backward from the striking distance.

Obviously, both the starting distance and striking distance will vary individually, depending upon your height and the reach of your arms while swinging the sword, the distance you cover in one stride, and the speed at which you can close that distance. It is therefore something you will learn and determine through practice and develop a feel for as your experience grows.

The final and perhaps most important distance involved in *iaijutsu* is that by which the opponent's blade should miss you during an attempted attack. This distance determines how far you move when evading an adversary's strike. It is important to dodge an opponent's strike so that it misses by just the slightest margin. If you move too far out of an opponent's reach, you will also have moved out of counterattacking range, so it is crucial to practice this aspect of *maai* diligently.

The Japanese say: *"Issun no maai o mikiru,"* which means to ascertain a distance of one inch. This entails observing the opponent's attack to determine how close his attacking momentum will carry him and how far his sword will reach toward his intended target. If you can cause your opponent to miss by just one inch, then you are well within counterattacking range immediately afterward.

To attain skill in judging the opponent's striking distance demands countless hours of training in the *dōjō*. By trial and error—often painful error—you will eventually be able to instinctively retreat just a hairsbreadth beyond an attacker's reach, and in a single fluid motion step in for a counterattack which is both too quick for your adversary to block and too close for him to avoid. The highest ideal of this *maai* is sometimes called *kami hitoe*—the thickness of a single sheet of paper—in which the opponent's sword would cut your garment but not quite graze your skin. If you reach this level of skill, you have truly mastered *maai*.

KIHAKU

Intensity

It is axiomatic that *iaijutsu* techniques executed with insufficient power and focus will be ineffective. However, as we have previously mentioned, power involves far more than simply applying muscle strength. In fact, muscle strength will often thwart the *iaijutsu* student who is attempting a powerful cutting technique. From the physical point of view, *te no uchi,* the subtleties of technique, will provide far more cutting power than sheer muscle strength.

But power is more than simply good technique, as well. The driving force behind a truly powerful technique is predominantly mental. It comes from developing a single-minded focus and intensity the Japanese call *kihaku.*

Kihaku is a combination of several mental factors, including self-confidence, determination, belief in the cause for which we are fighting *(shinnen),* and all-out commitment. It stems from an unremitting resolve *not to lose.* As we explained in detail in Chapter Two, you are more likely to achieve a victory if you are determined not to lose rather than trying to win. Thus, the best way for a martial artist to win is simply not to lose!

If we focus on winning, we place an expectation on ourselves that can induce unnecessary tension. The desire to win also tends to make us the aggressor, and this aggressiveness can easily lead to mistakes in our efforts to win. Conversely, if our sole objective is not to lose, we can unleash an indomitable spirit that is unencumbered by anxiety, heroic expectations, and the pressure

to succeed. Instead, our mind and body are free to react naturally and instinctively to our opponent—guided by our training—and with this kind of *kihaku* we are more likely to prevail.

These factors, in fact, all work together. If we have trained arduously, we can have justifiable faith in our physical ability. Based on this self-confidence, we can make the determination not to lose the battle we are facing. And knowing that we are fighting out of sincere and right motives for a just cause, we can make an all-out commitment to the battle without the slightest hesitation or reservation. This unrestrained fighting spirit—*kihaku*—then becomes the driving force behind the physical techniques.

Kihaku manifests itself in the dignity with which we conduct ourselves, knowing our cause to be just, the intensity with which we move *(kibi-kibi to shita dosa),* and the sincerity of heart *(kokoro no koma)* which is evident in our respect and poise. These are the qualities which set apart the advanced *iaijutsu* practitioner from the beginning student.

ZANSHIN
Warrior Spirit

Zanshin is a term which appears to be unique to the Japanese language; there is certainly no adequate translation of it in English. Taken literally, it means "remaining spirit," "leftover spirit," or "excess spirit," but it is usually explained as "leaving your spirit focused on the opponent." None of these terms does *zanshin* justice, however. Unfortunately, there is no easy way to define or explain *zanshin*. It is simply a state of mind that must be experienced to be understood. And once understood, it defies accurate description.

"Warrior Spirit" may be the easiest way for Westerners to conceptualize *zanshin*. It is a complex state of mind that encompasses indomitable will— the will not to lose we have explained earlier—a projection of fighting spirit that should be almost palpable to the opponent, mental and physical readiness to respond to attack, and an intense state of alertness, all of which are tempered with a complete lack of fear, worry, excitement, or tension. *Zanshin* is almost a paradox in itself, since it combines the fiercest possible fighting spirit with the calm peace-of-mind of *heijōshin*.

When practicing *iaijutsu* technique, *zanshin* should arise as you begin inhaling your *kokyū* cleansing breaths. This would correspond to the moment a threat is perceived. This intense state of mind then continues throughout *nukitsuke, kirioroshi, chiburi,* and even *nōtō.* In fact, by its very nature, *nōtō* is one of the most crucial times in which to retain *zanshin.* It is natural for almost anyone to maintain fighting spirit while drawing the sword, blocking a strike, or cutting. But one of the most vulnerable moments for the *samurai* is when the battle appears to be over and the sword is being resheathed.. The best time for a wounded opponent to make a dying effort to defeat you is at the midpoint of *nōtō*—the point at which the *kissaki* is just entering the *koiguchi.* From this point you cannot draw with any power or effect, but you do not have time to complete *nōtō* and draw again. So *chiburi* and *nōtō* are the times when your *zanshin* should be most evident.

When the *tsuba* first contacts the left hand there should still be a very strong sense of your *zanshin,* since your sword is still not completely in the *saya.* As a practical matter, you would not fully close the *tsuba* against the *saya,* wedging the *habaki* tightly into the *koiguchi* where it will be difficult to redraw, until you were certain your opponent was finished. Your *zanshin* should continue, just as evident as at the height of battle, until your right hand is removed from the *tsukagashira* at the end of the *waza.*

It is probably because so much attention is paid to *zanshin* after the opponent has been defeated that many people have the misconception that the "remaining spirit" of *zanshin* refers only to the martial spirit which is remaining *after* the fight. Although *zanshin* is most noticeable during *chiburi* and *nōtō*—that is, "after the fight"—it must be present from the moment the technique begins.

Just as there is no simple way to describe this state, there is no simple way to learn *zanshin.* It is a state of mind that can only be developed by dedicated training. It may have been easier for the *samurai* of old to practice *zanshin,* because there was the very real and imminent possibility that his training would be put to the test with his life at stake. For the modern *samurai,* however, it takes a bit of imagination to develop *zanshin.*

Visualization helps many people practice and develop their fighting spirit. By imagining that you are actually facing an opponent while performing *iaijutsu* techniques, you can more readily enter a mental state of alert concentration. By pretending that your life is at stake you can imitate the fierce resolve and willpower necessary to win the imaginary battle. And if you finish each *waza* anticipating that your defeated foe might spring up for one final attack, you can more easily practice that state of calm yet wary preparedness that is *zanshin*.

Zanshin would hardly qualify as an aspect of *iaijutsu* if it did not have a somewhat paradoxical nature—fortunately, *zanshin* readily meets this criterion. As already mentioned, *zanshin* literally means "remaining spirit," and is often associated with the warrior spirit remaining after combat, yet it is to be present *at all times,* before, during, and after the battle. On the other hand, the Japanese have a saying, *"Meijin ni zanshin nashi"* ("The master-of-masters needs no *zanshin*"). This suggests that at the highest levels of training, you no longer exhibit *zanshin*.

What this really means is that the highly advanced master has so much *zanshin* active every moment of his or her life—even during sleep—that to the untrained eye it appears that *zanshin* is absent. Instead, however, what is absent is not *zanshin,* but the *lack* of *zanshin,* so that in such a master there is no noticeable difference between being at rest or at the peak of mortal combat.

A final word about *zanshin* is that it underlies every other aspect of *iaijutsu*. It is the driving force behind all of the physical techniques. Its courage is manifest in the erect posture of *shisei*. It is the nearly palpable resolve-crushing spirit evident in *kamae*. It shines from the eyes to challenge the opponent in *chakugan*. It energizes every breath in *kokyū*. It emboldens the *samurai* to maintain correct, opponent-pressuring *maai*. And it provides the ferocious, singleminded focus of *kihaku*.

MACHIGAI
Mistakes

In *iaijutsu,* a confrontation ends in the blink of an eye and one of the combatants lies dead on the ground. The *samurai* could not afford to make a mistake. Mistakes, very simply, meant death.

On the other hand, the only way to learn an art as difficult and complex as *iaijutsu* is to make mistakes. So in one respect you must train with an intensity of *kihaku* as if there is no room for mistakes—as if they would be fatal—

while in another respect, you must accept the fact that mistakes are a normal part of the learning process.

It is important, therefore, not to dwell on your mistakes, whether they are simply training errors in the *dōjō* or mistakes that have a serious impact in your life. If you allow errors in your past to affect your future attempts, at the very least you will find yourself losing confidence and going into a slump. At the worst, you can become so paralyzed by the fear of failure that you will no longer even try!

Furthermore, your mind will inevitably try to achieve whatever you visualize. So if you keep visualizing yourself making that same old mistake over and over, you are effectively programming your subconscious to repeat it.

Instead, pay attention to your mistakes without dwelling on them. Try to determine what caused the error and how it can be corrected or avoided in the future, then visualize yourself acting correctly. In this way, rather than being a setback or hindrance, each mistake becomes an investment in your future success.

Remember, too, that it is far better to have tried and failed—and learned from the experience—than never to have tried, never to have learned, and never to have truly *lived!*

Chapter 8

初伝正座

Ōmori-Ryū Seiza Waza

Shoden Waza

Originally, *Hayashizaki-Ryū,* and subsequently *Eishin-Ryū, Iaijutsu* consisted only of techniques performed from the *tatehiza* (crouching) and *tachiwaza* (standing) positions. However, with the establishment of the Tokugawa Shōgunate in 1603, the status of the *samurai* class was further elevated, making it essential that techniques be devised to address situations which might arise during occasions of great formality or courtly ritual.

A seventeenth-century expert *(Tatsujin)* in *Shinkage-Ryū Kenjutsu,* Ōmori Rokurōzaemon, combined five *kenjutsu katachi* (formal partner exercises) and *battōjutsu* (sword drawing techniques) with the social rituals of *Ogasawara-Ryū Seiza Reihō* (the etiquette of tea ceremonies) to create a series of formal *Seiza Waza,* which begin in this traditional Japanese kneeling/seated position. The ninth-generation grandmaster of *Eishin-Ryū,* Hayashi Rokudayū, also studied *kenjutsu* under Ōmori Rokurōzaemon and incorporated these *Seiza Waza* into *Eishin-Ryū Iaijutsu.* In recognition of their origin, these *waza* are known as the *Shoden Ōmori-Ryū Seiza Waza.*

We often explain the term *Shoden* as "initial level." The Japanese word *den,* however, carries a much deeper and more interesting meaning than simply "level" or "stage." It is a complex concept with no single-word equivalent in English which does it justice. In essence, *den* is *personally* passing knowledge and information from one generation to the next in parental fashion. Even "heritage," "transmission," or "legacy," at least in their current usage, fail to impart the richness of nuance that we find in *den*.

The *Ōmori-Ryū Seiza Waza* are normally the first *waza* taught to beginning *iaijutsu* students, probably because so many of them are merely variations and practical applications of *iaijutsu* fundamentals.

Prior to the succession of 17th Grandmaster, Ōe Masamichi, all but one of the *Shoden waza* bore names different from those by which they are presently known, as shown below:

Present Name	Previous Name
1. *Mae*	*Shohattō* ("First Draw")
2. *Migi*	*Satō* ("Left Sword")
3. *Hidari*	*Utō* ("Right Sword")
4. *Ushiro*	*Atari-tō* ("Striking Sword")
5. *Yaegaki*	*Inyō Shintai* ("*Yin-Yang* Mind and Body")
6. *Ukenagashi*	*Ryūtō* ("Flowing Sword")
7. *Kaishaku*	*Juntō* ("Assisting Sword")
8. *Tsukekomi*	*Gyakutō* ("Reverse Sword")
9. *Tsukikage*	*Shinchūtō* ("True-Motives Sword")
10. *Oikaze*	*Korantō* ("Running Tiger Sword")
11. *Nukiuchi*	*Nukiuchi* ("Sudden Attack")

A notable feature of the *Shoden waza* is the use of the *Ōmori-Ryū*, or "Wet Umbrella," *chiburi*. Reread the detailed description of this *chiburi* in Chapter Seven, and practice it several times until you can perform it smoothly and without major noticeable flaws before practicing the *waza* in this chapter.

Another characteristic of this group of *waza* is the *Shoden*-type *nōtō*, also described in detail in Chapter Seven. This style of *nōtō* features broad, gracefully unhurried sweeping motions of the sword.

MAE

The first *waza*, *Mae* ("Front") or *Seiza Mae*, contains all the major elements of *kihon* in their most basic form. The simplicity of this *waza* is deceptive: while it is the easiest *waza* to learn and perform, it takes true mastery to perform it with the necessary power and precision.

Mae begins facing straight ahead in *seiza* posture (Figure 8–1a) while taking the three preparatory breaths.

As you finish inhaling the third time, raise your hands to the *tsuka*, with the left hand gripping the *saya* just before your right hand grasps the *tsuka* (Figure 8–1b), and perform *koiguchi no kirikata*.

Figure 8–1a
Seiza Posture

Figure 8–1b
Koiguchi no Kirikata

Begin to draw the *tsuka-gashira* directly toward your imaginary opponent's eyes as you rise on your knees. *It is essential that you simultaneously rise onto the balls of your feet* as you perform *nukitsuke*. If your toes remain extended, you will be unable to push forward with your rear foot. Finish *nukitsuke* by stepping forward with your right foot as shown in Figure 8–1c.

Perform *furikaburi* while remaining on one knee. The left hand remains poised at the left hip after having pulled the *saya* back during *nukitsuke* as shown in Figure 8–1d until raising the sword overhead (Figure 8–1e), at which point it also grasps the *tsuka*.

During *kirioroshi*

Figure 8–1c
Nukitsuke

Figure 8–1d
Begin *Furikaburi*

Figure 8–1e
Finish *Furikaburi*

the arms reach full extension when the blade is just above the target, at a 45-degree upward angle as shown in Figure 8–1f, then fall naturally as the cut is completed (Figure 8–1g).

To increase the power of *kirioroshi,* you shuffle forward during the cut by pushing with the left foot while stepping farther forward with the right foot, then allowing the left foot to slide forward so that it resumes the same spacing as before. This shuffle should draw you forward some six to twelve inches.

Ōmori-Ryū ("Wet Umbrella") *chiburi,* described in detail in Chapter Seven, follows *kirioroshi* as shown in Figures 8–1i through 8–1k. Rise to your feet during the downward stroke, drawing your left foot up even with your right foot as you do so. It is not necessary to reach full standing posture at the exact moment the sword snaps downward. Usually, the sword completes *chiburi* just a moment before you fully rise. Also remember to remain in *iaigoshi* when rising.

While maintaining *zanshin,* slide your right foot slowly and steadily back (Figure 8–1l).

As described in Chapter Seven, perform *Shoden nōtō* while gradually lowering to one knee (see figures 8–1m through 8–1o). Time this movement so that your right knee

Figure 8–1f

Figure 8–1g
Kirioroshi I

Figure 8–1i
Chiburi I

Figure 8–1j
Chiburi II

Figure 8–1k
Chiburi III

touches the floor at the exact moment the *tsuba* touches your left hand at the *koiguchi* (Figure 8–1o).

Hook your left thumb over the *tsuba,* then slide your right hand to the *tsuka-gashira* (Figure 8–1p), and rise to a standing position.

Then take two steps back to reach your original starting position. At this point, now standing fully erect, remove your right hand from the *tsuka-gashira* and return it to your right side while your left hand releases the *saya* and *tsuba* and returns to your left side.

The *bunkai* (step-by-step application) of *Mae* is defense against a single opponent, who is attacking from directly in front of you. The central concept of this *waza* is simply the use of *iaijutsu* fundamentals in their most basic form: *nukitsuke* to slice across the opponent's eyes, blinding the attacker while he is dispatched with *kirioroshi.* While this appears elementary, in actual application it requires extreme sensitivity to the attacker's intentions in order to beat him to the draw.

Figure 8–1l
Nōtō I

Figure 8–1m
Nōtō II

Figure 8–1n
Nōtō III

Figure 8–1o
Nōtō IV

Figure 8–1p
Nōtō V

MIGI

The second *waza*, *Migi* ("Right") is nearly identical to *Mae*, except that it begins turned 90 degrees to the right-front, and therefore includes a 90-degree turn to the left during *nukitsuke*, and its foot positions are the mirror-image of *Mae*. Earlier this *waza* was called *Satō* ("Left Sword") because of this initial pivot, but the name was subsequently changed to *Migi* because it was less confusing to students to name it for its starting orientation.

Figure 8–2a
Nukitsuke

Begin by turning 90 degrees to your right as you assume the initial *seiza* posture (Figure 8–1a), then take the three preparatory breaths. At the top of the third breath, begin *nukitsuke*. As you rise, set your toes so that you are on the balls of your feet, then complete *nukitsuke* by pivoting 90 degrees to your left and stepping forward with your *left* foot (Figure 8–2a).

Just as in *Mae*, except with the *left* foot leading, perform *furikaburi* while remaining on one knee, and shuffle forward while performing *kirioroshi*. Again perform *Ōmori-Ryū* ("Wet Umbrella") *chiburi*, rising to a standing posture (in *iaigoshi*)—with your feet together—during the downward stroke of *chiburi*.

While maintaining *zanshin*, slide your *left* foot slowly and steadily back, then do *Shoden nōtō* while lowering onto your left knee. Hook your left thumb over the *tsuba*, then slide your right hand to the *tsuka-gashira* (Figure 8–2b).

Figure 8–2bl
Nōtō IV

Rise to a standing position, then take two steps back to reach your original starting point and return your hands to their sides.

The *bunkai* of *Migi* is defense against a single opponent attacking from your left while seated. Again, the core concept is utilization of *iaijutsu* fundamentals at their most basic.

HIDARI

The third *waza, Hidari* ("Left") is also nearly identical to *Mae,* except that it begins turned 90 degrees to the left-front, making it the mirror image of *Migi.* Therefore, it begins with a 90-degree turn to the *right* during *nukitsuke.* Earlier this *waza* was called *Utō* ("Right Sword") because of this initial pivot, but the name was subsequently changed to *Hidari,* again because it was less confusing to students to name it for the starting direction.

Begin by turning 90 degrees to your left as you take the initial *seiza* posture, then draw the three preparatory breaths. At the top of the third breath, begin *nukitsuke.* As you rise, set your toes so that you are on the balls of your feet, then complete *nukitsuke* with a 90-degree turn to your right and step forward with your right foot (Figure 8–3a).

Figure 8–3a
Nukitsuke

From this point, the ***waza*** is performed ***exactly*** the same as ***Mae,*** with *furikaburi,* shuffling-forward *kirioroshi, Ōmori-Ryū* ("Wet Umbrella") *chiburi* as you stand up with feet together, and *Shoden nōtō* while lowering onto your left knee. After securing the *tsuba* with your left thumb, then slide your right hand to the *tsuka-gashira,* rise, and step back to your original starting position.

The *bunkai* of *Hidari* is defense against a single opponent who attacks from your right while seated. The core concept is once more simply the utilization of *iaijutsu* fundamentals at their most basic.

USHIRO

Ushiro ("Rear") is the fourth in the initial series of *waza,* completing the four possible directions of attack, so it begins facing backward from your original orientation.

Take the three cleansing breaths while in this rear-facing *seiza* posture, then begin *nukitsuke.* As you rise, set your toes so that you are on the balls of your feet, then complete *nukitsuke* while pivoting 180 degrees to your left and step-

Figure 8–4a
Nukitsuke

Figure 8–4b
Nōtō IV

ping forward with your left foot (Figure 8–4a).

From there, *exactly* as in *Migi*, perform *furikaburi, kirioroshi,* and *Ōmori-Ryū* ("Wet Umbrella") *chiburi,* followed by *Shoden nōtō* while lowering onto your left knee, ending as shown in Figure 8–4b.

Rise to a standing position, then take two steps back to your original starting point and place your hands at your sides.

The *bunkai* of *Ushiro* is defense against a single opponent who attacks from your rear while seated.

As with the previous three *waza,* the concept focused on is the utilization of *iaijutsu* fundamentals at their most elementary level.

YAEGAKI

The fifth *waza, Yaegaki* ("Barriers within Barriers"), displays an increased level of complexity over the first four *Shoden waza.* In addition are two similar but distinct versions of *Yaegaki, Omote* and *Ura.*

The nuances of *Omote* and *Ura* are difficult to translate into simple terms. As a general rule, *Omote* and *Ura* denote opposite sides of the same object, such as the "head" and "tails" of a coin, or the two sides of a sheet of paper or door. This meaning carries with it the notion of one side being readily visible, and the other side being hidden from view. So, while we use the simple translation of "Front" and "Back" for *Omote* and *Ura,* it might as well be "Apparent" and "Hidden," or any number of similar meanings.

YAEGAKI OMOTE

Yaegaki Omote ("Front") begins facing straight ahead in *seiza* position (Figure 8–5a).

As you inhale the third cleansing breath, perform *koiguchi no kirikata,* then step forward with your right foot while rising to one knee during *nukitsuke,* as shown in Figure 8–5b.

Rise almost to fully standing position during *furikaburi* (Figure 8–5c).

Then step forward with your left foot and drop to one knee while performing *kirioroshi,* ending as shown in Figure 8–5d.

As described in detail in Chapter Seven, use an *Eishin-Ryū* ("Flick") *chiburi* (Figure 8–5e).

While performing *Shoden nōtō,* slide your left foot backward at the same pace the sword is entering the

Figure 8–5a
Seiza

Figure 8–5b
Nukitsuke

Figure 8–5c
Standing *Furikaburi*

Figure 8–5d
Kirioroshi

Figure 8–5e
Chiburi I

Figure 8–5f
Nōtō I

Figure 8–5g
Redraw I

Figure 8–5h
Redraw II

Figure 8–5i
Furikaburi

Figure 8–5j
Kirioroshi

Figure 8–5k
Chiburi I

Figure 8–5l
Chiburi II

Figure 8–5m
Chiburi III

saya, until about two-thirds of the blade is sheathed, as depicted in Figure 8–5f. Begin to rise while drawing the sword at a slight downward angle as shown in Figure 8–5g. And finish using the back of the blade *(mine)* to guard in front of your right leg as shown in Figure 8–5h. Drop to one knee with your right foot forward (Figure 8–5i) during *furi-kaburi.* With the same lunging shuffle as in *Mae,* perform *kirioroshi* (Figure 8–5j). Follow with by *Ōmori-Ryū chiburi* (Figures 8–5k and 8–5l). After rising, slide your right foot back (Figure 8–5m). And finish with *Shoden nōtō* (Figures 8–5n, 8–5o, and 8–5p).

At the completion of the *waza,* rise to your feet (remaining in *iaigoshi*), then

Figure 8–5n
Nōtō I

Figure 8–5o
Nōtō II

Figure 8–5p
Nōtō III

Figure 8–5q
Seiza

step three steps back to your starting place and return your hands to your sides.

The basic *bunkai* of *Yaegaki Omote* is a defense against a single attacker directly in front of you. As with *Mae, nukitsuke* and *kirioroshi* are used to first blind, then finish, this opponent. However, the opponent was able to evade the brunt of your first *kirioroshi* and "plays possum" until you are vulnerable during *nōtō,* then makes a surprise attempt to sever your right leg. You use the second *nukitsuke* to block this slash to the leg, and a second *kirioroshi* to be certain he will not make another such attempt.

Figure 8–5r
Standing *Nukitsuke*

YAEGAKI URA

Yaegaki Ura ("Back") begins facing straight ahead in *seiza* position (Figure 8–5a) just as in *Yaegaki Omote.*

This *waza* is identical in every respect to *Yaegaki Omote,* except that rather than blocking downward on the second draw as shown in Figure 8–5h, *nukitsuke* swings horizontally at shoulder level (Figure 8–5r, above).

From this point, *Yaegaki Ura* continues in exactly the same manner as *Yaegaki Omote,* by dropping to one knee during *furikaburi,* shuffling forward *kirioroshi,* then *Ōmori-Ryū chiburi,* rise to *iaigoshi* standing height, slide your right foot back, and finish with *Shoden nōtō.*

At the completion of the *waza*, rise to your feet (again remaining in *iaigoshi*), then step three steps back to your initial position.

The *bunkai* for *Yaegaki Ura* is essentially the same as that of *Omote*, except that rather than the first attacker laying in wait for a second attack, a second attacker appears from concealment behind the first. Thus, the second *nukitsuke* and *kirioroshi* are identical to the first set.

UKENAGASHI

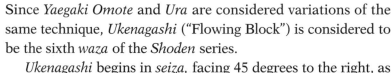

Figure 8–6a
Seiza

Since *Yaegaki Omote* and *Ura* are considered variations of the same technique, *Ukenagashi* ("Flowing Block") is considered to be the sixth *waza* of the *Shoden* series.

Ukenagashi begins in *seiza*, facing 45 degrees to the right, as shown in Figure 8–6a. As you inhale the final cleansing breath, look 45 degrees to your left, then raise your hands to the *tsuka* for *koiguchi no kirikata*. Begin to rise, stepping forward with your left foot as you draw about one-third to one-half of the sword (Figure 8–6b).

Rise to a standing position (with *iaigoshi*) as you complete *nukitsuke*, drawing the sword overhead, with the *kissaki* angled downward to your left as shown in Figure 8–6c.

In a continuously flowing movement, twist your body 90 degrees to your left without moving your feet, then grasp the *tsuka* with your left hand, turning the blade about 90 degrees to complete *furikaburi*, and perform *kirioroshi* with a small shuffle-step (moving your left foot first, then your right foot) bringing your feet together while maintaining *iaigoshi* (Figure 8–6d).

Figure 8–6b
Nukitsuke I

Figure 8–6c
Nukitsuke II

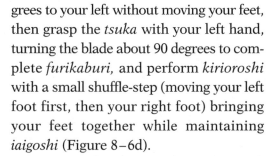

With *zanshin*, step back with your left foot into a wide, low stance (similar to a "side stance") while tilting the sword down and to the right at about a 45-degree angle until the *mine* rests against the top of your right thigh just above the knee as shown in Figure 8–6e.

Hold this "drip" *chiburi* steady while reversing the grip of your right hand on the *tsuka*. Release your left hand, still holding the sword in place with your right hand, and grasp the *saya* at the *koiguchi*. Swing the sword in a wide arc to your left side and place it, edge up, on top of your left forearm in preparation for *nōtō*. Pivot 45 degrees to your right as you draw the sword forward (Figure 8–6f).

Lower to one knee while inserting the sword in the *saya*, so that the *tsuba* touches your left hand just as your left knee touches the floor. Hook your left thumb over the *tsuba* and slide your right hand down the *tsuka* to the *tsuka-gashira* (Figure 8–6g).

Rise to a standing position and step back to your starting point, standing fully erect with your hands at your sides.

Bunkai for *Ukenagashi* is more subtle and intricate than the previous *waza*. Here, the attacker's sword is already drawn and ready, so there is no chance to beat him to

Figure 8–6d
Kirioroshi

Figure 8–6e
Drip *Chiburi*

Figure 8–6f
Nōtō

Figure 8–6g
Nōtō

the draw. Instead, by appearing vulnerable to attack as you begin to draw (Figure 8–6b), you lure the opponent into a premature attack, then rise with the "Flowing Block" for which the technique is named. By stepping to the side and allowing the opponent's strike to slide obliquely down your angled sword, his balance is momentarily lost, allowing you to finish him with the *kirioroshi* into which the block flows.

KAISHAKU

The seventh *Shoden waza* is *Kaishaku* ("Suicide Assistant"). This *waza* contains proper technique and etiquette for assisting a fellow *samurai* in committing suicide by *seppuku*. It is easiest to understand and practice if described and illustrated in its proper context.

Figure 8–7a
Seiza

Figure 8–7b
Nukitsuke I

Kaishaku begins facing straight ahead in *seiza* with the customary three cleansing breaths (Figure 8–7a).

Step forward with your right foot while beginning *nukitsuke* (Figure 8–7b).

It is crucial to draw the blade slowly and quietly, so as not to disturb the concentration of the person committing *seppuku*. As you finish *nukitsuke,* rise and step back with your right foot into a broad stance with both knees flexed ("side stance") and the sword held level overhead, then slowly lower the sword behind your head until the *kissaki* is at eye level. As shown in Figure 8–7c, the *kissaki* should be at the edge of your left eye's peripheral vision. This is the equivalent of *furikaburi*.

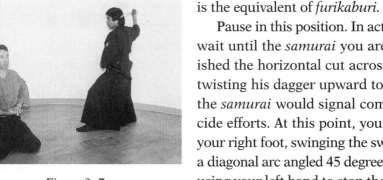

Figure 8–7c
Furikaburi

Pause in this position. In actual use, you would wait until the *samurai* you are assisting has finished the horizontal cut across his abdomen. By twisting his dagger upward toward his sternum, the *samurai* would signal completion of his suicide efforts. At this point, you step forward with your right foot, swinging the sword one-handed in a diagonal arc angled 45 degrees to your lower-left, using your left hand to stop the *tsuka* and halt the travel of the blade precisely (Figure 8–7d).

In actual practice, stopping the blade in this manner would prevent it from completely severing the *samurai*'s neck, so his head would not roll or bounce away disgracefully.

Chiburi and *nōtō* are identical to those in *Ukenagashi*. While maintaining *zanshin,* step back with your left foot into a wide, balanced stance (similar to a "side stance") and tilt the sword down and to the right at about a 45-degree angle until the *mine* rests against the top of your right thigh just above the knee as shown in Figure 8–7e.

Hold this "drip" *chiburi* steady while reversing the grip of your right hand on the *tsuka*. Release your left hand, still holding the sword in place with your right hand, and grasp the *saya* at the *koiguchi*. Swing the sword in a wide arc to your left side and place it edge up on top of your left forearm in preparation for *nōtō*. Pivot 45 degrees to your right as you draw the sword forward (Figure 8–7f).

Lower to one knee while inserting the sword in the *saya,* so that the *tsuba* touches your left hand just as your left knee touches the floor. Hook your left thumb over the *tsuba* and slide your right hand down the *tsuka* to the *tsuka-gashira* (Figure 8–7g).

Rise to a standing position and step back to your starting point, standing fully erect with your hands at your sides.

Figure 8–7d
Kirioroshi

Figure 8–7e
Drip *Chiburi*

Figure 8–7f
1/2 *Nōtō*

Figure 8–7g
End *Nōtō*

TSUKEKOMI

The eighth *Shoden waza* is *Tsukekomi* ("Seize Opportunity"), which begins in *seiza* position facing straight ahead (Figure 8–8a).

At the completion of your three cleansing breaths, begin *nukitsuke*, stepping forward with your right foot and leaning slightly forward to deliberately expose your head to attack, as shown in Figure 8–8b, while drawing one-third to one-half of the blade.

Rise quickly to full height (in *iaigoshi*), completing *nukitsuke* as an *ukenagashi*-type block (Figure 8–8c).

From this position, grasp the *tsuka* with your left hand during *furikaburi* as part of a continuous motion leading into a *partial kirioroshi*, stopping with the blade angled upward at about 45 degrees. This *kirioroshi* is performed with a shuffle-step forward (right foot, then left foot) ending with the feet together as shown in Figure 8–8d and with *iaigoshi* posture.

Raise the sword overhead in a second *furikaburi*, then shuffle-step forward again with a complete *kirioroshi* (Figure 8–8e), also with feet together in *iaigoshi* standing posture.

Step back with the right foot into *shizentai* —natural upright stance—holding the sword in *jōdan no kamae* as shown in Figure 8–8f.

Figure 8–8a
Seiza

Figure 8–8b
Nukitsuke I

Figure 8–8c
Nukitsuke II

Figure 8–8d
Kirioroshi I

Figure 8–8e
Kirioroshi II

After a brief pause, lower onto one knee, bringing the sword down in front of yourself, using the blade to protect your face and torso, as depicted in Figure 8–8g.

Holding this posture, first invert your grip on the *tsuka* with your right hand, then cup your left hand beneath the *tsuba* as shown in figure 8–8h.

Swiveling the sword on its *tsuba* in your left hand, use your right hand to turn it edge upward, pointing down and to your left at about a 45-degree angle, then draw the *tsuka* toward your right shoulder, letting the *mine* slide across the base of the fingers in your left hand as shown in Figure 8–8i.

This motion, mimicking wiping the blade on a cloth or the hem of your *hakama,* substitutes for *chiburi.* Use your left hand to guide the *kissaki* to your left side and the *mine* into the crook of your arm, then perform *nōtō* as shown in Figures 8–8j and 8–8k.

Hook your left thumb over the *tsuba* and slide your right hand down the *tsuka* to the *tsuka-gashira.* Rise to a standing position and step back to your starting point, standing fully erect with your hands at your sides.

Here again is a *waza* whose *bunkai* is subtle and somewhat complex. As with *Uke-*

Figure 8–8f
Jodan

Figure 8–8g
Kneeling I

Figure 8–8h
Kneeling II

Figure 8–8i
Chiburi

Figure 8–8j
Nōtō I

Figure 8–8k
Nōtō II

nagashi, your opponent's sword is already drawn and ready to strike. Your apparent vulnerability as you begin *nukitsuke* (Figure 8–8b) lures the attacker into striking prematurely. Again, as you rise with an *Ukenagashi*-type block (Figure 8–8c), his attack is thwarted, giving you the opportunity for counterattack (Figures 8–8d and 8–8e). In this case, either your first *kirioroshi* is not fully effective, requiring a second, or—as in the case of *Yaegaki Ura*—a second attacker was lurking behind the first.

TSUKIKAGE

Figure 8–9a
Seiza

Figure 8–9b
Tsukikage

Figure 8–9c
Kirioroshi

Figure 8–9d
Chiburi

Tsukikage ("Moon Shadow"), the ninth *waza* in the *Shoden* series, begins in *seiza* facing 45 degrees to the left. As you finish your cleansing breaths, look to your right as you grasp the *tsuka* in preparation for *nukitsuke* (Figure 8–9a).

Rise to a standing position (in *iaigoshi*) during *nukitsuke,* stopping with the blade angled upward at about a 45-degree angle as shown in Figure 8–9b.

Maintaining *iaigoshi* and holding the sword in this upward-angled position—with the feeling that you are keeping your head protected by the blade—step forward with your left foot. As you step forward next with your right foot, perform *furikaburi* then *kirioroshi* in a continuous motion so that the blade completes the downward cut as your right foot lands (Figure 8–9c).

Ōmori-Ryū ("Wet Umbrella") *chiburi* is performed from a standing position in *Tsukikage* by swinging the sword level to your right side and raising it overhead, then snapping it downward while drawing the right foot forward (Figure 8–9d).

Step back with your right foot and also do *Shoden nōtō* in a standing position. *Do not* lower onto one knee during *nōtō* in *Tsukikage*. After you have hooked your left thumb over the *tsuba* and extended your right hand to the *tsuka-gashira*, slide your right foot forward to meet your left foot in *iaigoshi*. Then, beginning with your left foot, step back to your starting point.

The *bunkai* for *Tsukikage* is another instance in which the attacker is already bearing down on you. As he strikes at your unguarded head, you use *nukitsuke* to slash his arms as they swing his sword down at you (Figure 8–9b). After pushing ahead to off-balance him, you finish the attacker with *kirioroshi*.

OIKAZE

Oikaze ("Chase the Wind"), the tenth *Shoden waza,* is the only one which begins from a standing position. As you inhale the third cleansing breath, rise onto your tiptoes as you grasp the *tsuka* in preparation for *nukitsuke*, then crouch slightly forward as you perform *koiguchi no kirikata* (Figure 8–10a).

Run forward in tiny, rapid steps as you begin *nukitsuke*, taking two or three normal size steps as you complete the level draw after covering a distance of about ten to fifteen feet (Figure 8–10b).

Step forward with the left foot during *furikaburi*, then another step with the right foot during *kirioroshi*, as shown in Figure 8–10c.

Ōmori-Ryū ("Wet Umbrella") *chiburi* is again performed from a standing position in *Oikaze* by swinging the sword level to your right side and raising it overhead, then snapping it downward while drawing the right foot forward (Figure 8–10d).

Figure 8–10a
Crouch

Figure 8–10b
Nukitsuke

Figure 8–10c
Kirioroshi

Figure 8–10d
Chiburi

Step back with your right foot and also do *Shoden nōtō* in a standing position. After you have hooked your left thumb over the *tsuba* and extended your right hand to the *tsuka-gashira,* slide your right foot forward to meet your left foot in *iaigoshi.* Then, beginning with your left foot, step back to your starting point.

The *bunkai* for *Oikaze* can be troubling to Westerners, because it is obvious that you are chasing someone and cutting them down from behind. However, *Oikaze* involves a situation known as *jōiuchi* ("Orders from Above"), in which you have been instructed to execute an enemy who flees at the sight of you. Here *nukitsuke* would either be used to hamstring the opponent as he runs, or blind him as he turns to fight. *Kirioroshi* of course follows to finish him with dignity.

Figure 8–11a
Seiza

Figure 8–11b
Furikaburi

Figure 8–11c
Kirioroshi

Figure 8–11d
Chiburi

NUKIUCHI

Last in the *Shoden* series, *Nukiuchi* ("Sudden Attack") begins facing straight ahead in *seiza* posture (Figure 8–11a).

On your third cleansing breath, grasp the *tsuka* and perform *koiguchi no kirikata,* then draw the sword straight up so that *nukitsuke* and *furikaburi* occur in a single motion as you rise up tall on your knees and get set on the balls of your feet (Figure 8–11b).

During *kirioroshi,* spread your knees wide for balance and stability while remaining on the balls of your feet. *Do not allow your sword to strike the floor during kirioroshi* (Figure 8–11c).

Use a "flick" *(Eishin-Ryū) chiburi* (Figure 8–11d).

Follow with *Shoden nōtō.* Remain on the balls of your feet during *nōtō* and gradually settle back onto your heels just as the *tsuba* meets your left hand. After you slide your right hand to the *tsuka-gashira,* rise up slightly, draw your knees back to the proper separation for *seiza,* flatten your feet against the floor, and lower yourself into *seiza* position.

The *bunkai* for *Nukiuchi* may also seem troubling at first to Western minds. In this *waza,* it is readily apparent that you are slaying someone who is bowing to you. As with *Oikaze,* however, this again is an instance of *jōiuchi* ("Orders from Above"). In this example, however, rather than flee—either being ignorant of, or accepting his fate—the enemy bows, giving you the opportunity to end his life with merciful speed.

Chapter 9

中伝立膝

Chūden Tatehiza Waza

Chūden Waza

The techniques that comprised *Hayashizaki-Ryū* during its formative years were predominantly those we now refer to as the *Okuden Waza,* including both the *Okuden Suwariwaza* performed from *tatehiza* (crouching) and most of the *Okuden Tachiwaza* (standing) techniques.

However, with the adaptation of *Hayashizaki-Ryū* techniques to the slightly shorter *katana* by the 7th generation Grandmaster, Hasegawa Eishin, additional techniques were added to the style. The *Chūden Tatehiza Waza*—or at least most of them—were among those added by Hasegawa Eishin when the style took on his name. Unlike the *Shoden Waza,* the *Chūden Waza* were not renamed by the 17th Grandmaster, Ōe Masamichi.

In Chapter Eight we explained the meaning of *den,* as in *Shoden* and *Chūden.* Just as we usually refer to *Shoden* as "initial level" or "beginning level" techniques, we describe *Chūden Waza* as "middle level" techniques.

One characteristic of *Chūden Waza* is that all but one *(Makkō)* begin in *tatehiza* posture. *Tatehiza* ("Standing Knee") is a posture which most Westerners find particularly uncomfortable, but which the *samurai* of feudal Japan frequently used when relaxing while wearing *yoroi,* the wide-woven bamboo armor common to that age. A *samurai* could not comfortably sit in *seiza* or cross-legged in *yoroi*, which probably accounts for the use of *tatehiza* in nearly half the techniques of *Eishin-Ryū*.

To assume the *tatehiza* position, squat as though preparing to sit in *seiza* and use your right hand to swat your *hakama* free of your left leg as you lower onto your left knee. Tuck your left foot beneath you and sit on it with the ankle-bone centered between your buttocks. The right foot remains flat on the floor, with the knee elevated. At the beginning of a *waza*, your hands should be resting in loosely clenched fists atop your knees while you perform your preparatory breathing.

Because *tatehiza* was a position used for resting, most of the techniques in the *Chūden* series are noticeably more *defensive* in nature than those found in *Shoden* or *Okuden Waza*, since they involve responses to a surprise attack. This is apparent in the fact that many of the techniques begin by moving *away* from the direction of attack, rather than toward the attacker as is more common in the *Shoden waza*.

Two other characteristics of this series of *waza* are that *Eishin-Ryū chiburi* —the "flicking" type—is used exclusively, and *nōtō* is performed a bit differently than in the *Shoden Waza*.

Chūden nōtō differs from *Shoden nōtō* in that when the *mine* is placed along the left forearm, only one-half to two-thirds of the blade is aligned on the arm, rather than the entire blade. From this point the blade is drawn forward more quickly than in *Shoden nōtō*. Once the *kissaki* drops into the *koiguchi*, however, the blade is sheathed at about the same steady pace as in *Shoden nōtō*.

Although the *Chūden Waza* are now sometimes taught earlier in a student's training, traditionally they were taught about the time the student entered the "*Ha*" stage of *Shu•Ha•Ri* (see Chapter Five), while during the "*Shu*" phase the student trained predominantly in the *Shoden Waza* (Chapter Eight) and *Tachi-uchi no Kurai* (Chapter Twelve).

YOKOGUMO

The first *Chūden waza*, *Yokogumo* ("Cloud Bank"), is essentially a *tatehiza* equivalent of *Seiza Mae*. *Yokogumo* begins facing straight ahead in *tatehiza* posture (Figure 9–1a) while taking the three preparatory breaths.

As you finish inhaling the third time, raise your hands to the *tsuka*, with the left hand gripping the *saya* just before your right hand grasps the *tsuka* (Figure 9–1b), and perform *koiguchi no kirikata*. Begin to draw the *tsuka-gashira* directly toward your imaginary opponent's eyes as you rise. *It is essential that you simultaneously raise the toes of your left foot, placing the ball of the foot on the floor* as you perform *nukitsuke*. If your toes remain extended, you will be unable to push forward with your rear foot. Finish *nukitsuke* by stepping forward with your right foot as shown in Figure 9–1b.

(NOTE: As a *variation* of this *waza,* you may step *backward* with the left foot during *nukitsuke*. *Yokogumo* is usually practiced with the forward step described here, since it is easier to perform in this fashion, but the backward step is more consistent with the nature of a defense against a surprise attack.)

Perform *furikaburi* while scooting your left knee forward for a better purchase (Figure 9–1c).

Then shuffle forward to increase the power of *kirioroshi,* while remaining in a kneeling position as shown in Figure 9–1d.

Eishin-Ryū ("Flick") *chiburi,* follows *kirioroshi* as shown in Figure 9–1e, and you remain in the kneeling posture rather than rising to your feet as in the *Shoden waza*.

While maintaining *zanshin,* perform *Chūden nōtō* while sliding your right foot slowly and steadily back (Figure 9–1f) at about the same rate the sword is entering the *saya*.

As your right heel comes into line with your left knee, the

Figure 9–1a
Tatehiza Posture

Figure 9–1b
Nukitsuke

Figure 9–1c
Furikaburi

Figure 9–1d
Kirioroshi

Figure 9–1e
Chiburi

Figure 9–1f
Nōtō I

Figure 9–1g
Nōtō II

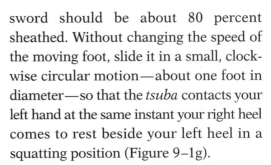

sword should be about 80 percent sheathed. Without changing the speed of the moving foot, slide it in a small, clockwise circular motion—about one foot in diameter—so that the *tsuba* contacts your left hand at the same instant your right heel comes to rest beside your left heel in a squatting position (Figure 9–1g).

Notice from the illustration that your body will have turned slightly to the right as your right foot made this circular motion. Try to minimize this twisting action, so you remain facing as directly as possible to the front. You should now be squatting on your heels as your left thumb hooks over the *tsuba*, and your right hand slides to the *tsuka-gashira*.

Step forward with your right foot, reaching much the same position as at the end of *nukitsuke* (Figure 9–1h).

Then rise to a standing position (in *iaigoshi*), sliding your left foot forward to meet your right.

Take two or three steps back to reach your original starting position. At this point, now standing fully erect, remove your right hand from the *tsuka-gashira* and return it to your right side while your left hand releases the *saya* and *tsuba* and returns to your left side.

Figure 9–1h
Nōtō III

As with *Seiza Mae*, the *bunkai* of *Yokogumo* is deceptively simple. You are being attacked by a single opponent directly in front of you. By anticipating his action, you are able to draw more quickly, slashing his eyes to blind him, thus gaining the time to prepare for and execute *kirioroshi*.

TORA NO ISSOKU

The second *Chūden waza*, *Tora no Issoku* ("One Leg of a Tiger") begins facing straight ahead in *tatehiza* posture (see Figure 9–2a), then take the three preparatory breaths.

Figure 9–2a
Tatehiza

Figure 9–2b
Nukitsuke

At the top of the third breath, begin *nukitsuke.* As you rise, set your toes so you are on the balls of your feet as you draw the *tsuka* at a *downward* angle. Complete *nukitsuke* by rising as you draw—stepping *back* with your left foot—and blocking in front of your right leg (with the blade edge forward) as shown in Figure 9–2b.

During *furikaburi,* drop to one knee with your right foot leading, then shuffle forward while performing *kirioroshi.*

Tora no Issoku ends identically to *Yokogumo,* with *Eishin-Ryū* ("Flicking") *chiburi* and *Chūden nōtō,* slid-

Figure 9–2c
Furikaburi

ing your right foot back and circling it beneath yourself as you resheath the sword. Rise to standing position and step back to your starting point, then place your hands at your side.

Bunkai for *Tora no Issoku* is only slightly different than that for *Yokogumo.* Your attacker is directly in front of you. In this case, you have not beaten him to the draw, however. Instead, you must use *nukitsuke* to block his *nukitsuke* attack to your leading leg, then follow with *kirioroshi.*

INAZUMA

The third *waza*, *Inazuma* ("Lightning") begins facing straight ahead in *tatehiza* posture (Figure 9–3a), then take the three preparatory breaths.

At the top of the third breath, begin *nukitsuke*. As you rise, set your toes so you are on the balls of your feet, then complete *nukitsuke* by rising as you draw and cut straight upward in line with your right shoulder (Figure 9–3b).

Drop to one knee, right foot leading, during *furikaburi*, then shuffle forward while performing *kirioroshi*.

Inazuma also ends identically to *Yokogumo*, with *Eishin-Ryū* ("Flicking") *chiburi*, and *Chūden nōtō*, sliding your right foot back and circling it beneath yourself as you resheath the sword. Rise to standing position and step back to your starting point, then place your hands at your side.

In *Inazuma* your opponent is again attacking from your front. This time, however, his sword was already drawn and he is attacking with *kirioroshi*. Your upward *nukitsuke* slashes his arms just as they reach full extension during *kirioroshi*, then you finish him with a *kirioroshi* of your own.

Figure 9–3a
Tatehiza

Figure 9–3b
Nukitsuke

Figure 9–3c
Furikaburi

UKIGUMO

Ukigumo ("Floating Clouds") is the fourth in this second series of *waza,* and begins in *tatehiza* posture facing 90 degrees to the left of your normal orientation.

Take the three cleansing breaths, then grasp the *tsuka* with your left hand and rise, stepping to your left as you twist the *tsuka* a half-circle counterclockwise, ending back at your left hip as shown in Figure 9–4b. Your right hand should still be resting at your right thigh.

While stepping across with your left foot in front of your right, grasp the *tsuka* with your right hand and circle it clockwise, beginning *nukitsuke* as the *tsuka* rises past "six o'clock" the *second* time (Figures 9–4c and 9–4d).

As you complete *nukitsuke,* turn your body slightly to the left, aligning your shoulders with the blade and lowering your center of gravity by bending both knees slightly and twisting your left ankle so your weight rests on the outer edge of the foot (Figure 9–4e).

Without allowing the blade to move, turn your body one quarter-turn to the right (see Figure 9–4f) and place the palm of your left hand against the *mine* as you step back with your right foot and drop to one knee, as shown in Figure 9–4g.

Figure 9–4a
Tatehiza

Figure 9–4b
Side Stance

Figure 9–4c
Cross-Foot Stance

Figure 9–4d
Cross-Foot
Stance/Half-Drawn

Figure 9–4e
Cross-Foot Drawn

Figure 9–4f
Standing
Half-Turned

Figure 9–4g
Kneeling Reinforced

Figure 9–4h
Furikaburi

Figure 9–4i
Kirioroshi

Turning your body another quarter-turn, push the blade downward to your right until it is pointing almost straight out from your right knee. Use your left hand to gently "flip" the blade upward during *furikaburi* (Figure 9–4h), then perform *kirioroshi* at a 45-degree angle down and to the left, ending at the position shown in Figure 9–4i.

With your left foot still forward, perform *Eishin-Ryū* ("Flicking") *chiburi,* and *Chūden nōtō,* sliding your *left* foot back and circling it beneath yourself as you resheath the sword. Rise to standing position and step back to your starting point, then place your hands at your side.

Figure 9–4j: Seated in Crowd

Much of the circular movement that gives *Ukigumo* its name ("Floating Clouds") is used to avoid striking other people seated around you as you retreat from an opponent's attempt to grab your *tsuka* (Figure 9–4j).

Draw (Figure 9–4k).

And counterattack (Figure 9–4d).

Without these movements, it is likely that your sword would be-

Figure 9–4k:
Grabbing for Sword

Figure 9–4l: Cutting to Neck

come entangled with the bystanders, delaying your response just long enough for your opponent to defeat you.

YAMAOROSHI

The fifth *Chūden waza*, *Yamaoroshi* ("Mountain Wind"), begins facing 90 degrees to the left in *tatehiza* (see Figure 9–5a).

Figure 9–5a
Tatehiza

As you inhale the third cleansing breath, look to your right (at about a 45-degree angle) as you grasp the *tsuka* with both hands, then step at a 45-degree angle to your right as you rise to one knee, twisting the *tsuka* in a clockwise circle and striking with the *tsukagashira*. This action avoids an opponent's attempt to grab your *tsuka* (see Figure 9–5b) and strikes the opponent in the face, as shown in Figure 9–5c.

Nukitsuke is performed by drawing all but the last few inches of the blade, then using a powerful snap of your right wrist with a simultaneous leftward twist of your hips as your left foot slides forward almost to your right foot, *nukitsuke* is completed with the blade angled upward at about 45 degrees as depicted in Figure 9–5d.

Figure 9–5b
Opponent Grabbing

Without allowing the sword to move from the finish of *nukitsuke,* place the palm of your hand on the *mine* at about midway along the blade, turn your body 90 degrees to the right, extend your right leg, then push the blade horizontally to the right while shifting your body weight onto your right leg, as depicted in Figure 9–5e.

Use your left hand to gently "flip" the blade upward during *furikaburi,* while sliding your body and left foot to the right so that you scoot *beneath* the

Figure 9–5c
Tsuka-ate

Figure 9–5d
Standing *Nukitsuke*

Figure 9–5e
Kneeling Side-slash

Figure 9–5f
Kirioroshi

overhead blade, then perform *kirioroshi* straight downward with a small step forward with your right foot (Figure 9–5f).

From this position, perform *Eishin-Ryū* ("Flicking") *chiburi* and *Chūden nōtō,* sliding your right foot back and circling it beneath yourself as you resheath the sword. Rise to standing position and step back to your starting point, then place your hands at your side.

The *bunkai* for *Yamaoroshi* is another defense against an attempt to grab your *tsuka.* This time, rather than being seated to your right, as in *Ukigumo,* your opponent is seated diagonally in front and to the right of you. As he reaches for your *tsuka,* you twist the *tsuka* away from—or out of— his grasp, then strike his face with the *tsukagashira* (Figure 9–5c), stunning him just long enough for you to counterattack with *nukitsuke* (Figure 9–5d), slash the blade free (Figure 9–5e), and finish him with *kirioroshi* (Figure 9–5f). This swirling, slashing counterattack brings to mind the harsh, icy winds that blow down the slope of a mountain, hence the name *Yamaoroshi.*

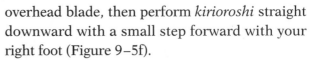

IWANAMI

Iwanami ("Waves Breaking Against the Rocks") is the sixth *waza* of the *Chūden* series. It begins in *tatehiza,* facing 90 degrees to the right (Figure 9–6a).

As you inhale the final cleansing breath, look 90 degrees to your left, then raise your hands to the *tsuka* for *koiguchi no kirikata.* Begin to rise, stepping back with your left foot as you draw about three-fourths of the sword (Figure 9–6b).

Place the fingertips of your left hand against the *mine* to guide the last few inches of the blade from the *saya,* then pivot 90 degrees

Figure 9–6a
Tatehiza

to your left while using both hands to turn the blade over as you rise to a standing position (with *iaigoshi*), as shown in Figure 9–6c.

Figure 9–6b
Nukitsuke I

Figure 9–6c
Nukitsuke II

Use a stutter-step with your right foot to confuse your opponent's timing, then step forward with your right foot while dropping to one knee and thrusting the blade forward with an upward rolling motion, using your left hand to steady and guide the blade, as depicted in Figure 9–6d.

Figure 9–6d
Thrust

Figure 9–6e
Kneeling Side-slash

Leaving your left hand in position against the *mine*, twist the blade 90 degrees to your right, step sideways with your right foot and shuffle to your right while pushing the blade horizontally to tear it free of your opponent (Figure 9–6e).

As in *Ukigumo* and *Yamaoroshi*, use the fingers of your left hand to "flip" the blade overhead during *furikaburi*, while simultaneously sliding your body beneath the upraised sword. Then, with a slight forward step of the right foot, perform *kirioroshi* straight down to finish your attacker (Figure 9–6f).

Figure 9–6f
Kirioroshi

Once again, perform *Eishin-Ryū* ("Flicking") *chiburi*, and *Chūden nōtō*, sliding your right foot back and circling it beneath yourself as you resheath the sword. Rise to standing position and step back to your starting point, then place your hands at your side.

Bunkai for *Iwanami* involves an attack initiated from your left side. You draw and prepare to thrust (Figure 9–6c), then use a stutter-step to throw his timing off as you perform a reinforced thrust (Figure 9–6d), slash the blade free (Figure 9–6e) and finish the attacker with *kirioroshi* (Figure 9–6f).

UROKOGAESHI

The seventh *Chūden waza* is *Urokogaeshi* ("Sudden Turn"). This *waza* is the *Chūden* equivalent of *Seiza Migi* from the *Shoden* series, so it begins facing 90 degrees to the right in *tatehiza* posture.

As you finish your third cleansing breath, look 90 degrees to your left, then raise your hands to the *tsuka* for *koiguchi no kirikata* (Figure 9–7b).

Begin to rise, stepping *back* with your left foot as you rise and draw with a level *nukitsuke,* as shown in Figure 9–7c.

Drop to one knee, with your right foot forward during *furikaburi,* then shuffle-step forward during *kirioroshi* (Figure 9–7d).

As with most of the previous *Chūden waza,* perform *Eishin-Ryū* ("Flicking") *chiburi,* and *Chūden nōtō,* sliding your right foot back and circling it beneath yourself as you resheath the sword. Rise to standing position and step back to your starting point, then place your hands at your side.

As with *Iwanami,* the attack in *Urokogaeshi* is coming from your left side. However, this time the *bunkai* is essentially the same as in *Seiza Migi:* you turn and slash across the opponent's eyes with *nukitsuke,* then finish with *kirioroshi.*

Figure 9–7a
Tatehiza

Figure 9–7b
Nukitsuke I

Figure 9–7c
Nukitsuke II

Figure 9–7d
Kirioroshi

Our translation of the name *Urokogaeshi* as "Sudden Turn" really fails to capture the imagery of the original Japanese, and thereby inadequately portrays the character of this *waza*. *Uroko*, literally, means "fish scales," and *Uroko-gaeshi* refers to the way a fish twists itself nearly in half, its scales flashing in the water, as it turns from peril. This is the character of *Urokogaeshi:* a quick, twisting turn and the bright flash of *nukitsuke* at the onslaught of danger.

NAMIGAESHI

The eighth *Chūden waza* is *Namigaeshi* ("Returning Wave"), the *tatehiza* equivalent of the *Shoden waza*, *Seiza Ushiro*. Thus, *Namigaeshi* begins facing to the rear.

At the completion of your three cleansing breaths, begin *nukitsuke*, pivoting 180 degrees to your left on the balls of your feet as you rise. *Nukitsuke* finishes as a level, standing draw (Figure 9–8b).

Drop to one knee, with your right foot forward during *furikaburi*, then shuffle-step forward during *kirioroshi* (Figure 9–8c).

As before, perform *Eishin-Ryū* ("Flicking") *chiburi*, and *Chūden nōtō*, sliding your right foot back and circling it beneath yourself as you resheath the sword. Rise to standing position and step back to your starting point, then place your hands at your side.

Since this is basically the *Chūden* equivalent of *Seiza Ushiro*, *bunkai* is essentially the same. As you sense an attack from the rear, you peek over your shoulder, turn during *nukitsuke* and slash your opponent's eyes, then finish him with *kirioroshi*.

Figure 9–8a
Tatehiza

Figure 9–8b
Nukitsuke

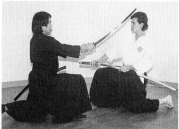

Figure 9–8c
Kirioroshi

TAKIOTOSHI

Takiotoshi ("Cascading Waterfall"), the ninth *waza* in the *Chūden* series, begins in *tatehiza* facing to the rear. This *waza* is a defense against an attacker who grabs the end of your *saya* (the *kojiri*) and raises it so you will be unable to draw.

Figure 9–9a
Koiguchi no Kirikata

As you finish your cleansing breaths, look over your left shoulder as you grasp the *tsuka* while stepping back with your left foot (Figure 9–9a) and performing *koiguchi no kirikata*.

Rise to a standing position (in *iaigoshi*) with a shuffle to the rear while thrusting sharply *downward* on the *tsuka* to break the opponent's grip, as shown in Figure 9–9b.

Still looking over your shoulder at your opponent, draw your left foot slightly ahead of your right foot, while twisting the *tsuka* in a clockwise direction to wrench the *kojiri* completely free of the attacker's grasp (Figure 9–9c).

Figure 9–9b
Standing

Take a step forward with your right foot while performing *nukitsuke*. As the sword is nearly drawn, pivot on the balls of both feet, so that the twist of your hips pulls the last couple of inches of blade from the *saya*. Keep the blade close by your right hip, held flat with the edge turned away from your body, as depicted in Figure 9–9d.

With a left-right shuffle-step forward, execute a one-handed thrust to the opponent's solar plexus, as shown in Figure 9–9e.

Withdraw the *kissaki* from the opponent by pulling your right hand

Figure 9–9c
Pull Free

Figure 9–9d
Nukitsuke

slightly back while twisting the blade a quarter-turn counter-clockwise, so the *mine* is upward (Figure 9–9f).

Figure 9–9e
Thrust

Figure 9–9f
Withdrawal

Then perform *furikaburi* while beginning to step forward with the right foot, so that the sword is directly overhead, poised for *kirioroshi* just as the right foot passes the left foot. Complete the step forward by dropping to one knee during *kirioroshi* as depicted in Figure 9–9g.

This is followed with customary *Eishin-Ryū* ("Flicking") *chiburi*, and *Chūden nōtō*, sliding your right foot back and circling it beneath yourself as you resheath the sword. Rise to standing position and step back to your starting point, then place your hands at your side.

Figure 9–9g
Kirioroshi

The name *Takiotoshi* comes from the swirling, dancing movements of the sword as you evade the grasp of your attackers, turn, thrust, and slash downward—motions reminiscent of the weaving path of a cascading mountainside waterfall.

MAKKO

Last in the *Chūden* series, *Makkō* ("Face to Face") is nearly identical to the *Shoden waza*, *Nukiuchi*. Like *Nukiuchi*, *Makkō* begins facing straight ahead in *seiza* posture (Figure 9–10a).

On your third cleansing breath, grasp the *tsuka* and perform *koiguchi no kirikata*, then draw the sword straight up so that *nukitsuke* and *furikaburi* occur in a single motion as you rise up tall on your knees and get set on the balls of your feet (see Figure 9–10b).

In *Makkō*, *kirioroshi* is *identical* to that performed in *Nukiuchi*, except that *nukitsuke*, *furikaburi*, and *kirioroshi* are per-

Figure 9–10a
Seiza

Figure 9–10b
Furikaburi

Figure 9–10c
Kirioroshi

Figure 9–10d
Chiburi

formed almost as a single action, and more quickly than in *Nukiuchi.* As before, *do not allow your sword to strike the floor* during *kirioroshi* (Figure 9–10c).

Use a "flick" *(Eishin-Ryū) chiburi* (Figure 9–10d).

In *Makkō,* the *chiburi* is followed by *Chūden nōtō.* Remain on the balls of your feet during *nōtō* and gradually settle back onto your heels just as the *tsuba* meets your left hand. After you slide your right hand to the *tsuka-gashira,* rise up slightly, draw your knees back to the proper separation for *seiza,* flatten your feet against the floor, and lower yourself into *seiza* position.

Bunkai for *Makkō* is identical to that of *Nukiuchi* in the *Shoden* series, a case of *jōiuchi* ("orders from above"). You are facing your enemy in formal *seiza* posture; as he bows, you draw and strike in a sudden and continuous motion.

Chapter 10

奥伝立業

Okuden Tachiwaza

Tachiwaza

The *Okuden Tachiwaza* (standing) techniques—or at least most of them—were part of *Hayashizaki-Ryū* during its formative years. With the adaptation of *Hayashizaki-Ryū* techniques to the slightly shorter *katana* by 7th generation Grandmaster Hasegawa Eishin, most or all of the *tachiwaza* had to be modified in some respect to accommodate the newer sword design.

Following the progression from *Shoden* ("initial level") to *Chūden* ("middle level"), we have now reached *Okuden,* or "deep level" techniques. It was once customary to begin training in the *Okuden Waza* late in the "*Ha*" period of *Shu•Ha•Ri,* so that mastery of the *Okuden* techniques occurred during "*Ri,*" when the student was already considered a master of swordsmanship. In more recent times, it is not unusual for students to begin learning *Okuden Waza* shortly after becoming *yudansha,* the equivalent of a black belt.

As we find in translating many Japanese words, *Oku* holds some interesting nuances, and "deep" really does not convey its full flavor. *Oku* actually describes the "innermost," that which lies at the very core or heart of a matter. So, in a real as well as literal sense, the *Okuden waza* are truly the core curriculum of *Musō Jikiden Eishin-Ryū Iaijutsu.*

One characteristic of the *Okuden Tachiwaza* is that all except the three *Itomagoi waza* are performed from a standing or walking posture. *Tachiwaza* begin from a standing position and most of the responses to attack are bolder, since you have greater mobility and power while standing. A standing *samurai* is also less suseptible to a surprise attack than when sitting in *seiza* or relaxing in *tatehiza*.

Most *Tachiwaza* employ a "standard" pattern of footwork. Begin standing erect, with your feet together as if at "Attention," while taking your three cleansing breaths. As you finish inhaling the third breath, hold that breath and step forward with your right foot. As you step with your left foot, both hands rise simultaneously to grasp the *tsuka* and perform *koiguchi no kirikata*. Then, as you take your third step (right foot again), you perform *nukitsuke.**

The stance used during *kirioroshi* is also different from that used in the *Shōden* and *Chūden waza*. Rather than finishing with your hips squarely forward in a stance similar to the *zenkutsu dachi* ("front stance") used in *karate*, with the back leg straight and heel slightly off the ground, *Okuden Tachiwaza* use what we will call a "power stance." Unique to the *Tachiwaza*, this power stance is a modified version of the "front stance" used in the *Shōden* and *Chūden waza*. The front leg is bent and bears most of your weight, but your hips and shoulders are turned about 30 degrees from forward. Your rear leg is bent slightly, with the foot pointing directly sideways and flat on the floor. This

Figure 10–1
Power Stance

stance, illustrated in Figure 10–1 at left, generates greater cutting power than that used in *Shōden* and *Chūden waza*.

Two other characteristics of this series of *waza* are that the "flicking" type *Eishin-Ryū chiburi* is used exclusively, and *nōtō* is performed differently than in either the *Shōden* or *Chūden waza*.

In *Okuden nōtō*, instead of placing most or all of the *mine* along the left forearm, only the last few inches are placed atop the left hand. The sword is then drawn *very* quickly forward until the *kissaki* drops into the *koiguchi*, then one-half to two-thirds of the blade is *very* rapidly sheathed. The remaining portion of the blade is sheathed at the slow, steady pace used in *Shōden* and *Chūden nōtō*.

---

*As an alternative to the three-step footwork pattern, five steps may be taken in most *Okuden waza*.

YUKIZURE

The first *Okuden waza, Yukizure* ("Escorted"), is a defensive technique used when walking in the custody of two opponents, one at either shoulder. In such a situation, you are likely being taken to be executed or interrogated, so you are under obligation to your lord to escape if at all possible.

As you finish inhaling the third time, take your first step forward with your right foot. Your second step (left foot) is made with a distinct movement toward your left side as you raise your hands to the *tsuka*. With the left hand gripping the *saya* at the same moment your right hand grasps the *tsuka*, perform *koiguchi no kirikata*. As you take your third step, turn 45 degrees to your right as you perform *nukitsuke*, drawing the sword in a downward arc in "power stance," ending with the *kissaki* pointing upward at about a 45-degree angle, as shown in Figure 10–2a.

Perform *furikaburi* while turning 90 degrees to your left as you step forward with your right foot, and perform *kirioroshi* in a "power stance." (Figure 10–2b)

Follow this with *Eishin-Ryū* ("Flick") *chiburi*, then *Okuden nōtō* while remaining in "power stance," exhibiting *zanshin*. After your right hand slides to the *tsukagashira*, maintain *iaigoshi* while sliding your left foot up to meet your right foot, then pivot 45 degrees to your right and step back to your original starting position. At this point, now standing fully erect, remove your right hand from the *tsuka-gashira* and return it to your right side while your left hand releases the *saya* and *tsuba* and returns to your left side.

The *bunkai* of *Yukizure* is more abrupt and bold than that of the *Shōden* and *Chūden waza*. In *Yukizure*, you are being escorted by two opponents, who are taking you to be executed or interrogated by your enemies. As you take the second step of the *waza* (with your left foot) you lurch against the

Figure 10–2a
Nukitsuke

Figure 10–2b
Kirioroshi

opponent on your left to temporarily off-balance him. This causes the opponent on your right to get a half-step ahead of you, so you seize the opportunity to dispatch him with *nukitsuke* (Figure 10–2a), turning quickly to finish the opponent on your left with *kirioroshi* (Figure 10–2b) before he can regain the initiative.

TSUREDACHI

The second *Okuden waza, Tsuredachi* ("Companions"), involves a situation similar to that in *Yukizure*. In this case, however, your opponents are escorting you at an angle; the one to your left is a half-step behind you, and the one to your right is a half-step ahead.

As you finish inhaling the third time, take your first step forward with your right foot. As you take your second step (left foot) raise your hands to the *tsuka,* with the left hand gripping the *saya* at the same moment your right hand grasps the *tsuka*. Then, as you take your third step, perform *koiguchi no kirikata* while turning 45 degrees to your right and thrusting forward with both hands, as if performing *tsuka-ate* (a strike with the *tsukagashira*). Next pull the *saya* back, performing *nukitsuke,* and take a half step to your rear while turning your left shoulder aside and making a one-hand chest-level thrust to the rear (Figure 10–3a).

As illustrated in Figure 10–3a, the thrust should be horizontal, with the blade turned sideways—edge away from you— and with the underside of your right forearm reinforcing the *tsuka*.

Raise the sword in *furikaburi* and take a shuffle-step forward as you execute *kirioroshi* in "power stance" at a 45 degree angle to your right-front, as depicted in Figure 10–3b.

Next is *Eishin-Ryū* ("Flick") *chiburi,* followed by *Okuden nōtō* while remaining in "power stance" and exhibiting *zanshin*. After your

Figure 10–3a
Rear Thrust

Figure 10–3b
Kirioroshi

right hand slides to the *tsukagashira,* maintain *iaigoshi* while sliding your left foot up to meet your right foot, then pivot 45 degrees to your left and step back to your original starting position. At this point, now standing fully erect, remove your right hand from the *tsuka-gashira* and return it to your right side while your left hand releases the *saya* and *tsuba* and returns to your left side.

Bunkai for *Tsuredachi* is only slightly different than that for *Yukizure*. You are again dealing with two opponents, only they are escorting you at an angle, rather than at your sides. This time, your action begins as you take your third step of the *waza* (with your right foot). You lunge toward the opponent to your right-front, knocking him temporarily off balance. Then, by merely pulling back the *saya,* you perform *nukitsuke.* The shuffle-step toward your left-rear not only ensures that you are within striking distance for the thrust which dispatches the opponent behind you, but also blocks him from making a normal *nukitsuke* and distances you from the enemy to your front. Before the opponent at your front can recover, you lunge ahead and finish him with *kirioroshi.*

SŌMAKURI

The third *waza, Sōmakuri* ("All Around"), is the most complex of the *Tachiwaza,* earning its name with a total of five cutting strokes which attack nearly every major target on the body.

At the top of your third cleansing breath, take your first step forward with your right foot. As you take your second step (left foot) raise your hands to the *tsuka,* with the left hand gripping the *saya* at the same moment your right hand grasps the *tsuka.* When your right foot takes the third step, perform *koiguchi no kirikata* and draw about half the blade, then step abruptly back with the right foot, completing *nukitsuke* overhead as an *ukenagashi*-type block (Figure 10–4a).

Next, take a shuffle-step forward—right foot, then left foot—while performing *furikaburi* and an angular *kirioroshi* aimed at your opponent's temple (see Figure 10–4b).

With another shuffle-step forward, *kirioroshi* at neck level on the opposite side of the opponent, as

Figure 10–4a
Nukitsuke

shown in Figure 10–4c.

Your next step forward lands in a "power stance," with an angular cut— slanting about 45 degrees down to your left—at rib level on your opponent's left side (Figure 10–4d).

Without moving your feet, and chiefly using a twist of your wrists, flip the sword back next to your left side at waist level, then take another shuffle-step

Figure 10–4b
First Cut

forward—lunging with the right foot, then letting your left foot "drag" forward—as your perform a *yoko ichi-mon-ji* (level horizontal) cut from left to right. Figure 10–4e shows the point at which the blade strikes the opponent, but in practice the blade should travel a complete half-circle arc to your right.

Allow your follow-through from *yoko ichimon-ji* to carry the blade around and up into *furikaburi* in a single, fluid motion, drawing your left foot forward to meet your right foot. Then take another step forward with your right foot as you finish with *kirioroshi* in "power stance" (Figure 10–4f).

End this *waza* with *Eishin-Ryū* ("Flick") *chiburi*, followed by *Okuden nōtō* while remaining in "power stance" and exhibiting *zanshin*. After sliding your right hand to the *tsukagashira*, maintain *iaigoshi* while drawing your left foot up to meet your right foot, then step back to your original starting position. At this point, now standing fully erect,

Figure 10–4c
Second Cut

Figure 10–4d
Third Cut

Figure 10–4e
Yoko Ichimon-ji

Figure 10–4f
Kirioroshi

remove your right hand from the *tsuka-gashira* and return it to your right side while your left hand releases the *saya* and *tsuba* and returns to your left side.

Bunkai for *Sōmakuri* includes several possible interpretations. The photographs accompanying the description show application against a single attacker who is back-pedaling to escape after his first unsuccessful attack. Because of his evasive movements, your first four counterattacks do not finish him.

Another application of *Sōmakuri* is against up to five opponents who rush at you single-file. This is not as unlikely as it may at first seem, since a single-file onslaught has the strategic advantage of making it difficult to determine the number of attackers, and the timing and nature of their attacks.

SŌDOME

Sōdome ("Stop Everything") is the fourth in the *Oku-den* series of *waza,* and contains techniques which are extremely awkward and difficult to master.

As you finish your third cleansing breath, take your first step forward with your right foot. Raise your hands to the *tsuka* as you take your second step (left foot), gripping the *saya* with your left hand at the same moment your right hand grasps the *tsuka.* Then, as you take your third step, perform *koiguchi no kirikata* followed by *nukitsuke,* landing in a "power stance" as shown in Figure 10–5a.

Figure 10–5a
Nukitsuke I

Note that the blade is angled upward at about a 45-degree angle. The power for this strike is derived from the reverse rotation of your hips, snapping them to your left—opposite from the direction of the travel of the sword.

Step forward with your left foot—just slightly ahead of your right foot—as you perform *nōtō,* twisting your hips forward once again, as depicted in Figure 10–5b.

When you have nearly completed *nōtō,* with only

Figure 10–5b
Nōtō I

Figure 10–5c
Nukitsuke II

Figure 10–5d
Nōtō II

Figure 10–5e
Nukitsuke III

a couple of inches of blade unsheathed, step forward with your right foot again and perform *nukitsuke* exactly as before (Figure 10–5c).

Again step forward with your left foot—just slightly ahead of your right foot—as you perform *nōtō*, twisting your hips forward once again, as depicted in Figure 10–5d.

Perform a third *nukitsuke,* exactly as before (Figure 10–5e).

This time, shift to a "front stance" as you do *Eishin-Ryū* ("Flick") *chiburi*, followed by *Okuden nōtō*. Once your right hand has reached the *tsuka-gashira,* maintain *iaigoshi* while sliding your left foot up to meet your right foot, then step back to your original starting position. At this point, now standing fully erect, remove your right hand from the *tsuka-gashira* and return it to your right side while your left hand releases the *saya* and *tsuba* and returns to your left side.

Sōdome is another *waza* with several possible *bunkai* of a similar nature. It is most commonly interpreted as a defense against an ambush while walking along an *azemichi,* the narrow path which separates one rice paddy from another and is often bordered by a low hedge in which enemies could conceal themselves. As each opponent springs from concealment, you use the downward-slicing *nukitsuke* before he has a chance to complete his attack.

An equally appropriate use of *Sōdome* is against a series of opponents rushing up at you as you descend a flight of temple steps. In such a case, you would use the advantage of being uphill to cut your opponents down before they could achieve proper purchase on the stairs as they rush upward.

SHINOBU

The fifth *Chūden waza*, *Shinobu* ("Stealthy"), is quite unique in nature, and its apparent simplicity is characteristically deceptive.

As you finish inhaling your third cleansing breath, take your first step forward with your right foot and raise your hands to the *tsuka*, gripping the *saya* with your left hand at the same moment your right hand grasps the *tsuka*. Perform *koiguchi no kirikata* and begin *nukitsuke* as you take your second step (left foot) at about a 45-degree angle to your left (Figure 10–6a). *Nukitsuke* should be slow and very quiet.

Figure 10–6a
Nukitsuke

Complete *nukitsuke* while taking your third step, crossing your right foot in front of your left. Bend both knees, lowering your body while maintaining erect posture as you turn 90 degrees to your right. Extending your arm almost fully, lightly tap the floor twice with the *kissaki*, as depicted in Figure 10–6b.

Still facing 45 degrees to your right, step forward with your right foot into "power stance" with *kirioroshi* (Figure 10–6c).

Remain in "power stance" as you do *Eishin-Ryū* ("Flick") *chiburi*, followed by *Okuden nōtō*. Once your right hand has reached the *tsukagashira*, maintain *iaigoshi* while sliding your left foot up to meet your right foot, then step back to your original starting position. At this point, now standing fully erect, remove your right hand from the *tsuka-gashira* and return it to your right side while your left hand releases the *saya* and *tsuba* and returns to your left side.

Bunkai for *Shinobu* reflects the uniqueness of this *waza*. It is a dark, moonless, or overcast night. You can sense your enemy approaching from your front, but you cannot see him. Knowing that both of you are operating by sound, you

Figure 10–6b
Tap Floor

Figure 10–6c
Kirioroshi

step to your left and silently draw your sword, then reach far to your right—near your starting position, where your opponent expects to find you—and make a slight noise. Your enemy will attack at the sound, and—guided by the *whoosh* of his sword—you defeat him with *kirioroshi*.

YUKICHIGAI

Yukichigai ("Passing By") is the sixth *waza* of the *Okuden* series, and deals with another common type of ambush. In this instance, your attackers are walking toward you, one behind the other, passing on your left—your more vulnerable side. Just as the first opponent passes, he turns to attack from your rear quarter, while his accomplice simultaneously attacks from your front.

As you finish inhaling the third time, take your first step forward with your right foot. As you take your second step (left foot) raise your hands to the *tsuka*, with the left hand gripping the *saya* at the same moment your right hand grasps the *tsuka*. Then, as you take your third step, perform *koiguchi no kirikata* while turning slightly to your left and thrusting forward with both hands, performing *tsuka-ate* (striking with the butt of the handle) at face height (Figure 10–7a).

Figure 10–7a
Tsuka-ate

Next, pull the *saya* back, performing *nukitsuke* as you pivot—without changing the position of your feet—180 degrees to your left, completing *nukitsuke* as an *ukenagashi*-type overhead block, as depicted in Figure 10–7b.

In a continuous motion—still without moving your feet—raise your left hand to the *tsuka* during *furikaburi*, then strike downward with *kirioroshi*, as shown in Figure 10–7c.

Raise the sword into *furikaburi* as you pivot—still without moving your feet—180 degrees to your right and finish with another *kirioroshi* (Figure 10–7d).

Complete the *waza* with *Eishin-Ryū* ("Flick")

Figure 10–7b
Ukenagashi

chiburi, followed by *Okuden nōtō.* After moving your right hand to the *tsukagashira,* maintain *iaigoshi* while sliding your left foot up to meet your right foot, then step back to your original starting position. At this point, now standing fully erect, remove your right hand from the *tsuka-gashira* and return it to your right side while your left hand releases the *saya* and *tsuba* and returns to your left side.

The *bunkai* for *Yukichigai* involves elements of timing and speed, as well as economy of motion. With two enemies attacking simultaneously, there is no time to lose and no room for error. In the fraction of a second it takes for the attacker to your rear to turn in preparation for his strike, you must drive your *tsukagashira* into the face of the assailant to your front. By pivoting as you draw, your sword is protecting your body from the attacker behind you even before your draw is complete. Your *uke-nagashi* and *kirioroshi* must follow only a split-second apart, so you will be able to pivot and finish the attacker to your front before he can recover from the blow to his face and resume his assault.

Figure 10–7c
Kirioroshi I

Figure 10–7d
Kirioroshi II

SODE SURIGAESHI

The seventh in this series is *Sode Surigaeshi* ("Brushing Sleeves") which, like many of the *Okuden waza,* has quite a unique character.

As you finish inhaling your third cleansing breath, take your first step forward with your right foot. As you take your second step (left foot) raise your hands to the *tsuka,* with the left hand gripping the *saya* at the same moment your right hand grasps the *tsuka.* Then, as you take your third step, perform *koiguchi no kirikata* and draw most of the sword (Figure 10–8a).

Figure 10–8a
Nukitsuke

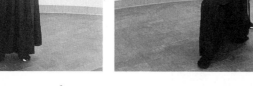

Figure 10–8b
Arms Crossed

Figure 10–8c
Arms Spread

Figure 10–8d
Kirioroshi

As you complete *nukitsuke,* step *back* with your right foot, rising on tip-toe and crossing your arms in front of you, so that the sword is pointing straight back behind you, as illustrated in Figure 10–8b.

Lower your hips and take a long step forward with your right foot, spreading your arms to the sides. As shown in Figure 10–8c, the sword should now be pointing straight ahead, edge upward.

Slide your left foot up to meet your right foot as you raise the sword to *furikaburi,* then step forward with your right foot into a "power stance" and perform *kirioroshi* (figure 10–8d).

Without changing your stance, perform *Eishin-Ryū* ("Flicking") *chiburi,* then *Okuden nōtō.* After moving your right hand to the *tsukagashira,* maintain *iaigoshi* while sliding your left foot up to meet your right foot, then step back to your original starting position. At this point, now standing fully erect, remove your right hand from the *tsuka-gashira* and return it to your right side while your left hand releases the *saya* and *tsuba* and returns to your left side.

The situation in *Sode Surigaeshi* is as interesting as the technique used to overcome it. You are faced by a single attacker who is lurking amid a crowd of innocent bystanders, using them as human shields as he prepares to attack you. To protect these bystanders, you draw your sword and fold your arms (Figure 10–8b above), and as shown from the rear in Figure 10–8e on the following page.

Figure 10–8e
Arms Folded

Figure 10–8f
Pushing Crowd

By lowering your hips and lunging forward, you gain the leverage needed to push the crowd aside, which is the purpose of the motion performed in Figure 10–8c. By keeping your sword edge-up, you avoid accidentally slashing any of the bystanders as you push your way clear of them, as depicted in Figure 10–8f.

Figure 10–8g
Kirioroshi

Once free of the crowd, you locate and dispose of your attacker with *kirioroshi* (Figure 10–8g).

By not waiting for your opponent to burst through the crowd at you, you have seized the initiative and are able to catch him off guard.

Obviously, this *waza* takes its name from the act of pushing aside the innocent bystanders—your sleeves brushing theirs—as you clear a path to your opponent.

MONIRI

The eighth *Okuden waza* is *Moniri* ("Entrance Gate"), which portrays an effective defense against another ambush attempt. In *Moniri*, your enemies are laying in wait at an entrance gate. Passing through such a gate is a vulnerable moment for a *samurai*, since its sides hamper a normal drawing motion and its low crossbeam prevents *kirioroshi*. Two ambushers are waiting on the far side of the gate, while a third stalks you from behind.

Figure 10–9a
Thrust

Figure 10–9b
Kirioroshi I

Figure 10–9c
Kirioroshi II

At the completion of your three cleansing breaths, take your first step forward with your right foot. As you take your second step (left foot) raise your hands to the *tsuka,* with the left hand gripping the *saya* at the same moment your right hand grasps the *tsuka,* and perform *koiguchi no kirikata.* On your third step, draw most of the sword and complete *nukitsuke* on your fourth step (left foot) by pulling the sword back to your right side, parallel to the floor and edge away from you next to your hip. Step forward with your right foot into a "power stance" and perform a one-handed thrust (figure 10–9a), supporting the *tsuka* against the underside of your forearm and the blade horizontal.

Pivot 180 degrees to your left as you grasp the *tsuka* with both hands and perform *furikaburi,* then step forward with your right foot in "power stance." Normally, you would use the momentum of your stride to add power to *kirioroshi.* In this case, however, make sure you have taken a complete step, *then* perform *kirioroshi* (Figure 10–9b).

Again pivot 180 degrees to your left during *furikaburi,* and step forward with your right foot in "power stance." As in the previous *kirioroshi,* make sure you have taken a complete step, then perform another *kirioroshi,* as shown in Figure 10–9c.

Without shifting your stance, perform *Eishin-Ryū* ("Flicking") *chiburi,* then *Okuden nōtō.* After moving your right hand to the *tsukagashira,* maintain *iaigoshi* while sliding your left foot up to meet your right foot, then step back to your original starting position. Once you are standing fully erect, remove your right hand from the *tsuka-gashira* and return it to your right side while your left hand releases the *saya* and *tsuba* and returns to your left side.

There are many subtle aspects of the *bunkai* for *Moniri* which warrant explanation. The unusual *nukitsuke,* for instance, is used to prepare for a straight thrust. The sword must be fully drawn and ready on the fourth step (left foot in front). When you step forward with the right foot and thrust, you are stepping *through* the gate, thus using it for *your* protection and gaining an advantage on the first ambusher (Figure 10–9a). Next, you must step completely clear of the gate before using *kirioroshi* on the attacker who was behind you (Figure 10–9b). If you try to use your body's momentum for a more powerful cut, you risk striking the top of the gate on the upswing. With your blade wedged deep in the wood and your hands overhead exposing your entire torso, you will almost certainly lose the battle. Similarly, as you pivot and step back through the gate to perform *kirioroshi* on the last assailant, you must complete your step first, *then* swing the sword.

When done at full speed, this subtle difference in timing is difficult to see. Yet correctly performing this *Moniri* makes all the difference in the world—a life-or-death difference in application—so it must be given close attention in your practice.

KABEZOE

Kabezoe ("Against the Wall"), the ninth *waza* in the *Okuden* group, contains an unusual-looking defense designed for a situation which was not uncommon in feudal Japan. By Western standards, Japanese streets and alleys seem narrow, even today. Four centuries ago, before automobiles or even bicycles, this was even more the case. It was not unusual for a *samurai* to find himself walking down a narrow alley that was little more than the width of his own shoulders.

At the completion of your cleansing breaths, step forward with your right foot, then as you take your second step (left foot), raise your hands to the *tsuka,* with the left hand gripping the *saya* at the same moment your right hand grasps the *tsuka,* and perform *koiguchi no kirikata*. On your third step, draw your right foot even with your left foot and rise onto tiptoe as you draw almost straight upward, as shown in Figure 10–10a.

Figure 10–10a
Nukitsuke

Figure 10–10b
Furikaburi

Figure 10–10c
Kirioroshi

Figure 10–10d
Chiburi

Figure 10–10e
Nōtō

Allow the *kissaki* to swing around just past your shoulder and behind you as you raise your left hand to the *tsuka* for *furikaburi,* as illustrated in Figure 10–10b.

While still on tiptoe, perform *kirioroshi,* allowing the *kissaki* to swing down to about knee level, rather than stopping its travel level with your navel as you normally would (Figure 10–10c).

Remaining on tiptoe, perform an abbreviated *chiburi* with a snap and twist of your right wrist (Figure 10–10d).

Then a modified *Okuden nōtō,* keeping your left elbow snug against your side and raising the *tsuka* to face level during the rapid portion of *nōtō,* as depicted in Figure 10–10e.

While completing the slow portion of *nōtō,* lower yourself to a flat-footed stance (in *iaigoshi*) as you lower both hands to a normal finishing position. After moving your right hand to the *tsukagashira,* step back to your original starting position. Once you are standing fully erect, remove your right hand from the *tsuka-gashira* and return it to your right side while your left hand releases the *saya* and *tsuba* and returns to your left side.

The narrow alleyways that *Kabezoe* anticipates were another favorite trap, since the cramped space prevents a normal *nukitsuke.* The unusual, compressed *nukitsuke* and *kirioroshi* of *Kabezoe* allows you to draw and defeat your opponent in these narrow confines. Likewise, the *chiburi* and *nōtō* peculiar to this *waza* permitted resheathing of the sword in such limited space.

UKENAGASHI

Last of the *Okuden Tachiwaza, Ukenagashi* ("Flowing Block") follows the basic principle of its *Shōden* namesake—the continuous-motion draw, block, and counterattack—performed only while standing or walking, rather than seated.

As you finish inhaling your third cleansing breath, take your first step forward with your right foot. On your second step, your left foot crosses in front of your right, so you are turned about 45 degrees to the right as you perform *koiguchi no kirikata* and draw about one-third to one-half of the sword (Figure 10–11a).

Your right foot now steps a little farther to the right and to the rear of your left— in a triangular pattern much like that used in the *Shōden* version of *Ukenagashi*—as you twist your upper body 45 degrees to your left and complete *nukitsuke* as a rising *ukenagashi* (see Figure 10–11b).

Twist your upper body another 45 degrees to your left as the sword swivels into *furikaburi*, grasp the *tsuka* with your left hand, and shuffle-step (left foot, then right foot) forward with *kirioroshi*. As shown in Figure 10–11c, *kirioroshi* is completed with the feet together in *iaigoshi*.

Remain facing 45 degrees to the left of your original direction, step back with your left foot into a "power stance" as you perform *Eishin-Ryū chiburi* (Figure 10–11d).

After *Okuden nōtō*, having moved your right hand to the *tsukagashira*, maintain *iaigoshi* while sliding your left foot up to meet your right foot, pivot 45 degrees to your right, then step back to your original starting position. Once you are standing fully erect, remove your right hand from

Figure 10–11a
Nukitsuke

Figure 10–11b
Ukenagashi

Figure 10–11c
Kirioroshi

Figure 10–11d
Chiburi

the *tsuka-gashira* and return it to your right side while your left hand releases the *saya* and *tsuba* and returns to your left side.

The *bunkai* for this variation of *Ukenagashi* is identical to that for the *Shōden* version, except that it occurs in a standing position. Your opponent is directly in front of you, with his sword drawn and ready as you approach. As you come within his striking range, you step to your right and begin to draw, apparently exposing yourself to attack. As your opponent strikes at what he perceives as your vulnerability, you draw, block, and counterattack in a single motion.

The sidestepping and twisting motion employed in the blocking phase of *Ukenagashi* is called *tenshin* ("position shift"), and is used to throw the opponent off balance by suddenly removing the resistance he expects to meet with his powerful *kirioroshi*. This is the reason you must turn and step to your left during *kirioroshi*, since your opponent's momentum will carry him stumbling forward to about this point after failing to meet the anticipated resistance of your block.

ITOMAGOI

The aptly named *Itomagoi* ("Farewell Visit") *waza* are three slightly different variations of a single theme. They are conceptually the same as the *Shōden waza Nukiuchi*, or the *Chūden waza Makkō*, differing only in nuances of their execution.

One difference common to all three *Itomagoi waza* is that the continuous-motion *nukitsuke—furikaburi—kirioroshi* is performed even more quickly than in *Makkō*.

Another shared difference, of course, is that the *Itomagoi waza* employ Oku-den *nōtō*.

Although they are normally included as *"Tachiwaza,"* the *Itomagoi waza* are all performed in *seiza* position, just as their *Shōden* and *Chūden* counterparts. They are differentiated from each other simply by being numbered *Ichi* ("One"), *Ni* ("Two"), and *San* ("Three").

ITOMAGOI ICHI

Begin in *seiza* posture (Figure 10–12a) by taking the customary three cleansing breaths.

As you finish inhaling the third time, begin to bow by leaning slightly forward and touching the fingertips of your left hand to the floor. Then, immediately grasp the *tsuka* and perform *koiguchi no kirikata,* then draw the sword straight up so that *nukitsuke* and *furikaburi* occur in a single motion as you rise up tall on your knees and get set on the balls of your feet (Figure 10–12b).

Remember that *nukitsuke, furikaburi,* and *kirioroshi* are performed almost as a single action. As in *Nukiuchi* and *Makkō,* do not allow your sword to strike the floor during *kirioroshi* (Figure 10–12c).

Use a "flick" *(Eishin-Ryū) chiburi* (Figure 10–12d).

Follow with Okuden *nōtō.* Remain on the balls of your feet during *nōtō* and gradually settle back onto your heels just as the *tsuba* meets your left hand. After you slide your right hand to the *tsuka-gashira,* rise up slightly, draw your knees back to the proper separation for *seiza,* flatten your feet against the floor, and lower yourself into *seiza* position.

Bunkai for *Itomagoi Ichi* is identical to that of *Nukiuchi* or *Makkō.* You are on a mission of *jōiuchi*

Figure 10–12a
Seiza

Figure 10–12b
Furikaburi

Figure 10–12c
Kirioroshi

Figure 10–12d
Chiburi

("orders from above"), so you are facing your enemy in formal *seiza* posture. Suspecting that you may be under orders to execute him, he waits for *you* to bow. As you begin to bow, he follows, giving you the split-second opportunity to draw and strike in a sudden and continuous motion.

ITOMAGOI NI

Itomagoi Ni is identical to *Itomagoi Ichi* except the extent to which you begin to bow. From *seiza* posture (Figure 10–12e) begin by taking the customary three cleansing breaths.

Figure 10–12e
Seiza

Figure 10–12f
Furikaburi

As you finish inhaling the third time, begin to bow by leaning slightly forward by placing your left hand on the floor, just as you would for a normal *seiza rei,* then follow soon after with the fingertips of your right hand. The moment your right hand touches the floor, immediately grasp the *tsuka* and perform *koiguchi no kirikata,* rise, and draw the sword straight up so that *nukitsuke* and *furikaburi* occur in a single motion as you rise up tall on your knees and get set on the balls of your feet (Figure 10–12f).

Follow with *kirioroshi* (Figure 10–12g), and then *Eishin-Ryū chiburi* (Figure 10–12h), ending with *Okuden nōtō.* Remain on the balls of your feet during *nōtō* and gradually settle back onto your heels just as the *tsuba* meets your left hand. After you slide your right hand to the *tsuka-gashira,* rise up slightly, draw your knees back to the proper separation for *seiza,* flatten your feet against the floor, and lower yourself into *seiza* position.

Figure 10–12g
Kirioroshi

Figure 10–12h
Chiburi

Bunkai for *Itomagoi Ni* is identical to

that of *Itomagoi Ichi*, except that your enemy is even *more* suspicious of you than his counterpart in *Itomagoi Ichi*. In this case, he hesitates until your right hand touches the floor, so that you have bent half to two-thirds down in your bow, before he returns your bow. Once again, you have a split-second opportunity to draw and strike in order to carry out your orders.

ITOMAGOI SAN

Itomagoi San is likewise identical to *Itomagoi Ichi* and *Ni*, except the extent of your initial bow. From *seiza* posture (Figure 10–12i) take the customary three cleansing breaths.

As you finish inhaling the third time, you bow *fully*, first placing your left hand on the floor, then follow with your right hand and bend at the waist in a normal *seiza rei*. Pause for a moment, then grasp the *tsuka* and perform *koiguchi no kirikata*, rise, and draw the sword straight in a combination *nukitsuke* and *furikaburi* as you rise up tall on your knees and get set on the balls of your feet (Figure 10–12j).

Perform *kirioroshi* (Figure 10–12k), then *Eishin-Ryū chiburi* (Figure 10–12l), and finish with *Okuden nōtō*. Remain on the balls of your feet during *nōtō* and gradually settle back onto your heels just as the *tsuba* meets your left hand. After you slide your right

Figure 10–12i
Seiza

hand to the *tsuka-gashira*, rise up slightly, draw your knees back to the proper separation for *seiza*, flatten your feet against the floor, and lower yourself into *seiza* position.

Bunkai for *Itomagoi San* is identical to that of *Itomagoi Ichi* and *Ni*, except

Figure 10–12j
Furikaburi

Figure 10–12k
Kirioroshi

Figure 10–12l
Chiburi

that in this case your enemy is *completely* distrustful of you. He therefore waits until you have performed a full bow before he follows suit. But honor requires that he return your bow, giving you a split-second chance to fulfill your *jōiuchi* mission.

Conclusion

As with the *Ōmori-Ryū Seiza Waza,* many of the *Okuden Tachiwaza* had different names prior to changes made by Grandmaster Ōe Masamichi (the 17th grandmaster of *Eishin-Ryū*):

Present Name	Previous Name
1. *Yukizure*	*Yukizure* ("Escorted")
2. *Tsuredachi*	*Tsuredachi* ("Companions")
3. *Sōmakuri*	*Gohōgiri* ("Five-Way Cut")
4. *Sōdome*	*Hanashiuchi* ("Severing Strikes")
5. *Shinobu*	*Yoru no Tachi* ("Night Sword")
6. *Yukichigai*	*Yukichigai* ("Passing By")
7. *Sode Surigaeshi*	*Ken no Koto* ("Brushing Sword")
8. *Moniri*	*Kakuresute* ("Ambushed")
9. *Kabezoe*	*Hito Naka* ("In the Middle")
10. *Ukenagashi*	*Yurumi Nuki* ("Relaxed Draw")
11. *Itomagoi*	*Itomagoi* ("Farewell Visit")

Chapter 11

奥伝坐業

Okuden Suwariwaza

Suwariwaza

The *Okuden Suwariwaza* (crouching techniques), like the *Okuden Tachiwaza*, were part of *Hayashizaki-Ryū* during its formative years. They too were modified by Hasegawa Eishin to adapt their techniques to the modern shorter sword design.

All of the *Okuden* ("deep level") *Suwariwaza* begin in *tatehiza* ("standing knee") posture. If you have practiced the *Chūden waza* for several months before moving on to the *Okuden* series, you may by now find *tatehiza* less uncomfortable than before. For a detailed description of the *tatehiza* position, please refer to the introductory material in Chapter Nine.

Like all other *Okuden* techniques, the *Suwariwaza* exclusively employ *Eishin-Ryū chiburi* (the "flicking" type) and *Okuden nōtō*, as described in Chapter Ten.

KASUMI

The first *Okuden waza*, *Kasumi* ("Haze") begins facing straight ahead in *tatehiza* posture (see Figure 11–1a) while taking the three preparatory breaths.

As you finish inhaling the third time, raise your hands to the *tsuka*, with the left hand gripping the *saya* just before your right hand grasps the *tsuka*, and perform *koiguchi no kirikata* and *nukitsuke*. In this instance, rather than finishing *nukitsuke* with the *kissaki* pointing back toward your opponent's position, allow the blade's momentum to carry it well to your right, as shown in Figure 11–1b.

With a small shuffle-step forward, turn the sword and sweep it back to your left side at knee level, in a movement called *kirikaeshi* ("Returning Cut"), as illustrated in Figure 11–1c.

Figure 11–1a
Tatehiza Posture

Perform *furikaburi* while scooting your left knee forward for a better purchase (Figure 11–1d).

Then shuffle forward to increase the power of *kirioroshi*, while remaining in a kneeling position as shown in Figure 11–1e.

Eishin-Ryū ("Flick") *chiburi*, follows *kirioroshi* as shown in Figure 11–1f.

While maintaining *zanshin*, perform *Okuden nōtō*, beginning to slide your right foot back after you have finished the rapid stage of *nōtō*, thence keeping pace with the slow and steady insertion of the *katana* into its *saya*. As your right heel comes into line with your left knee, the sword should be about 80 percent sheathed. Without changing the speed of the moving foot, slide it in a small, clockwise circular motion—about one foot in diameter—so that the *tsuba* contacts your left hand at the same instant your right heel comes to rest beside your left heel in

Figure 11–1b
Nukitsuke

Figure 11–1c
Kirikaeshi

Figure 11–1d
Furikaburi

Figure 11–1e
Kirioroshi

a squatting position (Figure 11–1g).

Step forward with your right foot, reaching much the same position as at the end of *nukitsuke* (Figure 11–1h).

Then rise to a standing position (in *iaigoshi*), sliding your left foot forward to meet your right.

Figure 11–1f
Chiburi

Figure 11–1g
Finish *Nōtō*

Figure 11–1h
Prepare to Rise

Take two or three steps back to reach your original starting position. At this point, now standing fully erect, remove your right hand from the *tsuka-gashira* and return it to your right side while your left hand releases the *saya* and *tsuba* and returns to your left side.

The *bunkai* of *Kasumi* is simpler than its technique is to perform. You are being attacked by an opponent who is directly in front of you. Anticipating his action, you are able to draw more quickly than he, but he recoils, avoiding your attempted slash at his eyes, so you immediately shift to *kirikaeshi*, cutting his leg to immobilize him while you prepare for and execute *kirioroshi*.

Kasumi, translated here as "Haze," possibly gets its name from the blur of motion in which *nukitsuke* flows into *kirikaeshi*, and then into *furikaburi* and *kirioroshi* in a continuous sequence.

SUNEGAKOI

The second *Okuden waza*, *Sunegakoi* ("Shin Protection") begins facing straight ahead in *tatehiza* posture (Figure 11–2a) while you take your three preparatory breaths.

At the top of the third breath, begin *nukitsuke*. As you rise, set your toes, so you are on the balls of your feet, as you draw the *tsuka* at a *downward* angle. Complete *nukitsuke* by rising as you

Figure 11–2a
Tatehiza

Figure 11–2b
Nukitsuke

Figure 11–2c
Furikaburi

draw—stepping *back* with your left foot—and blocking in front of your right leg (with the blade edge forward) as shown in Figure 11–2b.

Drop to one knee, right foot leading, during *furikaburi* (Figure 11–2c, then shuffle forward while performing *kirioroshi*, as depicted in Figure 11–2d.

Sunegakoi ends identically to *Kasumi*, with *Eishin-Ryū chiburi* and *Okuden nōtō*, sliding your right foot back and circling it beneath yourself as you resheath the sword. Rise to standing position and step back to your starting point, then place your hands at your side.

Bunkai for *Sunegakoi* is identical to that for the *Chūden waza* "*Tora no Issoku.*" In fact the only differences between the two are that *Sunegakoi* is performed more quickly than *Tora no Issoku,* and uses *Okuden*

Figure 11–2d
Kirioroshi

nōtō. In both instances, your attacker is directly in front of you, and you have not beaten him to the draw. Instead, you must use *nukitsuke* to block his *nukitsuke* attack directed at your leading leg, then counterattack with *kirioroshi.*

SHIHŌGIRI

Figure 11–3a
Tatehiza

In the third *Suwariwaza, Shihōgiri* ("Four-Way Cut"), you begin by facing straight ahead in *tatehiza* posture (Figure 11–3a), then take the three preparatory breaths.

At the top of the third breath, begin *nukitsuke*. As you rise, set your toes so you are on the balls of your feet during *koiguchi no kirikata*, then step at a 45-degree angle to your right-front as you begin *nukitsuke,* and finish *nukitsuke* with a level thrust at a 45-degree angle to your left-rear, as shown in Figure 11–3b.

Turn your upper body back toward the right-front during *furikaburi*, then shuffle forward while performing *kirioroshi* at 45 degrees to your right-front (Figure 11–3c).

Turn 90 degree to your left while raising the sword in *furikaburi*, and step forward (right foot front) with *kirioroshi* at 45 degrees to your left-front (Figure 11–3d).

Perform *furikaburi* again, while turning 45 degrees to your right, and step forward (right

Figure 11–3b
Thrust

Figure 11–3c
Kirioroshi I

Figure 11–3d
Kirioroshi II

Figure 11–3e
Kirioroshi III

foot front) with *kirioroshi* in the direction you were originally facing (Figure 11–3e).

Complete *Shihōgiri* with *Eishin-Ryū chiburi* and *Okuden nōtō*, sliding your right foot back and circling it beneath yourself as you resheath the sword. Rise to standing position and step back to your starting point, then place your hands at your side.

Interestingly, *bunkai* for *Shihōgiri* is usually explained differently than the way in which the *waza* is performed, and this difference deserves detailed examination.

In *Shihōgiri*, you are surrounded by attackers on four sides: right-front, left-front, left-rear, and right-rear, whom you must dispatch in order of the imminence of their threat. Their plan of attack is to have the opponent to your right-front grab your *tsuka* to prevent you from defending yourself, while the enemies to your rear attack, followed by the remaining attacker at your front-left.

Thus, although it is not usually practiced as a strike, the first movement—

rising to begin *nukitsuke*—is used as *tsuka-ate* ("handle-strike"), as shown in Figure 11–3f.

The next most dangerous foe is the one to your left-rear, so you make a lethal thrust past your left shoulder (Figure 11–3g).

The opponent at your right-rear is next in degree of threat, and is therefore next to receive *kirioroshi,* as depicted in Figure 11–3h.

Next comes the opponent to your

Figure 11–3f
Tsuka-ate

Figure 11–3g
Thrust

Figure 11–3h
Kirioroshi I

Figure 11–3i
Kirioroshi II

Figure 11–3j
Kirioroshi III

left-front, who has now had time to turn and begin his attack. You must quickly turn and deal him a *kirioroshi* (Figure 11–3i).

Lastly, having recovered from the agonizing blow to the face from your *tsuka*, the opponent to your right-front is now finished with *kirioroshi* (figure 11–3j).

TOZUME

Tozume ("Boxed-in by Doors") is the fourth in this series of *waza*, and begins in *tatehiza* posture facing straight ahead (Figure 11–4a).

Take the three cleansing breaths, then perform *koiguchi no kirikata* and rise, stepping firmly to your right as you complete *nukitsuke* with a downward cut that ends with the blade angled upward at about 45 degrees, as illustrated in Figure 11–4b.

During *furikaburi*, turn 90 degrees to your left and step strongly forward with your right foot with *kirioroshi* (Figure 11–4c).

After *kirioroshi*, perform *Eishin-Ryū chiburi* and *Oku-den nōtō*, sliding your right foot back and circling it beneath yourself as you resheath the sword. Rise to standing position, turn 45 degrees to your right while maintaining *iaigoshi*, then step back to your starting point and return your hands to your sides.

Figure 11–4a
Tatehiza

The *bunkai* for *Tozume* is somewhat subtle. Your two opponents are at angles to your right-front and left-front, but are crouching behind a pair of *byōbu* (folding decorative screens) or *fusuma* (interior sliding doors). The powerful forward step taken on *nukitsuke* and *kirioroshi* is designed to knock down each of these barriers, both hampering your enemy's attack and exposing him to counterattack.

Figure 11–4b
Nukitsuke

Figure 11–4c
Kirioroshi

TOWAKI

The fifth *Okuden waza*, *Towaki* ("Beside the Door"), involves a situation very similar to that dealt with in *Tozume*. Once again, you begin facing straight ahead in *tatehiza* (see Figure 11–5a).

Figure 11–5a
Tatehiza

As you inhale the third cleansing breath, look to your right (at about a 45-degree angle) as you grasp the *tsuka* with both hands, then step at a 45-degree angle to your right as you rise to one knee and draw the blade forward, then thrust back past your left shoulder at a 45-degree angle to your left-rear (Figure 11–5b).

Immediately turn to your right-front as you raise your sword in *furikaburi*, then step forward with your right foot and execute *kirioroshi*, as shown in Figure 11–5c.

Follow *kirioroshi* with *Eishin-Ryū chiburi* and *Okuden nōtō*, sliding your right foot back and circling it beneath yourself as you resheath the sword. Rise to standing position, turn 45 degrees to your left while maintaining *iaigoshi*, then step back to your starting point, and return your hands to your sides.

Figure 11–5b
Rear Thrust

The *bunkai* for *Towaki* is similar to that of *Tozume*. Once again, your opponents are hiding behind lightweight barriers, waiting for the ideal moment—or perhaps a signal—to attack. In this case, however, one is concealed behind you and one to your front at opposite corners, giving them the greatest advantage in a simultaneous attack. As you sense their presence and intent, you draw and stab to the rear, thrusting through one barrier, then step forward, knocking the second screen down onto the other attacker as you defend with *kirioroshi*.

Figure 11–5c
Kirioroshi

TANASHITA

Tanashita ("Beneath a Shelf") is the sixth *waza* of the *Okuden* series. It begins in *tatehiza,* facing directly to the right (Figure 11–6a). To perform this *waza* with the proper feeling, it is important to understand its *bunkai. Tanashita* takes its name literally, since you are crouching beneath a shelf, such as those common in Japanese gardens, or perhaps a raised porch of the type which customarily surrounded a Japanese home or teahouse in feudal times.

Figure 11–6a
Tatehiza

As you take your third cleansing breath, raise your hands to the *tsuka* for *koiguchi no kirikata.* As you begin to draw your sword, take a long, crouching step forward with your right foot, sliding it along the floor. As shown in Figure 11–6b, be sure to keep your head low, as if hunkered beneath a low overhang.

When the *kissaki* clears the *koiguchi,* remain crouched low and draw your left foot forward until your left knee is beside your right heel as you raise the sword over your back in a modified *furikaburi* (see Figure 11–6c).

Figure 11–6b
Nukitsuke

Push with your left foot as you take another long step forward with your right foot, straightening your back only as your weight comes to bear on your front leg and you perform *kirioroshi* (Figure 11–6d). As your momentum carries you onto your front leg, allow your rear leg to slide forward into the normal kneeling posture shown.

This crouching attack imitates the process of emerging from beneath the shelf or porch—

Figure 11–6c
Furikaburi

Figure 11–6d
Kirioroshi

stepping far enough clear of the overhang to have clear swinging space for your *katana*—and defeating your opponent with *kirioroshi.*

Once again, perform *Eishin-Ryū chiburi* and *Okuden nōtō,* sliding your right foot back and circling it beneath yourself as you resheath the sword. Rise to standing position and step back to your starting point, then place your hands back at your side.

RYŌZUME

The seventh *Okuden waza* is *Ryōzume* ("Boxed-in on Both Sides"). The situation in this *waza* is the equivalent of that found in the *Tachiwaza* called *Kabezoe.* You find yourself seated in *tatehiza,* sandwiched between two barriers, and confronted by an opponent directly ahead of you.

As you finish your third cleansing breath, raise your hands to the *tsuka* for *koiguchi no kirikata,* then draw the sword at an upward angle of about 45 degrees as you rise to one foot. When the *kissaki* leaves the *koiguchi,* pull the *tsuka* back toward your navel and grasp it with your left hand, as shown in Figure 11–7b.

With a shuffle-step forward, perform a two-handed thrust to the midsection (see Figure 11–7c).

Pull back on the *tsuka* again, then raise the sword in *furikaburi,* as depicted in Figure 11–7d.

With another shuffle-step forward, finish with *kirioroshi* (see Figure 11–7e).

Due to the tight confines for which this technique was designed, *chiburi* has been modified for *Ryōzume.* By bending your wrist upward, raise the *kissaki* a few inches while raising the *tsuka* enough to swing it from the inside to the outside of your right leg—keeping the *tsuba* even with your knee—and snap your wrist down,

Figure 11–7a
Tatehiza

Figure 11–7b
Nukitsuke

so the *kissaki* again drops slightly below level, finishing as shown in Figure 11–7f.

Nōtō in *Ryōzume* is also adapted to cramped quarters by raising the right hand to about face height during the rapid portion of *nōtō*, rather than keeping it level. Bearing in mind your high degree of vulnerability during *nōtō*, raising the *tsuka* in this fashion allows you to keep your right hand closer to the center of your body and away from the obstruction on your right. After the accelerated portion of *nōtō*, it is completed in the usual fashion.

Then rise to standing position and step back to your starting point, and place your hands back at your side.

In *Ryōzume*, you are boxed in by walls or obstacles on both sides, making a normal *nukitsuke* impossible. So, when your opponent begins his attack, you instead draw and thrust straight forward, inflicting an abdominal wound that delays your opponent's attack until you can finish with *kirioroshi*.

Figure 11–7c
Thrust

Figure 11–7d
Furikaburi

Figure 11–7e
Kirioroshi

Figure 11–7f
Chiburi

TORABASHIRI

The final *Okuden Suwariwaza* is *Torabashiri* ("Running Tiger"), a *tatehiza* technique with similarities to the *Shoden waza* called *Oikaze*. In *Torabashiri* your opponent begins a surprise attack, but when he realizes that you can successfully defend yourself, retreats as you rise to your defense.

Thus, as you complete your three cleansing breaths, grasp the *tsuka* for *koiguchi no kirikata*, rising on the balls of your feet as shown in Figure 11–8a.

In a manner similar to *Oikaze*, take a number of small stutter-steps forward, ending with a normal step with your left foot, then a normal step with your right foot as you complete *nukitsuke* in a standing position (Figure 11–8b).

Crouch down as you raise your *katana* in *furikaburi*, then take a shuffle-step forward as you perform *kirioroshi* (Figure 11–8c).

After *Eishin-Ryū chiburi*, begin *Okuden nōtō*, starting to slide your right foot back. Just before you would normally circle it beneath yourself, a second (concealed) attacker begins an assault (Figure 11–8d).

Draw both feet slightly together to gain the best possible footing, then take a number of stutter-steps *backward* as you begin *nukitsuke* again. Your last step back is a full step with your left foot as you complete *nukitsuke* (Figure 8e).

Crouch down as you again raise your *katana* in *furikaburi*, then take a shuffle-step forward as you perform another *kirioroshi* (Figure 11–8f).

Once again, perform *Eishin-Ryū chiburi* and *Okuden nōtō*, this time completing *nōtō* by sliding your right foot back and circling it beneath yourself as you resheath the sword. Rise to standing position and step back to your starting point, then place your hands back at your side.

Figure 11–8a
Koiguchi no Kirikata

Figure 11–8b
Nukitsuke I

Figure 11–8c
Kirioroshi I

Figure 11–8d
Nōtō I

Figure 11–8e
Nukitsuke II

Figure 11–8f
Kirioroshi II

Conclusion

Again, many of the *Suwariwaza* also had different names prior to changes made by Grandmaster Ōe Masamichi (the 17th grandmaster of *Eishin-Ryū*):

Present Name	Previous Name
1. *Kasumi*	*Mukōbarai* ("Sweep Opponent")
2. *Sunegakoi*	*Tsukadome* ("Stop Attack")
3. *Shihōgiri*	*Shisumi* ("Four Corners")
4. *Tozume*	*Misumi* ("Three Corners")
5. *Towaki*	*Mukōzume* ("Boxed-in by Opponents")
6. *Tanashita*	*Tanashita* ("Beneath a Shelf")
7. *Ryōzume*	*Ryōzume* ("Boxed-in on Both Sides")
8. *Torabashiri*	*Torabashiri* ("Running Tiger")

Chapter 12

太刀打之位

Tachiuchi no Kurai

Katachi

It is probable that some form of *kumitachi* ("practice fencing") has been part of the regimen of *Eishin-Ryū* from its earliest days, since partner training and contests using *bokken* ("wooden swords") in place of *shinken* ("live swords") has been common practice in most styles of swordsmanship for many centuries.

However, it is likely that the *Tachiuchi no Kurai*—prearranged *bokken* sparring involving two partners—that we currently practice in *Eishin-Ryū* are of relatively recent development, having evolved through alteration, augmentation, and simplification of earlier forms of *kumitachi* as they were passed from one generation to the next.

Each of these *Katachi* ("patterned drills") was created to promote practice of a key principle of *Eishin-Ryū* under controlled but reasonably realistic conditions.

Prior to practicing the *Tachiuchi no Kurai,* you should perform *Sa-hō* and *Rei-hō* just as if you were preparing for any other aspect of *iaijutsu* training. Treat your *bokken* just as you would treat an *iai-tō* or *shinken,* by performing *tōrei* as you take up your *bokken* and bowing to your partner.

In a formal setting, the highest level of sincerity and respect is shown by performing your preparation and etiquette in a *seiza* position, facing your partner. In the description of each *Katachi,* we are assuming that the partners have already performed these rituals of proper etiquette, so our narrative covers only the techniques in the *Katachi* itself.

In each *Katachi* one partner practices a key principle of *iaijutsu,* and the other partner provides the appropriate attack and defense to facilitate this training. The partner who practices the principle intrinsic to the *Katachi* is called *Shitachi* ("User") and the partner assisting is called *Uchitachi* ("Receiver"). Even though *Shitachi* is the one practicing the key technique of each *Katachi,* it is equally important to develop aptitude in the role of *Uchitachi,* both for development of your swordsmanship skills and the refinement of such character traits as humility, cooperation, and self-sacrifice.

Some characteristics common to all ten *Tachiuchi no Kurai* are the *chiburi* and *nōtō. Eishin-Ryū chiburi* is performed at the completion of each *Katachi.* This is followed by a simulated *nōtō,* using the left hand to simulate the *koiguchi,* and sliding the *bokken* through the opening of the hand as if sheathing it. It is not customary or necessary to slide the *bokken* through your belt to simulate it being in the *saya.*

Another characteristic not found in the *waza* of *Eishin-Ryū* is *kiai*—the loud shout that accompanies each striking motion in the *Katachi.* This means that sometimes only *Shitachi* or *Uchitachi* will *kiai,* since only one of the two is using an attacking technique, while the other is blocking. In several cases, however, such as the first attacks of *Deai, Tsukekomi, Ukenagashi, Ukekomi,* and others in which the partners are attacking simultaneously, *both* partners will *kiai.*

In the illustrations in this chapter, the models are performing the *Katachi* with *iai-tō* rather than *bokken,* because a steel blade better shows the proper angle of the sword in each of the attack and defense techniques depicted.

DEAI

The first *Katachi, Deai* ("First Meeting"), is designed to employ the *iaijutsu* fundamentals *nukitsuke* and *kirioroshi* in simulated attack and defense with a training partner.

Begin facing your partner at a distance of about eight paces. Both partners take their three cleansing breaths just as if preparing to perform a *waza* (see Figure 12–1a).

Figure 12–1a
Ready

Figure 12–1b
Furikaburi

Nukitsuke (Figure 12–1b)

Uchitachi (left): Reacting to *Shitachi*'s advance, take three simultaneous steps toward *Shitachi*. On the second step, grasp the *tsuka* with your right hand and use *nukitsuke* to block *Shitachi*'s strike to your knee.

Shitachi (right): Take three steps toward *Uchitachi*. On the second step, raise your right hands to the *tsuka,* and on the third step (right foot), perform *nukitsuke* aiming toward *Uchitachi*'s knee.

Kirioroshi (Figure 12–1c)

Uchitachi: Reacting to *Shitachi*'s advance, draw your right foot back in line with your left foot and point the *kissaki* toward your partner's eyes in *seigan no kamae.*

Shitachi: Draw your left foot even with your right as you perform *furikaburi.*

Uchitachi: Step back with your left foot and block *kirioroshi* with a level block, keeping both hands on your left side.

Shitachi: Step forward with your right foot and strike with *kirioroshi.*

Figure 12–1c
Kirioroshi

Figure 12–1d
Chiburi

Chiburi (Figure 12–1d)

Uchitachi: When your partner begins to withdraw, step back toward your own starting position, lowering your sword to *seigan no kamae.*

Shitachi: As you step back toward your initial starting position, lower your sword to *seigan no kamae.*

Uchitachi: While in *seigan no kamae,* push your hips slightly forward, then perform *Eishin-Ryū chiburi.*

Shitachi: While in *seigan no kamae,* push your hips slightly forward, then perform *Eishin-Ryū chiburi.*

Both partners then perform *nōtō,* draw their left foot even with their right foot in *iaigoshi,* slide their right hand down to the *tsuka-gashira,* then rise to a full standing position.

TSUKEKOMI

The second *Katachi, Tsukekomi* ("Take Advantage") provides practice of the principle of quickly seizing the initiative and advantage as an opponent attempts to withdraw from an unsuccessful attack.

Begin facing each other about eight paces apart while both partners take their three cleansing breaths, just as if preparing to perform a *waza* (Figure 12–2a).

Figure 12–2a
Ready

Nukitsuke (Figure 12–2b)

Uchitachi: Take three steps toward *Shitachi.* On the second step, raise your right hands to the *tsuka,* and on the third step (right foot), perform *nukitsuke,* aiming toward *Shitachi's* knee.

Shitachi: Reacting to *Uchitachi's* advance, take three steps toward *Uchitachi.* On the second step, grasp the *tsuka* with your right hand, and use *nukitsuke* to block *Uchitachi's* strike to your knee.

Reinforced Thrust (Figure 12–2c)

Uchitachi: Begin to withdraw from your unsuccessful strike, by leaning slightly away from *Shitachi*, leaving your sword in contact with *Shitachi*'s

Shitachi: Reacting to *Uchitachi*'s attempt to move away, step forward quickly with your left foot, grasp *Uchitachi*'s right hand with your left hand, controlling it while you perform a reinforced thrust to *Uchitachi*'s solar plexus.

Figure 12–2b
Nukitsuke

A close-up of the correct grip on *Uchitachi*'s wrist is shown in Figure 12–2d.

It is crucial to use your thumb and fingers, as shown in the close-up, to firmly control *Uchitachi*'s wrist to prevent *Uchitachi* from cutting you as you move in or deflecting your reinforced thrust.

Shitachi then pushes *Uchitachi*'s hand aside and steps back to the original starting point while taking a *seigan no kamae* posture. At the same time, *Uchitachi* also steps back into *seigan no kamae* at the starting point. After a brief pause, *Shitachi* and *Uchitachi* perform *chiburi* and *nōtō,* then rise to a full standing position.

Figure 12–2c
Reinforced Thrust

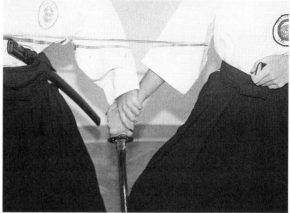

Figure 12–2d: Close-up/Reverse View

UKENAGASHI

Figure 12–3a: Ready

Figure 12–3b
Hasso no Kamae

The principle practiced in *Ukenagashi* ("Flowing Block") is that found in several *Eishin-Ryū waza*, allowing the opponent's attack to slide off the block, then counterstriking in a continuous flowing motion before the attacker can recover.

Begin facing each other about eight paces apart while both partners take their three cleansing breaths, just as if preparing to perform a *waza* (see Figure 12–3a).

Both *Shitachi* and *Uchitachi* draw their *bokken*, stepping forward with their right feet into *seigan no kamae*. Taking a step forward with their left feet, both then raise their swords to *hassō no kamae*, shown in Figure 12–3b.

When *Uchitachi* lifts his sword in *furikaburi*, *Shitachi* begins to follow suit, so that *Uchitachi* steps right foot forward while *Shitachi* steps left foot back, simultaneously striking toward each other's temple, so that their swords meet in the middle, as shown in Figure 12–3c.

Figure 12–3c
Attack/Defense I

Figure 12–3d
Attack/Defense II

Attack/Defense II (Figure 12–3d)

Uchitachi: Step away from *Shitachi*'s counterattack and block it with a strike of your own, swinging your sword in exactly the opposite motion as *Shitachi*'s attack.

Shitachi: Following *Uchitachi*'s attack, step toward *Uchitachi*, with a strike to the opposite temple, swinging your sword in an almost circular motion as you perform *furikaburi* and counterattack in a single motion.

Seigan/Jodan (Figure 12–3e)

Uchitachi: Shuffle away from *Shitachi,* moving your right foot then left foot back a full step, as you raise your sword to *jōdan no kamae.*

Shitachi: Slide your left foot slightly back as you lower your sword into *seigan no kamae.*

Figure 12–3e
Seigan/Jodan

Ukenagashi (Figure 12–3f)

Uchitachi: Step forward with your right foot and attack with *kirioroshi.*

Shitachi: Slide your left foot slightly to your left as your raise your sword to black *Uchitachi's* attack. Be sure your *kissaki* is angled downward, so *Uchitachi's* strike will slide off your blade harmlessly to your right.

A reverse view of Figure 12–3f is provided in Figure 12–3g. In Figure 12–3g, you can clearly note the downward slope of *Shitachi's* blade during *ukenagashi,* as well as the fact that *Shitachi* has shuffled slightly to her right to side-step the full force of *Uchitachi's* kirioroshi.

Ukenagashi (Figure 12–3h)

Uchitachi: Allow your *kirioroshi* to follow past *Shitachi's* ukenagashi.

Shitachi: In a continuous motion, swing your sword from the *ukenagashi* around over your head *(furikaburi)* finishing with *kirioroshi* to *Uchitachi's* head.

Both *Shitachi* and *Uchitachi* step back to their respective starting points as they take *seigan no kamae,* perform *chiburi* and *nōtō,* then rise to a full standing position.

Figure 12–3f
Ukenagashi

Figure 12–3g
Reverse View

Figure 12–3h
Kirioroshi

UKEKOMI

Figure 12–4a: Ready

Figure 12–4b
Hasso no Kamae

Ukekomi ("Block and Move In") is the fourth *Katachi*, and it employs a different type of defense to the same situation practiced in *Ukenagashi*.

Begin facing each other about eight paces apart while both partners take their customary three cleansing breaths (see Figure 12–4a).

Both *Shitachi* and *Uchitachi* draw their *bokken,* stepping forward with their right feet into *seigan no kamae.* Taking a step forward with their left feet, both then raise their swords to *hassō no kamae,* shown in Figure 12–4b.

When *Uchitachi* lifts his sword in *furikaburi, Shitachi* begins to follow suit, so that *Uchitachi* steps right foot forward while *Shitachi* steps left foot back, simultaneously striking toward each other's temple so that their swords meet in the middle, as shown in Figure 12–4c.

Attack/Defense II (Figure 12–4d)

Uchitachi: Step away from *Shitachi*'s counterattack and block it with a strike of your own, swinging your sword in exactly the opposite motion as *Shitachi*'s attack.

Shitachi: Following *Uchitachi*'s attack, step toward *Uchitachi,* with a strike to the opposite temple, swinging your sword in an almost circular motion as you perform *furikaburi* and counterattack in a single motion.

Figure 12–4c
Attack/Defense I

Figure 12–4d
Attack/Defense II

Kiriageru (Figure 12–4e)

Uchitachi: Shuffle away from *Shitachi,* moving your right foot then left foot back a full step, as you raise your sword to *jōdan no kamae.*

Shitachi: As *Uchitachi* shuffles backward into *jōdan no kamae* in preparation for a final attack, you step quickly forward with your right foot, moving slightly to the right of *Uchitachi,* and strike upward beneath *Uchitachi's* left armpit.

It is crucial for *Shitachi* to move *quickly* in, so the counterattack can be delivered before *Uchitachi*

Figure 12–4e
Kiriageru

can respond. Also, by shifting slightly to *Uchitachi's* left side, *Shitachi* is out of the line of *Uchitachi's* intended *kirioroshi.*

Both *Shitachi* and *Uchitachi* step back to their respective starting points as they take *seigan no kamae,* perform *chiburi* and *nōtō,* then rise to a full standing position.

TSUKIKAGE

The fifth *Katachi, Tsukikage* ("Moon Shadow"), primarily teaches a technique of dodging an opponent's strike, but it also provides valuable training in sensing and reacting to an opponent's strength.

Begin facing your partner at a distance of about eight paces apart and take your three cleansing (Figure 12–5a).

Both *Shitachi* and *Uchitachi* draw their *bokken,* stepping forward with their right feet into *seigan no kamae.* Taking a step forward with the left feet, *Uchitachi* assumes *hassō no kamae,* but *Shitachi* remains in *seigan.* After a brief pause, *Shitachi* drops the *kissaki* to *gedan no kamae,* as shown in Figure 12–5b.

When *Uchitachi* attacks toward *Shitachi's* temple, *Shitachi* raises her sword to block the attack

Figure 12–5a: Ready

Figure 12–5b
Hasso vs. *Gedan*

Figure 12–5c
Clashing Swords

Figure 12–5d
Tsuba-to-*Tsuba*

Figure 12–5e
Waki no Kamae

(see Figure 12–5c).

Both then shuffle slightly forward, pushing their swords *tsuba*-to-*tsuba*, as depicted in Figure 12–5d.

In this position, both partners must be sensitive to each other's strength. In a real battle, this would be a crucial opportunity for victory. If one slacks off slightly, the other could easily push through with a thrust or short slice to the throat. Therefore, each partner must exactly match the other's intensity. Using this sensitivity, both partners push away from each other, stepping back with their right feet into a sideways stance, with their swords in *waki no kamae*, as shown in Figure 12–5e.

Again, it is essential that both partners push simultaneously and with equal power. If either the timing or strength of the push is off, one partner will be toppled and the other will gain instant victory.

Furikaburi (Figure 12–5f)

Uchitachi: Step forward with the right foot and make a lateral cut toward *Shitachi* midsection.

Shitachi: As *Uchitachi* attacks, draw your left foot quickly back, even with your right, "sucking in" your stomach as you raise your sword in *furikaburi*.

Figure 12–4f : *Furikaburi*

Kirioroshi (Figure 12–5g)

Uchitachi: Complete your attempted cut just past *Shitachi.*

Shitachi: As *Uchitachi* misses, step forward with your right foot as you perform *kirioroshi* to *Uchitachi*'s head.

It is crucial for *Shitachi* to move quickly in, so the counterattack can be delivered before *Uchitachi* can recover from the missed attack.

Both *Shitachi* and *Uchitachi* step back to their respective starting points as they take *seigan no kamae,* perform *chiburi* and *nōtō,* then rise to a full standing position.

Figure 12–5g
Kirioroshi

SUIGETSŪTŌ

Suigetsūtō ("Solar Plexus Thrust") is the sixth *Katachi,* and is used to practice a deflection and continuous-motion counterattack against a thrust to the solar plexus.

Begin with both partners facing each other about eight paces apart while they take the three cleansing breaths (see Figure 12–6a).

Both *Shitachi* and *Uchitachi* draw their *bokken,* stepping forward with their right feet into *seigan no kamae.* Taking a step forward with their left feet, both then raise their swords to *hassō no kamae,* shown in Figure 12–6b.

Figure 12–6a: Ready

When *Uchitachi* lifts her sword in *furikaburi, Shitachi* begins to follow suit, so that *Uchitachi* steps right foot forward while *Shitachi* steps left foot back, simultaneously striking toward each other's temple so that their swords meet in the middle, as shown in Figure 12–6c.

Figure 12–6b: *Hasso no Kamae*

Figure 12–6c
Attack/Defense I

Figure 12–6d
Attack/Defense II

Attack/Defense II (Figure 12–6d)

Uchitachi: Step forward with your left foot and strike toward *Shitachi's* right temple.

Shitachi: Step away from *Uchitachi's* attack with your right foot, swinging your sword in an almost circular motion as you perform *furikaburi* and counterattack in a single motion.

Seigan/Seigan (Figure 12–6e)

Uchitachi: Step away from *Shitachi,* moving your left foot back, as you lower your sword to *seigan no kamae.*

Shitachi: Shuffle slightly forward as you lower your sword into *seigan no kamae,* keeping your right foot forward.

Parry (Figure 12–6f)

Uchitachi: Lunge forward with your right foot and make a two-hand thrust *(morote-zuki)* to *Shitachi's* solar plexus. Be sure to twist the blade a quarter-turn counterclockwise as you execute the thrust.

Shitachi: Parry *Uchitachi's* attack toward your right side, as shown in Figure 6f.

Figure 12–6e
Seigan/Seigan

Kirioroshi (Figure 12–6g)

Uchitachi: Allow your *morote-zuki* thrust to follow past *Shitachi's* parry.

Shitachi: Then, in a continuous motion, swing your sword from the parry around over your head *(furikaburi)* finishing with *kirioroshi* to *Uchitachi's* head.

Both *Shitachi* and *Uchitachi* step back to their respective starting points as they take *seigan no kamae,* perform *chiburi* and *nōtō,* then rise to a full standing position.

Figure 12–6f
Parry

Figure 12–6g
Kirioroshi

ZETSUMYŌKEN

The seventh *Katachi* is *Zetsumyōken* ("Unbeatable Sword"), which is used to practice a *tsuka-ate* (handle-strike) technique.

Begin facing each other about eight paces apart while both partners take the three cleansing breaths, just as if preparing to perform a *waza* (see Figure 12–5a).

Both *Shitachi* and *Uchitachi* draw their *bokken*, stepping forward with their right feet into *seigan no kamae*. Taking a step forward with the left foot, *Uchitachi* assumes *jōdan no kamae*, but *Shitachi* remains in *seigan*. *Uchitachi* should step forward while in *jōdan no kamae* to close within attacking distance. After a brief pause, *Shitachi* drops the *kissaki* to *gedan no kamae*, as shown in Figure 12–7b.

Figure 12–7a
Ready

When *Uchitachi* attacks toward *Shitachi*'s temple, *Shitachi* raises her sword to block the attack (Figure 12–7c).

Both then shuffle slightly forward, pushing their swords *tsuba*-to-*tsuba,* as depicted in Figure 12–7d.

In this position, both partners must be sensitive to each other's strength. In a real battle, this would be a crucial opportunity for victory. If one slacks off slightly, the other could easily push through with a thrust or short slice to the throat. Therefore, each partner must exactly match the other's intensity.

Figure 12–7b
Hasso vs. *Gedan*

Using the *tsuka* as a fulcrum against *Uchitachi*'s wrist, *Shitachi* steps left foot forward and pivots the sword suddenly, so its *kissaki* swings downward and the *tsuka* swings sharp-

Figure 12–7c
Clashing Swords

Figure 12–7d
Tsuba-to-*Tsuba*

Figure 12–7e
Tuska-ate

Figure 12–7f
Close-up/Reverse View

ly upward, pushing *Uchitachi*'s hands up with it (Figure 12–7e).

Shitachi immediately follows with a strike to *Uchitachi*'s face with the butt of the *tsuka*—a movement called *tsuka-ate*. A close-up of this strike is shown in Figure 12–7f.

The matched force of *Uchitachi tsuba*-to-*tsuba* against *Shitachi* provides the vulnerability that makes this technique work. The moment *Shitachi*'s sword pivots, *Uchitachi*'s own pushing force causes her sword to ride up over *Shitachi*'s. This, coupled with the leverage *Shitachi* gains, creates the break in *Uchitachi*'s balance and the opening to the face which allows *Shitachi* to make the strike. The *katachi* ends at this point, since the stunned *Uchitachi* could be easily finished by any technique of *Shitachi*'s choosing.

Both *Shitachi* and *Uchitachi* step back to their respective starting points as they take *seigan no kamae,* perform *chiburi* and *nōtō,* then rise to a full standing position.

DOKUMYŌKEN

Eighth in the *Tachiuchi no Kurai* is *Dokumyōken* ("Miraculous Sword"), which incorporates one of the most difficult techniques found in the *Katachi*.

Figure 12–8a
Ready

Begin at a distance of about eight paces from your partner as you both take three cleansing breaths (see Figure 12–8a).

Both *Shitachi* and *Uchitachi* draw their *bokken,* stepping forward with their right feet into *seigan no kamae.* Taking a step forward with their left feet, both then raise their swords to *hassō no kamae,* shown in Figure 12–8b.

When *Uchitachi* lifts her sword in *furikaburi, Shitachi* begins to follow suit, so that *Uchitachi* steps right foot forward while *Shitachi* steps left foot back, simul-

Figure 12–8b
Hasso no Kamae

Figure 12–8c
Attack/Defense I

Figure 12–8d
Attack/Defense II

taneously striking toward each other's temple so that their swords meet in the middle, as shown in Figure 12–8c.

Attack/Defense II (Figure 12–8d)

Uchitachi: Step forward with your left foot and strike toward *Shitachi's* right temple.

Shitachi: Step away from *Uchitachi's* attack with your right foot, swinging your sword in an almost circular motion as you perform *furikaburi* and counterattack in a single motion.

Overhead Block (Figure 12–8e)

Uchitachi: Step forward with your right foot, striking straight down to *Shitachi's* head with *kirioroshi*.

Shitachi: Step back with your left foot and use a reinforced block level overhead to stop *Uchitachi's* *kirioroshi*. Note that the blade is edge upward, so the left hand reinforces against the *mine*.

Figure 12–8e
Overhead Block

Sweep Aside (Figure 12–8f)

Uchitachi: Allow your hands to swing naturally back to your left, or the force of *Shitachi's* sweeping motion will cause you to strike your own left leg with your sword.

Figure 12–8f
Sweep Aside

Shitachi: Twist your hips powerfully to the right using your left hand to push your sword along *Uchitachi*'s, sweeping it aside.

Shitachi now steps left foot forward while performing a reinforced thrust to *Uchitachi*'s exposed right side, using the left hand along the *mine* to guide the *kissaki* to its target.

Since *Uchitachi* has driven *Shitachi* back with her repeated attacks, *Shitachi* takes one step forward with the right foot and assumes *seigan no kamae* as *Uchitachi* steps back to her respective starting point and takes *seigan no kamae.* Both simultaneously perform *chiburi* and *nōtō,* then rise to a full standing position.

SHINMYŌKEN

Shinmyōken ("Clear Mind Sword") is the ninth *Katachi,* and also presents a high degree of difficulty in terms of *Shitachi*'s timing.

Figure 12–9a
Ready

Figure 12–9b
Jodan no Kamae

Begin about eight paces from your partner, and take the usual three cleansing breaths (Figure 12–9a).

Uchitachi draws, stepping forward with the right foot into *seigan no kamae.* Taking a step forward with the left foot, *Uchitachi* raises the sword to *jōdan no kamae,* as shown in Figure 12–8b.

Uchitachi will probably have to take one or two steps forward, ending with a left foot lead, to close within attacking distance. After a brief pause, *Uchitachi* steps forward with the right foot and attacks with *kirioroshi* toward *Shitachi*'s head.

Shitachi draws and blocks the *kirioroshi* (Figure 12–9c).

And in a continuous, fluid motion parries *Uchitachi*'s strike to the right side (Figure 12–9d).

Then follows around in a circular motion, grasping the *tsuka* with the left hand during *furikaburi,* completing a cut to *Uchitachi*'s neck.

The temptation when performing this *Katachi,* is to begin the parry-and-counterattack motion before the

Figure 12–9c
Block

Figure 12–9d
Parry

block has been fully effective. If *Uchitachi* is performing the *kirioroshi* with realistic follow-through, this timing error can result in a painful knot on *Shitachi*'s head.

Both *Shitachi* and *Uchitachi* step back to their respective starting points as they take *seigan no kamae,* perform *chiburi* and *nōtō,* then rise to a full standing position.

UCHIKOMI

Uchikomi ("Clash Together") is the final technique of the *Tachiuchi no Kurai,* and it appears to be deceptively simple.

Begin facing your partner at a distance of about eight paces and take your three cleansing breaths (Figure 12–10a).

Both *Shitachi* and *Uchitachi* draw their *bokken,* stepping forward with their right feet into *seigan no kamae.* Taking a step forward with their left feet, both then raise their swords to *hassō no kamae,* shown in Figure 12–10b.

When *Uchitachi* lifts her sword in *furikaburi,* *Shitachi* begins to follow suit, so that *Uchitachi* steps right foot forward while *Shitachi* steps left foot back, simultaneously striking toward each other's temple so that

Figure 12–10a
Ready

Figure 12–10b
Hasso no Kamae

Figure 12–10c
Clashing Swords

Figure 12–10d
Tsuba-to-*Tsuba*

their swords meet in the middle, as shown in Figure 12–10c.

Both then shuffle slightly forward, pushing their swords *tsuba*-to-*tsuba*, as depicted in Figure 12–10d.

As with *tsukikage* and *Zetsumyōken*, it is essential that both partners be sensitive to each other's strength. In a real battle, this would be a crucial opportunity for victory. If one slacks off slightly, the other could easily push through with a winning thrust or slash. Therefore, each partner must exactly match the other's intensity.

Furthermore, because *Uchikomi* ends in a draw, this sensitivity and matching force are even more pronounced. Both partners gradually slacken the force of their pushing. In a real battle, each would be sensitive to the other's possible treachery, so they must recede from one another at exactly the same pace, feeling their partner's intentions as registered by the exertion against the clashed swords.

As the mutual force becomes minimal, *Uchitachi* and *Shitachi* simultaneously step apart, returning to their respective starting points in *seigan no kamae*. At this point, they perform *chiburi* and *nōtō*, then rise to a full standing position.

At the conclusion of *Tachiuchi no Kurai* practice, you should perform *Sa-hō* and *Rei-hō* just as you did at the beginning, but in reverse order.

To demonstrate the utmost mutual respect, the partners would sit in *seiza* posture, perform *tōrei* to their swords and *zarei* to each other, treating their *bokken* just as they would treat an *iai-tō* or *shinken*.

In less formal settings, it is sufficient to simply perform a standing bow to each other, followed by a standing *tōrei*, and *hairei* prior to leaving the *dōjō*.

Chapter 13

全日本剣道連盟 制定居合

Zen Nippon Kendō Renmai Seitei Iai Kata

Seitei Kata

The *Zen Nippon Kendō Renmei Seitei Iai* are presented separately in this book, because they are not technically part of the *Eishin-Ryū* system. They are a development of the Zen Nippon Kendō Renmei (All-Japan *Kendō* Federation) for use by its members. For this reason, we often refer to this series of techniques as the "*Seitei Kata*" ("standard patterns") to clearly distinguish them from the true *Eishin-Ryū waza*. Another term for these same techniques is *Ken-Ren Kata*—from a contraction of ***Kendō Renmei***.

The *Seitei Kata* were first formulated around 1968 to provide a series of *iaidō* techniques for practice by *kendō* students. The Zen Nippon Kendō Renmei invited the acknowledged heads of each of the major styles of *iaidō*, including *Musō Jikiden Eishin-Ryū, Hōki-Ryū, Eishin-Ryū, Tamiya-Ryū, Katori Shinden-Ryū,* and *Musō Shinden-Ryū*, to devise a set of standard techniques for practice by *kendō* students. These representatives selected seven techniques which represented their respective styles to comprise the *Seitei Kata*. Representing *Musō Jikiden Eishin-Ryū* at this meeting was its 18th Grandmaster, Masaoka Kazumi Shihan. After about a decade of use, around 1980, three more techniques were added to the *Seitei kata,* bringing their total to the ten currently in use. In addition to practice by *kendō* students, the *Seitei Kata* are frequently taught to students of martial arts with an interest in *samurai* swordsmanship, such as *aikidō,* and even occasionally in *karate* schools, as well many styles of *iaidō.*

The techniques used in the *Seitei kata* are not always performed exactly as they are practiced in the system from which they were borrowed. In several cases, substantial modifications were made for purposes of standardization, or to adapt an underlying principle to a different posture or situation. For this reason, they are often referred to as *kata* ("forms" or "patterns") to distinguish them from the *waza* ("techniques") of their respective styles.

As students of *Eishin-Ryū,* our principle reason for practicing the *Seitei kata* is not for their training value or their principles of attack and defense. In fact, we recommend *against* training in them for those reasons, because the principles of body movement are not uniform and are sometimes at variance with the theories and practice of *Eishin-Ryū.* Instead, they are included in the *Eishin-Ryū* curriculum—and this book—solely because they are so widely recognized and used frequently in martial arts tournaments in which *iaidō* events are included.

With each category of *Eishin-Ryū waza* we included a description of elements that characterize each series. However, due to their nature—as a collection of techniques from a variety of styles—there are few such characteristics with the *Seitei kata.* The principle characteristic of the *Seitei kata,* in fact, is probably that they have *no* singular characteristic! For instance, there is no characteristic method of performing *nōtō* in the *Seitei kata.*

Since the *Seitei kata* were drawn from several different styles, each having a different method of *nōtō,* it is generally held that *nōtō* should be performed in the manner usually followed in the style with which you are most familiar. For *Eishin-Ryū* students, this usually means using *Shoden nōtō* while performing the *Seitei kata.* It is not uncommon, however, to see advanced *Eishin-Ryū* practitioners using *Shoden nōtō* for the *seiza kata* and *Okuden nōtō* for the *tachiwaza* of *Seitei kata.*

As we introduce each of these *kata,* we will explain its origin and the key feature or principle to be practiced.

SEIZA MAE

The first *waza*, *Mae* ("Front") or *Seiza Mae*, also sometimes called *Seiza Shōmen* ("Facing Forward"), was derived from the *Musō Jikiden Eishin-Ryū Shoden waza* of the same name. As with its *Eishin-Ryū* namesake, the purpose for including *Mae* is for practice of the major elements of *kihon* in their most basic form. This *kata* is performed identically to its *Shoden* counterpart, with the exception of the footwork involved in *chiburi*.

Mae begins facing straight ahead in *seiza* posture (Figure 13–1a) while taking the three preparatory breaths.

As you finish inhaling the third time, raise your hands to the *tsuka*, with the left hand gripping the *saya* just before your right hand grasps the *tsuka* (Figure 13–1b), and perform *koiguchi no kirikata*.

Figure 13–1a
Seiza Posture

Figure 13–1b
Koiguchi no Kirikata

Begin to draw the *tsuka-gashira* directly toward your imaginary opponent's eyes as you rise on your knees. It is essential that you simultaneously rise onto the balls of your feet as you perform *nukitsuke*. If your toes remain extended, you will be unable to push forward with your rear foot. Finish *nukitsuke* by stepping forward with your right foot as shown in Figure 13–1c.

Perform *furikaburi* while remaining on one knee. The left hand remains poised at the left hip after having pulled the *saya* back during *nukitsuke* as shown in Figure 13–1d until raising the sword overhead (Figure 13–1e), at which point it also grasps the *tsuka*.

During *kirioroshi* the arms reach full extension when the blade is just above the target, at a 45-degree upward angle as shown in Figure 13–1f, then fall naturally

Figure 13–1c
Nukitsuke

Figure 13–1d
Furikaburi I

Figure 13–1e
Furikaburi II

Figure 13–1g
Kirioroshi I

Figure 13–1h
Kirioroshi II

Figure 13–1i
Chiburi I

Figure 13–1j
Chiburi II

as the cut is completed (Figure 13–1g).

To increase the power of *kirioroshi*, you shuffle forward during the cut by pushing with the left foot while stepping farther forward with the right foot, then allowing the left foot to slide forward so that it resumes the same spacing as before. This shuffle should draw you forward some six to twelve inches.

Ōmori-Ryū ("Wet Umbrella") *chiburi*, described in detail in Chapter Seven, follows *kirioroshi* as shown in Figures 13–1i through 13–1k. Rise to your feet during the downward stroke. Unlike *Eishin-Ryū's Mae*, your rear foot does not slide up to meet your front foot as you rise. Instead, you rise straight up, *keeping your feet in place.* For this reason, in the *Seitei* version of *Mae*, you should attempt to reach full standing posture (in *iaigoshi*, of course) at the same moment the sword snaps downward. Usually, the sword completes *chiburi* just a moment before you fully rise.

While maintaining *zanshin*, slide your left foot slowly and steadily forward until it is even with your right foot, then, with no noticeable shift in balance, slide your right foot back so that your relative foot positions have changed (Figure 13–1l).

As you perform *Shoden nōtō*, gradually lower to one knee (Fig-

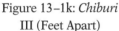

Figure 13–1k: *Chiburi* III (Feet Apart)

Figure 13–1l *Nōtō* I

Figure 13–1m *Nōtō* II

Figure 13–1n *Nōtō* III

ures 13–1m through 13–1o), timing this movement so that your right knee touches the floor at the exact moment the *tsuba* touches your left hand at the *koiguchi* (Figure 13–1o).

Hook your left thumb over the *tsuba*, then slide your right hand to the *tsuka-gashira* (Figure 13–1p), and rise to a standing position.

Then take two steps back to reach your original starting position. At this point, now standing fully erect, remove your right hand from the *tsuka-gashira* and return it

Figure 13–1o *Nōtō* IV

Figure 13–1p *Nōtō* V

to your right side while your left hand releases the *saya* and *tsuba* and returns to your left side.

The *bunkai* of *Mae* is defense against a single opponent who is attacking from directly in front of you. The central concept of this *waza* is simply the use of *iaijutsu* fundamentals in their most basic form: *nukitsuke* to slice across the opponent's eyes, blinding the attacker to provide the split second needed to safely perform *furikaburi*, then finish the opponent with *kirioroshi*.

SEIZA USHIRO

Like *Mae, Seiza Ushiro* ("Rear") was derived from the *Musō Jikiden Eishin-Ryū waza* of the same name and, like *Mae,* the only difference between the *Seitei* and *Shoden* versions is the footwork accompanying *chiburi.*

Take your three cleansing breaths while in a rear-facing *seiza* posture, then begin *nukitsuke.* As you rise, set your toes, so you are on the balls of your feet, then complete *nukitsuke* while pivoting 180 degrees to your left and stepping forward with your left foot (Figure 13–2a).

Figure 13–2a
Nukitsuke

Figure 13–2b
Chiburi

From there, perform *furikaburi* and *kirioroshi,* just as in *Mae,* except with the left foot leading. Use an *Ōmori-Ryū* ("Wet Umbrella") *chiburi,* but *do not* bring the feet together as you would in the *Eishin-Ryū* version of *Ushiro.* As shown in Figure 13–2b, the feet should remain *apart* as you rise during *chiburi.*

While maintaining *zanshin,* slide your right foot slowly and steadily forward until it is even with your left foot, then, with no noticeable shift in balance, slide your left foot back so that your relative foot positions have switched (Figure 13–2c).

Now perform *Shoden nōtō* while lowering onto your left knee, ending as shown in Figure 13–2d.

Rise to a standing position, then take two steps back to your original starting point and place your hands at your sides.

The *bunkai* of *Ushiro* is defense against a single opponent who attacks from your rear while you are seated in a formal setting.

Figure 13–2c
Nōtō I

Figure 13–2d
Nōtō II

UKENAGASHI

The principle technique practiced in *Ukenagashi*—the "Flowing Block" from which it takes its name—is common to *waza* from several styles, including *Musō Jikiden Eishin-Ryū, Hōki-Ryū,* and *Eishin-Ryū*. It is perhaps for this reason that there are more numerous differences between the *Seitei* and *Shoden* versions.

The *Seitei* variation of *Ukenagashi* begins in *seiza,* facing 90 degrees to the right, rather than 45 degrees, as in our *shoden* version. As you inhale the final cleansing breath, look to your left, then raise your hands to the *tsuka* for *koiguchi no kirikata.* Begin to rise, stepping forward with your left foot as you draw about one-third to one-half of the sword (Figure 13–3a).

Figure 13–3a
Nukitsuke I

Rise to a standing position (with *iaigoshi)* as you complete *nukitsuke,* drawing the sword overhead as you turn your body about 45 degrees to your left, with the *kissaki* angled downward to your left as shown in Figure 13–3b.

In a continuously flowing movement, twist your body another 90 degrees to your left as you grasp the *tsuka* with your left hand and perform *furikaburi,* then perform *kirioroshi* at a 45-degree angle down and to your left, gaining momentum by stepping back with your left foot into a wide, low stance (similar to a "side stance"), so that your direction has now turned 135 degrees from your original *seiza* orientation (Figure 13–3c).

With *zanshin,* maintain this stance as you tilt the sword down and to the right at about a 45-degree angle until the *mine* rests against the top of your right thigh just above

Figure 13–3b
Nukitsuke II

Figure 13–3c
Kirioroshi

Figure 13–3d
Drip *Chiburi*

Figure 13–3e
Begin *Nōtō*

the knee as shown in Figure 13–3d.

Hold this "drip" *chiburi* steady while reversing the grip of your right hand on the *tsuka*. Release your left hand, still holding the sword in place with your right hand, and grasp the *saya* at the *koiguchi*. Swing the sword in a wide arc to your left side and place it edge up on top of your left forearm in preparation for *nōtō* (Figure 13–3e).

Lower to one knee while inserting the sword in the *saya*, so that the *tsuba* touches your left hand just as your left knee touches the floor. Hook your left thumb over the *tsuba* and slide your right hand down the *tsuka* to the *tsukagashira*.

Rise to a standing position, swivel 45 degrees to your left, then step back to your starting point, standing fully erect with your hands at your sides.

Bunkai for *Ukenagashi* is essentially the same as for the *Shoden* version. Your attacker's sword is already drawn and ready, so there is no chance to beat him to the draw. Instead, by appearing vulnerable to attack as you begin to draw (Figure 13–3a), you lure the opponent into a premature attack, then rise with the "Flowing Block" for which the technique is named. By stepping to the side and allowing the opponent's strike to slide obliquely down your angled sword, his balance is momentarily lost, allowing you to finish him with the *kirioroshi* into which the block flows.

TSUKA-ATE

Tsuka-ate ("Handle-Strike") is a derivation of a *tatehiza waza* from *Eishin-Ryū* (not *Musō Jikiden Eishin-Ryū*), but it has several similarities to our *Chūden waza*. *Tsuka-ate* is the only *Seitei kata* performed from the *tatehiza* posture. It gets its name from the first defensive technique, which occurs even before *nukitsuke*.

In *Tsuka-ate*, you begin facing straight ahead in *tatehiza* (see Figure 13–4a).

As you inhale the third cleansing breath, grasp the *tsuka* with both hands, rise to one knee as you step forward with your right foot, circle the *tsuka* clockwise and strike at face level with the *tsuka-gashira*, as shown in Figure 14–4b.

Figure 13–4a
Tatehiza

Figure 13–4b
Tsuka-ate

Perform *koiguchi no kirikata*, then *nukitsuke* by drawing the *saya* back with your left hand, turning your shoulder to the left to draw the *kissaki* from the *koiguchi*, and—with a slight scoot to the rear—thrust one-handed past your left shoulder behind you (see Figure 13–4c).

Use the turn of your upper body to draw your *katana* slightly forward and raise it to *furikaburi*, grasping the *tsuka* now with both hands, then shuffle-step forward with *kirioroshi*, with your right foot front, as depicted in Figure 13–4d.

Figure 13–4c
Thrust

Follow *kirioroshi* with *Eishin-Ryū* ("Flicking") *chiburi* and *nōtō*, sliding your right foot back and circling it beneath yourself as you resheathe the sword. Rise to standing position, maintaining *iaigoshi*, then step back to your starting point, and return your hands to your sides.

The *bunkai* for *Tsuka-ate* should be somewhat familiar. You have opponents at both your front and rear. The one in front attempts to grab your *tsuka* in order to render you defenseless against the enemy attacking from behind.

Figure 13–4d
Kirioroshi

However, with the clockwise movement of the *tsuka*, you either evade the opponent's grasp or wrench the *tsuka* free, and pummel him in the face. With the sword in striking position, you need only pull the *saya* back and it is instantly drawn, allowing you to pierce the attacker behind you without delay. Then, before the enemy in front of you can recover from the stunning blow to his face, you finish him with *kirioroshi*.

KESAGIRI

Kesagiri ("Diagonal Cut") is a derivative of a similar technique found in *Hōki-Ryū*. It is the first of the *Seitei Tachiwaza*, or standing techniques. A *kesa* is the traditional robe of a Japanese monk, which covers only the left shoulder and arm. The lapel of the left shoulder runs diagonally across the chest and beneath the left armpit. *Kesagiri* takes its name from the fact that the angle of its finishing cut follows the line of a *kesa*'s lapel—cutting from the left shoulder toward the right hip.

Figure 13–5a
Sword Twisted

As you finish inhaling the third time, take your first step forward with your right foot. During your second step (left foot) raise your hands to the *tsuka,* with the left hand gripping the *saya* at the same moment your right hand grasps the *tsuka,* and perform *koiguchi no kirikata.* As you begin your third step, twist the *tsuka* and *saya* almost a half-turn counterclockwise (Figure 13–5a) as you prepare to draw.

Nukitsuke swings up and to your right at about a 45 degree angle, finishing with the *kissaki* pointing out and away from your body at about 45 degrees, as depicted in Figure 13–5b.

Twist your right wrist 180 degrees clockwise to reverse the direction of its cutting edge, then bend your right wrist performing a modified *furikaburi* over your right shoulder as you take a shuffle-step (right foot, then left foot) forward, grasp the *tsuka* with your left hand and perform a diagonal cut angled down and to your right at about a 45-degree angle, ending in the position shown in Figure 13–5c.

Step back with your right foot and raise the sword to *hassō no kamae,* as illustrated in Figure 15–5d.

Step back with your left foot as

Figure 13–5b
Nukitsuke

Figure 13–5c
Kesagiri

you swing the sword past your head, slightly to the left side, and perform *Eishin-Ryū* ("Flicking") *chiburi* (Figure 13–5e).

After *nōtō,* draw you left foot forward to meet your right foot (maintaining *iaigoshi*), then step back to your starting position, before placing your hands at your sides.

Bunkai for *Kesagiri* involves a confrontation with a single opponent, whose sword is already drawn. As the opponent attacks with *kiri-oroshi,* your rising *nukitsuke* slashes one or both of his arms as they

Figure 13–5d
Hasso no Kamae

Figure 13–5e
Chiburi

reach full extension. Your *kesa-giri* is then used to finish him. By stepping back into *hassō no kamae,* you are on-guard in case he is not quite finished or has accomplices nearby. If your opponent is still struggling for life, your tall, overwhelming posture and *zanshin* will serve to crush his resolve and break his spirit, thereby helping him expire and lessening his suffering.

MOROTEZUKI

Morotezuki ("Two-Handed Thrust") is based upon a common *kendō* technique, but its key principles can also be found in various *iaidō* styles, although normally practiced in a different manner.

As you complete your third cleansing breath, take your first step forward with your right foot. During your second step (left foot) raise your hands to the *tsuka* and perform *koiguchi no kirikata.* On your third step twist the *tsuka* and *saya* 45 degrees counterclockwise and perform *nukitsuke* as an angular cut at temple-height (Figure 13–5a).

Pull the *tsuka* back toward your navel and grip it with your left hand, then take a small shuffle-step forward and make a

Figure 13–6a
Nukitsuke

Figure 13–6b
Morotezuki

Figure 13–6c
Furikaburi I

Figure 13–6d
Kirioroshi I

Figure 13–6e
Furikaburi II

Figure 13–1f
Kirioroshi II

two-handed thrust to the solar plexus, as shown in Figure 13–6b.

Simultaneously pull the sword free and turn, pivoting on the balls of both feet without changing their relative positions, *furikaburi* as a natural by-product (Figure 13–6c).

Step forward with your right foot and perform *kirioroshi* to the rear opponent (Figure 13–6d).

Again pivot on the balls of both feet while raising the sword in *furikaburi*, as depicted in Figure 13–6e.

Step forward with your right foot and perform *kirioroshi* to the front opponent (Figure 13–6f).

While maintaining *zanshin*, use *Eishin-Ryū chiburi*, followed by *nōtō*, then step back to your original starting position.

Morotezuki is normally considered to be a defense against three attackers; two to your front (one behind the other) and one to your rear. *Nukitsuke* and *morotezuki* are used to first disable, then finish the first opponent in front of you, before turning and finishing the opponent to your rear with *kirioroshi*, then returning to the second frontal attacker with another *kirioroshi*.

SANPŌGIRI

Sanpōgiri ("Three-Way Cut") is found in various formats in numerous styles of *iaidō*. It is a defense against three attackers, coming at you from the front and each side.

On your third cleansing breath, take your first step forward with your right foot. During your second step (left foot) raise your hands to the *tsuka* and perform *koiguchi no kirikata,* then your third step is 90 degrees to your right, using *nukitsuke* as a downward cut to the top of the head, stopping with the blade angled upward at about a 45-degree angle (Figure 13–7a).

Figure 13–7a
Nukitsuke

Without changing the position of your feet, pivot 180 degrees to your left on the balls of both feet while raising the sword in *furikaburi,* completing your turn with *kirioroshi* to your left side, as shown in Figure 13–7b.

Turn 90 degrees to your right, raising the sword in *furikaburi,* then step forward with your right foot and perform *kirioroshi,* as depicted in Figure 13–7c.

Figure 13–7b
Kirioroshi I

Step back with your right foot into *jōdan no kamae.* After a moderate pause, step back with your left foot as you swing the sword slightly to the left side of your head and perform *Eishin-Ryū chiburi,* then *nōtō.*

Bunkai for *Sanpōgiri* is fairly straightforward: *nukitsuke* is used to dispatch the opponent to your most vulnerable side (right), turning almost instantly with *kirioroshi* to the opponent on your left. The opponent to your front is kept in view at all times, until you turn and finish him with *kirioroshi,* as well.

Figure 13–7c
Kirioroshi II

GANMEN-ATE

Ganmen-ate ("Face Strike") is based upon techniques used in the *Musō Jiki-den Eishin-Ryū waza, Yukichigai* and *Moniri.*

As you finish inhaling the third cleansing breath, take your first step forward with your right foot. During your second step (left foot) raise your hands to the *tsuka* and perform *koiguchi no kirikata.* As you take your third step (right foot), thrust the *tsuka* and *saya* forward to face height, striking with the *tsuka-gashira,* as shown in Figure 13–8a.

Pull the *saya* back with your left hand, then pivot on the balls of both feet, using the rotation of your hips to complete *nukitsuke,* holding the sword at waist level with your right hand, as illustrated in Figure 13–8b.

Figure 13–8a
Ganmen-ate

Figure 13–8b
Nukitsuke

Step forward with your right foot and make a one-handed thrust to the solar plexus, using the underside of your right forearm to reinforce and steady the blade. Note that the blade is turned flat, so its edge is facing outward, as shown in Figure 13–8c.

Pull the *tsuka* back toward your navel with your right hand to withdraw it, turning your hand one-quarter turn clockwise, so the *mine* is upward (Figure 13–8d).

Then pivot on the balls of both feet, and continue the motion of your hand, raising the sword into *furikaburi* as you grip it with your left hand, then step forward with your right foot, finishing with *kirioroshi* (Figure 13–8e).

Maintain *zanshin* during *Eishin-Ryū chiburi* and *nōtō,* then draw your left foot even with your right foot and step back to your starting position before dropping your hands to your sides.

Bunkai for *Ganmen-ate* is usually shown against two opponents: one each at your front and rear.

Figure 13–8c
Thrust

Since both are attacking simultaneously, you must use the *ganmen-ate* strike to the face to temporarily disable the enemy in front of you in order to have time to turn and impale the foe behind you. Before the first opponent can recover from the blow to his face, you must turn again and finish him with *kirioroshi*.

Figure 13–8d
Withdraw

Figure 13–8e
Kirioroshi

SOETEZUKI

Soetezuki ("Reinforced Thrust") is derived from one of the best known techniques found in *Hōki-Ryū*, containing precise and difficult footwork and movement.

As you finish inhaling the third time, take your first step forward with your right foot. During your second step (left foot) raise your hands to the *tsuka* and perform *koiguchi no kirikata*. As you begin your third step, twist your right foot inward as you turn to face 90 degrees to your left, as shown in Figure 13–9a.

Twist your body to the left as you begin *nukitsuke* (Figure 13–9b).

Step back with your left foot into a side stance as you complete *nukitsuke* as a downward arcing cut at about a 45-degree angle, as illustrated in Figure 13–9c.

Pull the *tsuka* back to your right hip, allowing your right foot to slide

Figure 13–9a
Koiguchi no Kirikata

Figure 13–9b
Nukitsuke I

Figure 13–9c
Nukitsuke II

Figure 13–9d
Reinforcing

Figure 13–9e
Reinforced thrust

Figure 13–9f
Pinching Blade

back about a half-step as you turn your body to the right, and align your left hand along the *mine*, with your thumb on top and finger parallel to the blade, as depicted in Figure 13–9d.

Step forward with your left foot and make a reinforced thrust, guiding the travel of the blade with your left hand, letting the *mine* slide along the groove between your thumb and forefinger (see Figure 13–9e).

Without moving your feet, raise and extend your right arm, pinching the *mine* between the thumb and index finger of your left hand as you tilt the blade at a 45-degree angle down to your left (Figure 13–9f).

Step back with your left foot as you flick the blade forward into an *Eishin-Ryū chiburi*, and follow this with *nōtō*. Bring your left foot even with your right foot, turn 90 degrees to your right, then step back to your starting position.

Soetezuki is normally practiced as a defense against a single opponent attacking from your left as you are walking. You turn and step back, cutting to the enemy's temple or neck, then thrust through the solar plexus to finish him. An alternative *bunkai* is against two opponents, both attacking from the side. *Nukitsuke* is then used to cut the first opponent's neck, and the reinforced thrust from which *Soetezuki* gets its name finishes his accomplice.

SHIHŌGIRI

Shihōgiri ("Four-Way Cut") is a *tachiwaza* (standing) version of similar *suwari-waza* (half-kneeling) techniques common to both *Musō Jikiden Eishin-Ryū* and *Hōki-Ryū*. Unlike its *Eishin-Ryū Suwariwaza* counterpart, the *bunkai* for *Seitei Shihōgiri* is identical to the way it is practiced.

In *Shihōgiri,* you are surrounded by four attackers (Figure 13–10a).

As you complete your third cleansing breath, take your first step forward with your right foot. During your second step (left foot) raise your hands to the *tsuka* and perform *koiguchi no kirikata.*

Turn 45 degrees to your right on the third step. Twist the *tsuka* and *saya* 45 degrees counterclockwise as you strike downward with the side of the *tsuka,* as shown in Figure 13–10b and 13–10c.

This strike to the wrist of the opponent to your front-right breaks his grip on his *tsuka,* giving you time to pull the *saya* back with your left hand and, with a shuffle-step to your left-rear, perform a thrust to the rear past your left shoulder. As shown in Figure 13–10d, the *tsuka* is braced against

Figure 13–10a
Surrounded

Figure 13–10b
Tsuka-ate

Figure 13–10c
Close-up

Figure 13–10d
Rear Thrust

Figure 13–10e
Kirioroshi I

Figure 13–10f
Kirioroshi II

Figure 13–10g
Kirioroshi III

the underside of your right forearm.

Raise the sword and grasp the *tsuka* with your left hand in *furikaburi* as you face back toward your right-front. Step forward with your left foot and use *kirioroshi* to finish the opponent whose wrist you first struck (see Figure 13–10e).

Turn 90 degrees to your right during *furikaburi* and step forward with your right foot as you employ *kirioroshi* against the opponent to your right-rear, as depicted in Figure 13–10f.

Pivot on the balls of both feet 180 degrees to your left during *furikaburi,* and step forward with your right foot as you perform *kirioroshi* on the remaining attacker (Figure 13–10g).

Step back with your right foot raising your sword to *jōdan no kamae.* Use the menace of your posture and the strength of your *zanshin* to suppress any remaining spirit in your opponents. Then, step back with your left foot as you swing the sword just to the left of your head into *Eishin-Ryū chiburi,* followed by *nōtō.* Slide your left foot even with your right foot, turn 45 degrees to your right while still in *iaigoshi,* and step back to your starting point.

Chapter 14

試し斬り

Tameshigiri

Practice Cutting

Iaijutsu training has three major components: *waza* (techniques), *tachiuchi no kurai* (partner exercises), and *tameshigiri* (practice cutting). Together these elements provide a balanced training program for the physical skills of *iaijutsu* in much the same way that *kata* (forms), *kumite* (sparring), and *tameshiwari* (breaking) promote well-rounded training in *karate-dō*.

The *waza* practice in *iaijutsu* develops the knowledge of appropriate techniques for the various types of attacks a *samurai* might encounter. It also trains the practitioner to block and cut with correct stance, balance, mental focus, and technique.

However, *waza* practice must be augmented with partner exercises, such as the *tachiuchi no kurai*, in order for the student to develop proper timing, distance, and footwork in their practical application.

Tameshigiri is essentially a means of determining if the student can apply the lessons learned in *waza* and *katachi* practice to the use of a live sword *(shinken)*. In order to cut the practice material, you must apply correct swinging technique, together with proper cutting distance *(kirima)*. If these elements are combined correctly, a clean test cut is the result. If not, the areas requiring further practice become readily apparent.

Often, *tameshigiri* is depicted as a technique only masters are capable of performing, requiring near superhuman ability and training to execute correctly. While *tameshigiri* is not particularly easy, it is also nothing mysterious or inordinately difficult with properly balanced training in *waza* and *katachi*.

The purpose of a *katana,* after all, is to cut! The curvature and balance of the blade are specifically designed to cause it to slice when the sword is swung correctly. Proper repeated practice of *waza* will develop the correct cutting stroke, and consistent training in *Tachiuchi no Kurai* will develop the proper footwork, balance, and cutting distance. The major elements on which to focus for a proper cutting stroke are *te no uchi* (grip), *hasuji o tosu* (straight alignment of cutting edge), and *enshin ryoku* (centripetal force). The key components of balance and distance are a stable stance, strong hip rotation at the finish, and striking with the *monouchi.*

The *monouchi* is a portion of the blade, about ten inches in length, which begins approximately six inches from the *kissaki,* as shown in Figure 14–1. This section of the blade provides the best possible combination of tensile strength and curvature for the cut. The striking portion of the blade must be past its center in order to obtain the natural slicing action for which its curvature was designed, but if impact occurs too close to the *kissaki* you risk either breaking the blade or not getting a deep enough cut.

monouchi

Figure 14–1

For cutting, correct technique is of course far more important than muscle strength. If you have solid *kihon,* you should not have difficulty cutting when the time comes. In fact, women and children can often perform *tameshigiri* earlier in their training than many men, because rather than trying to strike forcefully they tend to let the sword do what it was designed to do. A key fact to remember is:

The SWORD cuts; not you!

Once you have developed the proper swing, *tameshigiri* is merely a matter of correctly applying that swing to the target. In the following illustrations, we have diagrammed the major technical elements involved in cutting. We have based these illustrations on *kesagiri,* the downward diagonal cut which follows the line of a monk's *kesa,* the most basic cutting technique.

Generally, a *kesagiri* cut will be made along the line shown in Figure 14–2 below:

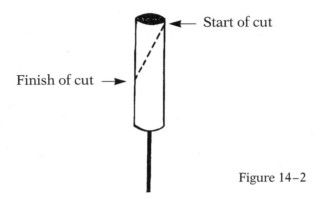

Start of cut

Finish of cut →

Figure 14–2

Seen from a top view, the path of the sword through the material should generally look like the illustrations in Figure 14–3:

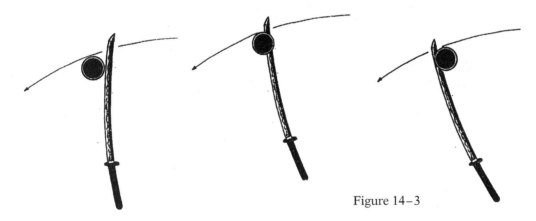

Figure 14–3

As shown in this series of three illustrations, the natural swing of the blade, combined with its curvature and the natural rotation of the hips at the completion of the swing, will cause the blade to slice cleanly and almost effortlessly through the target.

In contrast, a "baseball" swing—in which the arms and wrists do not reach full extension until after striking the target—will result in a clubbing action, as illustrated in Figure 14–4 below. A striking motion invariably causes the blade to wedge into the target like an ax. Such a cut is seldom completed, no matter how powerful the swing, and never leaves a clean, straight cut.

Figure 14–4

Although such a blow would certainly be fatal, it would be unthinkable for a *samurai* to hack an opponent to death in such a crude and ignominious manner. To act with respect for one's adversary by preserving his dignity in a swift and honorable death requires that the cut be clean and complete in a single stroke.

The most common materials for *tameshigiri* are *tatami* (straw matting) or a piece of bamboo from two to six inches in diameter. To prepare *tatami* for cutting, immerse and soak it in water overnight until it is thoroughly saturated. It then closely approximates the consistency of human tissue. Tightly roll the saturated mats around a wooden stick or PVC pipe inserted no more than one-third the length of the mat. To begin with, we suggest that you cut single mats. Later, you may wish to cut two *tatami* rolled together.

Cutting watermelons and similar rinded fruits requires almost no skill whatsoever, and such demonstrations are normally made by those without real training in *samurai* swordsmanship to impress spectators who have little, if any, martial arts knowledge. Cutting apples, potatoes, etc. tossed in the air does not require cutting skill per se, but can occasionally be useful for training in accuracy and eye-hand coordination.

We want to caution overly zealous students against turning your skills into some sort of carnival sideshow. If you are a true student of *iaijutsu*, you will have too much self-respect to waste your skills on flashy tricks for the sake of attracting a crowd of ignorant, but cheering, spectators.

Furthermore, there is little to be gained by attempting *tameshigiri* too early in your training. *Tameshigiri* should not be viewed as some form of showmanship, nor even as a test of your skill, but rather as a means of measuring or confirming your progress in developing a correct and natural swing. We seldom encourage students to attempt *tameshigiri* until they are approaching *dan* level, by which time they have first performed thousands of *kirioroshi* through thin air to refine their cutting stroke.

A final word of caution is that *tameshigiri* involves swinging a live sword with potentially lethal effect. We therefore strongly urge the reader never to attempt *tameshigiri* except under the supervision of a qualified instructor.

Chapter **15**

Eishin-Ryū no Yōten

Summary of the Eishin-Ryū System

The preceding chapters have detailed the forty-four *waza* and ten *katachi* of *Musō Jikiden Eishin-Ryū Iaijutsu,* together with the ten *Zen Nippon Kendō Renmei Seitei Iai Kata,* totalling sixty-four training drills. To help you picture the entire *Eishin-Ryū* system and better understand the progression from *Shoden* to *Chūden* to *Okuden,* we have prepared a chart listing all of the techniques in each level.

When instructing students in Western countries, we normally teach the *Seitei Kata* and *Tachiuchi no Kurai* first. This allows them to learn a variety of techniques early in their training and immediately begin practicing distance and footwork with a partner. While Japanese students are already accustomed to the *seiza* posture, and can spend long periods training exclusively in the *Shoden Waza,* most Westerners find that practicing the *Seitei Kata* first helps them gradually become comfortable sitting in *seiza* position and later progress to *tatehiza* with reduced discomfort. For those students desiring to enter tournament competition (see Chapter Seventeen), the *Seitei Kata* provide both variety of technique and relatively uniform recognition by tournament judges.

Eishin-ryū Iaijutsu Waza

Shoden Ōmori-ryū Seiza Waza ("Shoden Waza" or "Seiza Waza")

1. Mae
2. Migi
3. Hidari
4. Ushiro
5. Yaegaki
   a. Omote
   b. Ura
6. Ukenagashi
7. Kaishaku
8. Tsukekomi
9. Tsukikage
10. Oikaze
11. Nukiuchi

Chūden Tatehiza Waza ("Tatehiza Waza")

1. Yokogumo
2. Tora no Issoku
3. Inazuma
4. Ukigumo
5. Yamaoroshi
6. Iwanami
7. Urokogaeshi
8. Namigaeshi
9. Takiotoshi
10. Makkō

Okuden Tachi Waza ("Tachiwaza")

1. Yukizure
2. Tsuredachi
3. Sōmakuri
4. Sōdome
5. Shinobu
6. Yukichigai
7. Sode Surigaeshi
8. Moniri
9. Kabezoe
10. Ukenagashi

Okuden Itomagoi Waza ("Itomagoi Waza")

1. Itomagoi Ichi
2. Itomagoi Ni
3. Itomagoi San

Okuden Suwari Waza ("Suwariwaza")

1. *Kasumi*
2. *Sunegakoi*
3. *Shihōgiri*
4. *Tōzume*

5. *Tōwaki*
6. *Tanashita*
7. *Ryōzume*
8. *Torabashiri*

Tachiuchi no Kurai ("Katachi")

1. *Deai*
2. *Tsukekomi*
3. *Ukenagashi*
4. *Ukekomi*
5. *Tsukikage*

6. *Suigetsutō*
7. *Zetsumyōken*
8. *Dokumyōken*
9. *Shinmyōken*
10. *Uchikomi*

Zen Nippon Kendō Renmei Seitei Iai Kata* ("Seitei Kata")

1. *Seiza Mae*
2. *Seiza Ushiro*
3. *Ukenagashi*
4. *Tsuka-ate*
5. *Kesagiri*

6. *Morotezuki*
7. *Sampōgiri*
8. *Ganmen-ate*
9. *Soetezuki*
10. *Shihōgiri*

---

*The *Zen Nippon Kendō Renmei Seitei Iai Kata* are not truly *Eishin-ryū waza*, but a representative collection from different styles.

Chapter 16

審査

Shinsa ni Tsuite
Promotion Guidelines

Musō Jikiden Eishin-Ryū Iaijutsu awards *kyū* and *dan* ranking in a similar manner to most popular martial arts. A key difference is that in *iaijutsu* these ranks are not designated by colored belts, as is common in *karate-dō* or *jūdō*.

In addition to the *dan* ("Black Belt") and *kyū* (below "Black Belt") rankings, *Eishin-Ryū* also recognizes three highly coveted titles: *Renshi*, *Kyōshi*, and *Hanshi*. The meaning of these titles is very difficult to adequately translate into English. Literally, they translate roughly as: "Training Warrior," "Warrior Instructor," and "Exemplary Warrior" respectively. However, to convey the nuance of these titles, the terms "Master" *(Renshi)*, "Advanced Master" *(Kyōshi)*, and "Grandmaster" *(Hanshi)* convey the degree of respect accorded to those to whom they have been bestowed. These titles are specifically awarded by either the Nippon Kobudō Jikishin-Kai or the Dai Nippon Butoku-Kai in recognition of outstanding martial arts achievement.

The honorary titles of *Sensei* ("teacher") and *Shihan* ("master") are generally used as a matter of respect and are not specifically bestowed by an organization. Instead, those *yudansha* ("Black Belts") who give instruction are typically referred to as *Sensei*, and *yudansha* who are high ranking, have been teaching for a long time, or are deserving of special recognition are referred to as *Shihan*. In a smaller *dōjō* with only one instructor, he or she would usually be called *Sensei*, unless they are particularly high ranking or widely regarded. In a larger *dōjō*, several instructors would be *Sensei*, while the chief instructor would probably be called *Shihan*.

For ranks through *shodan* (First Degree "Black Belt"), the Nippon Kobudō Jikishin-Kai USA has specific requirements to be met for each successive promotion. In addition to specified elements to be performed *(waza* and *katachi)*, there are certain aspects of historical, technical, and philosophical knowledge *(gakka)* which must be demonstrated, as well as the instructor's ongoing evaluation of the student's respect and spirit during training.

While observing the student's performance of *waza* and *katachi*, promotion examiners customarily evaluate the student's *kihon* (fundamentals) by the following criteria:

1. *Nukitsuke*
   Koiguchi no kirikata, nukidashi (draw), *saya hiki* (pulling the saya), footwork precision, angle of blade, posture, and spirit.

2. *Furikaburi*
   Level movement of blade, position of *tsuba*, exposure of arm, and coordination of hands with sword.

3. *Kirioroshi*
   Hasuji o tōsu (straightness of cut), height of *kissaki* at finish, footwork, *tsuba* position, *tsuka no nigiri kata, enshin ryoku*, and spirit.

4. *Chiburi*
   Position of sword hand, angle of blade, timing of *chiburi* to footwork, and *iaigoshi*.

5. *Nōtō*
   Hand position at *koiguchi*, speed and timing, coordination of *nōtō* with footwork, and *zanshin*.

The examiners will also make an general assessment of the student's *jitsugi*, his overall presentation and demeanor, looking for the following key elements:

1. **Kibikibi to shita dosa**: Sharp, precise, spirited movement.

2. *Kokoro no koma*: Sincerity of respect showing from within.

3. *Katana no atsukai kata*: Method of handling the sword, showing familiarity, respect, and technical correctness.

Outlined below are the technical and knowledge requirements of the Nippon Kobudō Jikishin-Kai USA for promotion to the ranks *(kyu)* and *dan* grades shown:

Rokkyu: 6th Kyū
- *Waza*: *Seitei kata: Seiza Mae, Seiza Ushiro, Ukenagashi*
- *Katachi*: *Deai*
- *Gakka*: (1) Name of Style, (2) Name of Founder, (3) Age of Style, (4) Hasegawa Eishin was the ___th generation Grandmaster, (5) Name of present Grandmaster

Gokyu: 5th Kyū
- *Waza*: *Seitei kata: Tsukaate, Kesagiri, Morotezuki,* and *Sampōgiri*
- *Katachi*: *Tsukekomi, Ukenagashi*
- *Gakka*: Names of the major parts of the sword (in Japanese)

Yonkyu: 4th Kyū
- *Waza*: *Seitei kata: Seiza Mae, Tsukaate, Ganmen-ate, Soetezuki,* and *Shihōgiri*
- *Katachi*: *Ukekomi, Tsukikage*
- *Gakka*: Describe/explain *Nukitsuke, Kirioroshi,* and *Chiburi*

Sankyu: 3rd Kyū
- *Waza*: Any *Eishin-Ryū Seiza waza,** *Yaegaki, Ukenagashi, Kaishaku,* and *Tuskekomi*
- *Katachi*: *Suigetsūtō, Zetsumyōken*
- *Gakka*: Describe/explain *Metsuke, Zanshin,* and *Kokyū*

---

*Choice of *Mae, Hidari, Migi,* or *Ushiro*

Nikyu: **2nd Kyū**

Waza: *Tsukikage, Oikaze, Nukiuchi,* and any two "free" *waza*

Katachi: *Dokumyōken* and *Shinmyōken*

Gakka: Describe/explain *Koiguchi no kirikata, Maai,* and *Iaigoshi*

Ikkyu: **1st Kyū**

Waza: Two each "free" *Seiza waza, Tatehiza waza,* and *Tachiwaza*

Katachi: *Uchikomi* and *Tsubamegaeshi*

Gakka: Describe the origins of *Ōmori-ryū Seiza waza*

Shōdan-Ho: **Provisional 1st *dan***

Waza: Six *waza,* all "free" (at least one each of *Seiza, Tatehiza,* and *Tachiwaza*)

Katachi: Any three "free" *Katachi*

Gakka: Describe/explain the object of training in *Iaijutsu*

Training: Minimum one year consistent training

Shōdan: **1st *dan* ("Black Belt")**

Waza: Six *waza,* all "free" (at least one each of *Seiza, Tatehiza,* and *Tachiwaza*)

Katachi: Any three "free" *Katachi*

Gakka: Describe/explain *Heijōshin*

Training: Minimum six months at *Shōdan-Ho* (1½ years total)

Prior to advancement to *Rokkyū* (6th *Kyū*), students are generally referred to as *shoshinsha* ("beginners"). While the first promotion is usually to the rank of *Rokkyū,* it is not uncommon for lower ranks, such as *Kyūkyū* (9th *kyū*), etc., to be used by some *dōjō,* either to provide a more rapid sense of advancement for beginners or to give a more frequent sense of achievement for children.

After promotion to *Shodan* (1st *dan*), practitioners must show increasing knowledge of the *Eishin-Ryū* system and continuing refinement of technique. With higher ranks, examiners increasingly look for evidence of the *Dai•Kyō•Soku•Kei* progression (see Chapter Five) and exhibition of "personality" in the techniques performed during testing. They also place increasing emphasis on genuine, sincere respect and *heijōshin* being evident in a practitioner's performance as he rises in *dan* rank. Another key factor examiners look for in *yudansha* is *fūkaku* ("depth" or "strength") in such areas as *chakugan, kokyū, maai, kihaku,* and *zanshin.* Each of these elements most show the advanced student's deeper insight and application.

As a student progresses through stages of *Shu•Ha•Ri,* his technique passes through equivalent stages called *Jutsu•Waza•Ryaku,* and the promotion examiners will be watching for these progressive levels of expertise.

術 *Jutsu* is the most basic level of technique. The term *jutsu* refers to "technique" in almost a mechanical sense. It is purely the method of performance, devoid of personality and predominantly physical in nature.

技 *Waza* is a higher level of technical expertise, more akin to "skill." At the *Ha* stage of development, the practitioner should now be exhibiting a degree of finesse in his performance. His techniques should be a blend of both the physical and mental aspects of the art.

略 *Ryaku* is the highest level of technique. Here, the refinement of physical ability, mental prowess, and the infusion of the personality of a master at the *Ri* stage of development elevates every technique performed to the level of "art." *Ryaku* can be literally translated as "abridgement," an apt term for a stage at which all of the principles of the art are combined into each individual technique performed by a master of this caliber.

In addition to the improved skills and attitude needed for promotion after *Shodan,* the Jikishin-Kai prescribes minimum age and training time requirements for each subsequent advancement, as shown in the table below:

Dan Promotion Timing Guidelines

Rank Sought	Minimum Training Time	Age	Cumulative
Shodan (1st *dan*)	Six months at *Shodan-ho*	13	1½ years
Nidan (2nd *dan*)	One year at *Shodan*	16	2½ years
Sandan (3rd *dan*)	Two years at *Nidan*	18	4½ years
Yondan (4th *dan*)	Three years at *Sandan*	"	7½ years
Godan (5th *dan*)	Four years at *Yondan*	"	11½ years
Rokudan (6th *dan*)	Five years at *Godan*	"	16½ years

It may seem odd that the minimum age for *Yondan, Godan,* and *Rokudan* remains 18, rather than rising to 21, 25, and 30, respectively. However, there are cases in which a young student has reached *Shodan-Ho* at the age of 8 or 9 and subsequently risen no higher than *Nidan* due to his or her age. Upon reaching adulthood, such a student would be promoted to the rank, hypothetically as high as *Godan,* warranted by his or her skill, knowledge, and years of training.

Similar minimum age and training times apply to the titles which may be bestowed upon deserving *kodansha:*

Title	Minimum Training Time	Minimum Age
Renshi	Three years after *Godan*	24
Kyōshi	Seven years after *Renshi*	31
Hanshi	Twenty years after *Kyōshi*	55

While it is beneficial to students to have a means of measuring their progress and to feel a sense of accomplishment at their promotion to higher ranks, we should point out that there is also a danger inherent in the ranking system.

Occasionally, students become overly focused on advancing from rank to rank. Worse yet, some become fixated on outranking students they perceive as rivals in their quest for higher rank. For these students, rank becomes the objective of their training rather than perfection of their character and improvement of their skills.

While high rank does carry with it a certain degree of status, it is critically important to understand and accept the ranking system for what it is: a *tool,* a simple means to measure your progress toward your goal.

We do not want to minimize the importance of rank nor discourage anyone from seeking advancement. However, the knowledge, skill, and improved lifestyle should be the goals of your training, not merely your rank. Rank is best viewed simply as one barometer of the progress you are making toward your real goal of a victorious life.

Chapter 17

Taikai ni Tsuite
Tournament Information

U ntil recently there have been few tournaments outside Japan featuring *iaidō*. Occasionally, someone with a *samurai* sword wound up in the same "weapons" category at a *karate* tournament as those with *bō, sai, nunchaku, kama, eku,* and the like. In those rare cases, one of two things usually resulted: either the techniques did not have the showmanship qualities to garner good scores from the judges, or the performance looked like an audition for a "Ninja Turtles" movie, complete with whirling leaps and flourishes that would get you killed on a real battlefield.

As the popularity of authentic *iaidō* has increased in the last few years, a number of reputable *karate* tournament promoters have established separate *iaidō* divisions. With knowledgeable judges and uniform scoring criteria, these events have been growing in popularity with competitors and spectators alike.

To help ensure uniform standards of judging, the Nippon Kobudō Jikishin-Kai USA has established competition guidelines for tournament sponsors. These guidelines have also been submitted to the Amateur Athletic Union (AAU) for use in those AAU *karate* tournaments in which *iaidō* is now a sanctioned event.

Tournament competition offers a number of potential training benefits to the *iaijutsu* practitioner. Four hundred years ago, a *samurai*'s motivation to train diligently and intently was quite clear: there might be a battle tomorrow in which his life would be at stake. We no longer benefit from this such a powerful stimulus to practice. But an upcoming tournament offers an incentive with several parallels to a battle.

Likewise, life-or-death combat demonstrated with finality whether a *samurai* was able to apply the lessons learned in the *dōjō* while under intense pressure. Without risking your life, tournaments give you the opportunity to test your skills, and your *heijōshin,* under the pressures of competition, giving you some realistic and helpful feedback on your training progress.

For these reasons, we encourage students of *iaijutsu* to regularly participate in the *iaidō* events featured at many of the top-quality *karate* tournaments.

To help you prepare for tournament competition, this chapter includes an outline of the rules now used at most of the tournaments featuring *iaidō.*

Iaidō Tournaments
Tournament Director's Guidelines

These Tournament Director's Guidelines for tournament rules and classification of competitors by age and rank are intended to be *examples* for use by *iaidō* tournament directors. It is solely the tournament director's responsibility to ensure that the number and type of divisions allow for fair competition and that the rules adopted for the tournament provide for adequate safety for its participants. Likewise, it is solely the tournament director's responsibility to ensure that judges and referees are adequately trained and motivated to enforce all rules fairly and conduct the tournament professionally and safely.

Iaidō Tournament Divisions

Tameshigiri (Cutting) Events:

T-1   *Tameshigiri* (Cutting)—Junior (ages 13 to 17) *Yukyūsha*
Use one piece of cutting material[1] and make two cuts: one from right to left; one from left to right.

---

[1]Cutting materials, such as rolled *tatami* or bamboo, and the means of supporting them are to be furnished by the competitor.

T-2   *Tameshigiri* (Cutting)—Junior (ages 13 to 17) Advanced
(*Dan*-holders, or over twenty-four months' training)
Use one piece of cutting material and make two cuts: one from right to left; one from left to right.

T-3   *Tameshigiri* (Cutting)—Adult *Yukyūsha*
Use one piece of cutting material and make two cuts: one from right to left; one from left to right.

T-4   *Tameshigiri* (Cutting)—Adult Advanced
(*Dan*-holders, or over twenty-four months' training)
Use one piece of cutting material and make two cuts: one from right to left; one from left to right.

Special Note:

For safety purposes, it is strongly recommended *not* to allow *Tameshigiri* (Cutting) participation in the Youth (ages 8 to 12) category. Furthermore, tournament directors are cautioned to provide extra supervision in the Junior division during *Tameshigiri* competition.

Since *Tameshigiri* is not generally practiced by beginner and novice students, more divisions than those shown do not seem warranted under usual circumstances.

Individual *Kata* Events

K-1   Individual *Kata*—Beginner (up to 5th *kyū*; max. ten months'
training)
Youth (ages 8 to 12)
May perform up to two *waza* or *kata*.

K-2   Individual *Kata*—Intermediate (4th to 1st *kyū*; maximum twenty-four months' training)
Youth (ages 8 to 12)
May perform up to three *waza* or *kata*.

---

[2]Techniques performed are to be from the *Zen Nippon Kendō Renmai Seitei Iai (Seitei Kata)* or a recognized traditional (ie., ancient) style of *iaidō, iaijutsu,* or *battōjutsu.*

K-3   Individual *Kata*—Advanced (*Dan*-holders, or over twenty-four months' training)
Youth (ages 8 to 12)
May perform up to three *waza* or *kata*.

K-4   Individual *Kata*—Beginner (up to 5th *kyū*; maximum ten months' training)
Juniors (ages 13 to 17)
May perform up to two *waza* or *kata*.

K-5   Individual *Kata*—Intermediate (4th to 1st *kyū*; maximum twenty-four months' training)
Junior (ages 13 to 17)
May perform up to three *waza* or *kata*.

K-6   Individual *Kata*—Advanced (*Dan*-holders, or over twenty-four months' training)
Juniors (ages 13 to 17)
May perform up to three *waza* or *kata*.

K-7   Individual *Kata*—Beginner (up to 5th *kyū*; maximum ten months' training)
Adults
May perform up to two *waza* or *kata*.

K-8   Individual *Kata*—Intermediate (4th to 1st *kyū*; maximum twenty-four months' training)
Adults
May perform up to three *waza* or *kata*.

K-9   Individual *Kata*—Advanced (*Dan*-holders, or over twenty-four months' training)
Adults
May perform up to five *waza* or *kata*.

Special Note:

Tournament Directors are encouraged to consolidate these divisions in the event of few competitors, or expand the categories if there are many competitors. Since size is not a critical factor in *iaidō,* we suggest first expanding the categories by experience (either grouping by rank or cumulative training time).

We suggest using the term *kata,* even though it is somewhat a misnomer, since its meaning is more familiar to a broad spectrum of martial artists than *waza.*

Synchronized (Team) *Kata* Events

S-1   Synchronized *Kata*—Pre-Adult (under age 18) *Yukyūsha* (maximum twenty-four months' training)
3-person team may perform up to three *waza* or *kata.*

S-2   Synchronized *Kata*—Pre-Adult (under age 18) Advanced (*Dan*-holders, or over twenty-four months' training)
3-person team may perform up to three *waza* or *kata.*

S-3   Synchronized *Kata*—Adult (under age 18) *Yukyūsha* (maximum twenty-four months' training)
3-person team may perform up to three *waza* or *kata.*

S-4   Synchronized *Kata*—Adult (under age 18) Advanced (*Dan*- holders, or over twenty-four months' training)
3-person team may perform up to three *waza* or *kata.*

Special Note:

If a large number of Synchronized *Kata* competitors participate, particularly in the Youth (ages 8 to 12) and Junior (ages 13 to 17) categories, or a wide range of beginner and intermediate students compete, the Synchronized *Kata* divisions may be increased to correspond to the *Katachi* (Prearranged Sparring) [6 divisions] groupings or the Individual *Kata* [9 divisions], as appropriate.

Katachi (Prearranged Sparring) Events

KT-1   *Katachi* (Prearranged Sparring)—*Yukyūsha* Youth (ages 8 to 12)
Perform up to three *katachi*; maximum 1½ minutes.

KT-2   *Katachi* (Prearranged Sparring)—Advanced (*Dan*-holders, or over twenty-four months' training) Youth (ages 8 to 12)
Perform up to three *katachi*; maximum 1½ minutes.

KT-3   *Katachi* (Prearranged Sparring)—*Yukyūsha* Junior (ages 13 to 17)
Perform up to three *katachi*; maximum 1½ minutes.

KT-4 *Katachi* (Prearranged Sparring)—Advanced (*Dan*-holders, or over twenty-four months' training) Junior (ages 13 to 17)
Perform up to three *katachi*; maximum 1½ minutes.

KT-5 *Katachi* (Pre-arranged Sparring)—*Yukyūsha* Adult
Perform up to three *katachi*; maximum 1½ minutes.

KT-6 *Katachi* (Pre-arranged Sparring)—Advanced (*Dan*-holders, or over twenty-four months' training) Adult
Perform up to five *katachi*; maximum 1½ minutes.

Special Note:

If a wide range of beginner and intermediate students compete in this division, the *Katachi* (Prearranged Sparring) divisions may be increased to match the categories established for Individual *Kata* [9 divisions] above.

Rules

1. Each participant must furnish his/her own cutting material (bamboo, *tatami* mat, etc.) for *Tameshigiri* (Cutting) events. It will be permissible to borrow a sword from another *dōjō* or participant. In the event of a tie after the first two cuts, the tied participants will make a third cut *(yoko ichimon-ji)* on the same material as a tiebreaker.

2. For both individual and synchronized *kata,* participants must perform *waza (kata)* from a *traditional* style of *iaidō,* or from the standard *Zen Nippon Kendō Renmei Seitei Iai Kata.*

3. Participants in *Katachi* (Prearranged Sparring) events may use either a *shinai* (bamboo sword) or *bokken* (wooden sword). Both members of each pair must use the same type of sword. For safety, *shinai* are preferred for Youth divisions.

4. All participants are required to inspect their mekugi prior to their performance. For safety reasons, judges may inspect *mekugi* at random and will disqualify any contestant whose *mekugi* is loose, weak, or broken.

5. Both genders (boys and girls; men and women) compete together, since *iaijutsu* does not depend upon size or physical strength.

6. Etiquette will be to bow to the judges at the edge of the ring, proceed to your starting position in the ring, announce the name of your style and

the name(s) of the *waza* or *kata* you will perform, perform *hairei, tōrei,* and *taitō,** then begin your waza or kata performance. Upon completion, perform *tōrei, dattō,* and *hairei,** then wait for announcement of your score. After your score is given, step back to the edge of the ring and bow once before leaving.

7. It is permissible to wear a traditional white *karate* uniform, but an *iaidō* uniform (*iaidō-gi* with *hakama*), *kendō* uniform (*kendō-gi* with *hakama*), or *aikidō* uniform (*jūdō-gi* with *hakama*) is preferable. Only traditional uniform colors of white, black, gray, dark blue, dark brown, or *tatejima* (including traditional mixtures of the aforementioned) are permitted. Uniforms may bear traditional *kamon,* school patches or emblems, and/or *wappen.* Contestants whose uniforms are brightly colored, imprinted or embroidered with elaborate designs, or otherwise nonconforming may be disqualified. If in doubt, you are cautioned to check with the tournament director prior to competing.

Key Scoring Criteria

1. *Tameshigiri* will be judged by:
   a. The straightness of each cut.
   b. The difficulty of the cut (type and thickness of material, direction of cut, etc.).

2. Individual *Kata* will be judged by:
   a. Sincerity and correctness of *reigi* (etiquette).
   b. The spirit, demeanor, and personality of the participant during performance.
   c. Technical merits, especially sharpness of technique, focus, posture, eye contact, breathing, and straight travel of the sword.

3. Synchronized *Kata* will be judged by:
   a. Synchronization of movement with other team members.
   b. The judging elements of Individual *Kata* listed above.

---

*To save time in larger tournaments, it is recommended that the judges direct the participants to perform *hairei* (bow to the *dōjō* emblem/shrine) and *tōrei* (bow to the sword) as a group prior to and following each event.

4. *Katachi* will be judged by spirit of attack and defense, focus, maintaining proper attack and defense distance with opponent, unity of timing with opponent, sharpness of technique, and coordination of attack and defense with opponent.

Special Notes:

Tournament Directors are urged to hold judges' meetings prior to the events, to ensure that all judges are thoroughly familiar with the scoring criteria and how to apply them. Judges should be advised in advance the relative weight to apply to each of the scoring criteria. As long as all judges are generally applying the same standards, the outcome will be fair and impartial.

In smaller tournaments, divisions may be consolidated by first combining the Youth and Junior age divisions of contestants of equal rank. If this still produces too many categories for the number of competitors, then the Beginner and Intermediate divisions may be combined into a single *Yukyūsha* division for each event. If this still produces too many categories, then we suggest combining all ages together within the *Yukyūsha* and *Yudansha* categories for each event. The last combination recommended is to group both *yukyūsha* and *yudansha* into a single division for each event.

Jikishin-Kai Annual *Taikai*

One of the most exciting tournament events for *iaidō* aficionados is the Annual "Weapons-Only" Tournament, cosponsored by the Jikishin-Kai each year. *Iaidō* is the main event of this tournament which includes divisions for a variety of other weapons arts as well. The tournament is held in mid-October of each year at the University of California, San Diego (UCSD) and also features a number of instructional sessions for interested participants.

For information and details on this tournament, please contact:

> Mr. Alfonso Gomez
> Tournament Director
> U.C. San Diego Sports Facilities 0074
> La Jolla, CA 92093
> (619) 534–8906

First Jikishin-Kai sponsored weapons-only tournament,
University of California, San Diego

Chapter 18

勝利への道

Sho-ri e no Michi

The Way to Victorious Life

*"If you take the easy path, life is difficult;
if you take the difficult path, life is easy."*

This book contains enough instruction for several lifetimes. It will take a dozen years of training to become adept at the physical techniques alone, and decades more to master them and imprint them with your own personality and spirit. The philosophy contained in this book is condensed from the lives of many of Japan's greatest warriors, and it would be the height of arrogance for any of us to presume that we could assimilate all of it in a single lifetime. Bear in mind also that we have only presented the major tenets of *samurai* philosophy in this volume. An authoritative and exhaustive study on the philosophy of *samurai* swordsmanship would require a work of encyclopedic proportions.

This manual can serve you for a lifetime of training, enjoyment, and personal enrichment, and can then be passed on to your children and their children in much the same way the art of *iaijutsu* itself has been passed from generation to generation. We want to close by providing some practical ways to apply this book to your everyday life; to help you achieve true victory over the circumstances and adversities we all face in our family lives, jobs, and ambitions, and to bring you and those around you greater joy.

To begin with, here are twenty-one precepts distilled from ancient *samurai* philosophy:

武士の心得

SAMURAI NO KOKORŌE
Precepts of the Samurai

1. Know yourself. (*Jikō o shiru koto*)

The foundation of all personal growth is to truly know yourself, that which seems both good and bad in yourself. To understand your faults as well as your virtues allows you to begin working to remedy your faults, strengthen your virtues, and find ways to work around those aspects of your personality and character that you may be unable to change.

2. Always follow through on commitments. (*Jibun no kimeta koto wa saigo made jikkō suru koto*)

A commitment is essentially a promise you make to yourself. Commitments can be as shallow as going on a diet or as deep as marriage; the marriage *vow* is the promise you make to your spouse; the marriage *commitment* is the promise you make to *yourself*. Each unfulfilled commitment is a personal failure that can be deeply disappointing and damaging to your self-esteem. Think carefully before you make any commitment. Make only those commitments that are truly valuable to you. And don't overburden yourself with so many commitments that you are doomed to failure from the start.

3. Respect everyone. (*Ikanaru hito demo sonke suru koto*)

If you have gained nothing else from this book, the concept of *respect* should be indelibly etched into your mind. The true *samurai*, as we have often stated, respected even his enemies. Respect for others—for their ideas, beliefs, culture, and human rights—is the bridge to mutual understanding and ultimately to peaceful coexistence with others.

4. Hold strong convictions that cannot be altered by your circumstances.
(*Kankyō ni sayu sarenai tsuyoi shinnen o motsu koto*)

It's one thing to develop strong convictions; it's quite another to hold to those convictions even when it appears foolish in the eyes of the world to do so. We now live in an era in which welfare and insurance fraud are commonplace roads to financial success, where TV and movies have glamorized promiscuity to an extent that sexually transmitted diseases are epidemic, where the majority of deaths are the direct result of alcohol, drugs, and smoking, where easy money is more highly revered than hard work, and where commitment to family and religious values is publicly ridiculed.

Incredible strength of conviction is necessary to withstand such social and economic pressures—pressures that have led our present generation into a malaise of alcohol and drug abuse, immorality, greed, laziness, and self-indulgence that is out of control and bringing the entire world to ruin.

5. Don't make an enemy of yourself. (*Mizu kara teki o tsukuranai koto*)

Don't be your own worst enemy! Jealousy, greed, and self-pity will ensure that you have plenty of enemies if you try to accomplish something worthwhile with your life. If you treat people with respect and compassion you won't add to the number of your opponents by your own attitude.

6. Live without regrets. (*Koto ni oite kōkaisezu*)

This is a double-edged admonition. First, don't wallow in regret over your past mistakes. Take responsibility for them and learn from them. Accept the fact that the past cannot be undone, find something of value (such as a lesson learned) in your mistakes, and go forward with the knowledge that you have taken another step toward perfection of character.

Second, if you know—or even suspect—that you will regret an action you are considering, *don't do it!* Heed the warning of your conscience in advance. As you strive toward improving yourself and grow in compassion and self-awareness, you will find that your conscience allows you to make fewer and fewer regrettable decisions.

7. Be certain to make a good first impression. (*Hito to no deai o taisetsu ni suru koto*)

As the old saying goes, "First impressions are lasting impressions." A good first impression is a barometer of the kind of life you are leading. If you consistently leave good impressions on those you meet, it is likely that you are living a more fulfilling and positive life than someone who consistently leaves a poor first impression.

8. **Don't cling to the past.** (*Miren o motanai koto*)

This is more than simply not regretting the past; it means to let go of both the good and the bad. All to often we meet people who sacrifice their own present or future because they are still mired in the past. Their stories of "the good old days" are a telltale sign that nothing of import is occuring in their lives *now*.

Our past is a good history lesson, and it is as valuable as a road map to our future. But inorder to move ahead, we must let go of past glories as well as past failures.

9. **Never break a promise.** (*Yakusoku o yaburanai koto*)

To be a person of character you must say what you mean and mean what you say. It is really that simple. Don't make promises you can't or won't keep, and if you do make a promise, do whatever is necessary to keep it. Remember: the disappointment and distrust caused by only one broken promise can undo ten years of kept promises.

10. **Don't depend on other people.** (*Hito ni tayoranai koto*)

This precept is a bit paradoxical. We cannot succeed in life without the help of others. We cannot have fulfilling relationships with other people without allowing them to become deeply involved in our lives. Yet, we must not *depend* on them!

What this really means is that we must take personal responsibility for our lives. Children depend on their parents, but adults must be responsible for themselves. We cannot rely on family, friends, or the government to take care of us, direct us, or make us happy. With realistic expectations of others, we will feel genuine gratitude for their contributions and we will avoid anger and disappointment if others let us down.

11. **Don't speak ill of others.** (*Hito o onshitsu shinai koto*)

If you have a grievance with someone, the respectful and proper way to deal with it is to speak directly *with* that person, not *about* that person to others. Compassionate confrontation is the core of good relationships. It is easy to compliment people, but it takes real courage and true friendship to openly discuss with others the things that bother you. Yet we can only have deep friendships if we are willing to take the emotional risks of raising difficult issues and settling them. If we do, then both people benefit. If we don't, both will suffer.

12. **Don't be afraid of anything.** (*Ikanaku koto ni oite mo osorenai koto*)

Fear robs you of *heijōshin* and prevents you from thinking clearly and reacting naturally. It ignites the "fight or flight" reaction, yet often neither fighting nor fleeing is the most beneficial response. This is especially true of the flight response, since our avoidance of all but physical danger usually takes the form of emotional barriers or escapism into drug and alcohol use or submission to cult behavior.

It is always preferable to face your problems, whether they are physical dangers or the everyday obstacles and challenges of life. After all, as a *samurai,* you have already conquered the fear of death, and are instead pursuing a noble death (see Chapter Two). So, since you do not fear death, why should you fear anything that *life* might throw your way?

13. **Respect the opinions of others.** (*Hito no iken o soncho suru koto*)

The opinions of others have been shaped by a lifetime of experience and thought, just as yours have. It is important not to preconceive different opinions or ideas as "wrong." The other person's opinion may be just as well substantiated as your own—perhaps even more so. If you can set aside your desire to be "right" and focus only on the opinion which has the most value, you will find your attitude encourages others to share their ideas freely, which will in turn provide you with greater insight and more options from which to choose.

Don't forget the lesson of Takeda Shingen, who encouraged and rewarded dissent among his subordinates. It was that very trait that made him one of the greatest leaders in history!

14. **Have compassion and understanding for everyone.** (*Hito ni taishite omoiyari o motsu koto*)

True compassion cannot be achieved without deep understanding of human nature and motivations, so this precept implies the need to really know people.

This is especially crucial for leaders, and it can be seen in such examples as Takeda Shingen, Abraham Lincoln, and countless others. Those who take a genuine interest in people inspire great loyalty, dedication, and desire to succeed. There is great truth in the axiom: "People don't care how much you know until they know how much you care."

Compassion is the key to discovering what motivates people. If you sincerely care, you will be interested enough to learn their deepest desires, hopes, and fears and eventually grow to understand them. Compassion is also the key to developing healthy and harmonious relationships with family, friends, and your spouse, the key to appreciating and validating the points of view and feelings of others, even if they differ from yours.

15. Don't be impetuous. (*Karuhazumi ni koto o okosanai koto*)

The *samurai* of old were bound by a strict code of honor and lived in a society in which the slightest insult could result in a duel to the death. In addition, *iaijutsu* was founded during a tumultuous period of civil wars in which loyalties were constantly changing with the tides of shifting power among warlords and their vassals. In such times, the implications of every action had to be carefully considered beforehand. The slightest mistake could cost you your life and bring about the ruination of your family.

Even though the consequences are not as severe, it is not so different today. Rash decisions or words can cost a new job or a promotion; impulsive financial decisions can throw your family into bankruptcy. If you maintain *heijōshin* and do not allow your emotions and impulses to dictate your decisions, you will enjoy greater abundance in all aspects of life.

16. Even little things must be attended to. (*Chiisa na koto demo taisetsu ni suru koto*)

There is a common saying, "Take care of the little things and the big things will take care of themselves." There is a great deal of truth in this dictum. If unattended, the little things in life soon compound into big things. Just as small physical tasks, such as personal and financial details, can add up into serious problems if not taken care of, a series of seemingly insignificant emotional hurts will quickly escalate into major conflicts.

It is not always necessary to *personally* perform the little tasks; it is only important to see that they get done. If your lifestyle requires you to concentrate on major issues, then you must delegate the small tasks and ensure that they are done.

17. **Never forget to be appreciative.** (*Kansha no kimochi o wasurenai koto*)

A sincere word of thanks is often better than payment for a favor done. Most of us enjoy helping others and gain a sense of satisfaction in knowing that we have done something unselfish, but we also quickly grow tired of doing things for people who do not show any appreciation for our efforts. If we show genuine appreciation for the assistance of others, there will always be friends willing to help us through difficult times. But if we fail to show our appreciation, we will quickly become known as a "taker," and our acquaintances will lose all respect for us.

This is also a prime example of taking care of the little things. Just the simple courtesy of a "thank you" to a friend or loved one, if left unsaid, can build up into great anger and discontent with time and repetition. But that same simple courtesy, if never forgotten, will keep our friends and family steadfast by our side even through the darkest of times.

18. **Be first to seize the opportunity.** (*Hito yori sossenshi kōdō suru koto*)

We must not act impetuously. But once we have reached a well-considered decision we must act quickly and precipitously. As the old saying goes, "Opportunity knocks but once." We usually get only one chance, and that chance only lasts for a limited time.

This is a lesson we practice often in *iaijutsu*. Our opponent will give us few opportunities to win the encounter, and those opportunities will last only moments at best. So we must seize an opportunity the instant it arises. The same holds true in business and other areas of life. *True* opportunities will be rare and short-lived, so we must be prepared for them and act swiftly when they are presented.

19. **Make a *desperate* effort.** (*Isshō kenmei monogoto o suru koto*)

Here is another lesson direct from *iaijutsu* training. In important matters, a "strong" effort usually results in only mediocre results. Whenever we are attempting anything truly worthwhile, our effort must be as if our life is at stake, just as if we were under a physical attack! It is this extraordinary effort—an effort that drives us beyond what we thought we were capable of—that ensures victory in battle and success in life's endeavors.

20. Have a plan for your life. (*Jinsei no mokuhyō o sadameru koto*)

If you don't know where you are going, how will you know when you get there? To have a plan for your life is such an obvious admonition that it almost seems ludicrous to mention it here. Yet sadly, less than 10 percent of us have a clear, written plan for our lives. And of those who do have some kind of plan, less than 10 percent have planned for anything other than just the financial aspects. The average person spends more time planning a holiday weekend than in planning their whole life.

While financial matters are an important part of an overall life plan, it is equally—if not more—important to set goals for all the other areas of your life. The necessities of life keep economic matters at the forefront of our thoughts. Having specific goals for the other areas of our life helps prevent financial matters from crowding everything else out. Your life plan should also be written, so that you can use it as a road map to your achievements and to help keep you accountable for staying on track.

However, a good life plan does not have to be highly detailed. An outline is usually sufficient. At a minimum, it should include specific goals and timetables for achieving them, in the following areas:

1. **Family goals:** This broad category concerns such issues as family relationships, marriage, children, where you will live, and most other lifestyle decisions.

2. **Social involvement:** Your social life can include clubs, social status, political involvement, and will often affect such areas as recreation, charitable activities, and the like.

3. **Personal accomplishments:** These are your "trophies," how you want to leave your mark on the world, what you will be remembered by.

4. **Financial objectives:** This area should focus primarily on the income and expenses you generate. The things you purchase and own (cars, home, etc.) are planned under other categories. Your financial plan outlines how you will obtain the money needed to acquire those things that you have planned for elsewhere.

5. **Intellectual development:** This should include goals for both formal education (high school, college, advanced degrees, etc.) and informal areas

(topics you might study—even become expert in—outside of academic institutions).

6. **Emotional maturity:** Just as it helps to have definite, measurable objectives in financial areas, you should plan for your emotional maturation. How will you ensure that you continue to mature and improve your character? Will you attend courses, read self-help books, or join organizations which promote this? How will you establish an underlying philosophy or ethical basis by which to guide your behavior?

7. **Spiritual growth:** You will not be a whole person until you have resolved your quest for meaning in life. You must deal with the issues that most of us consider "religious": Is there a God? How does the existence or nonexistence of God affect my life and behavior? Is there a hereafter? What will become of my soul when my body dies? Do I need to make spiritual preparations for afterlife? What is my role in the universe? Why am I here? Is there a purpose to life beyond mere carnal pleasures? Are there moral absolutes? By what spiritual path can I find these answers? These questions require deep soul-searching and careful investigation. You must be careful to seek *truth*, rather than what is popular, self-serving, or convenient to believe. And your quest for the answers to such crucial spiritual questions should be at least as well-planned as your family vacation!

To help you focus on what is truly important to you, as opposed to those things that would merely be nice to accomplish if you had a chance, just ask yourself this question: "If I died at the end of this _____ (day, week, month, year, etc.), what accomplishments would leave me with absolutely *no* regrets?"

Ask this question for your long-term (five, ten, and twenty year) goals, medium-term (one to three year) goals, and short-term (weekly, monthly, quarterly) plans. Then, use the answers to set your truly important objectives for each of these planning periods.

This is truly a *samurai's* perspective—the perspective of a warrior who routinely faced the real possibility of untimely death. If you knew with certainty that you would die exactly one week from today, just think what you would really do during those final seven days. You would make sure that all your personal and financial affairs were as orderly as possible, so as not to inconvenience your heirs. Petty squabbles and hurt feelings would suddenly seem inconsequential, and you would spend hours cherishing the company of your closest friends and loved ones. And you would probably take the time to do one or two really important things that you always wished you had done. Those are precisely the types of things your short-term objectives should concentrate on.

On the other hand, if you knew you would die in exactly three years, you would plan more types of activities and goals. You would set aside money for events planned months ahead. You might schedule a dream vacation to some distant land, or devote several months to working for a cause you believe in deeply. These are appropriate medium-range goals.

Lastly, if you know you would die in exactly ten or perhaps twenty years, you would make other, more far-reaching plans and prioritize them differently. You might plan a dream home to share with your family for the last ten of those twenty years, or establish a fund for your children's college education, or set aside time to research and write a book, or plan a change of careers.

This is truly the secret of living without regrets. If you lived each day as if you were scheduled to die at midnight that night, you would make sure you spent every waking hour accomplishing only the most important things in life and you would devote the most time possible to the people who mean the most to you. At the end of such a day, you would have no regrets.

Regardless of whether the goals you set are lofty or simple, once you have established a plan for your life your next step is to begin applying the other principles in this book to accomplishing that plan. Chief among these is *always follow through on commitments.* Having made a commitment to achieve your written goals, don't stop working toward them, especially when you encounter setbacks.

Not everything you try in life will succeed. The more you try to accomplish, the more failures you will experience. The most successful people in the world are the ones who have failed the most often, because they have tried more things! You cannot allow failures, obstacles, and setbacks to affect your confidence and desire to succeed. Remember: the only people who never fail are the ones who never try.

In *iaijutsu* there is no such thing as a draw. In every battle, you either win or lose, and to lose is to die. The same is essentially true for your ambitions in life. There is no middle ground; you either succeed or fail.

You can think of your life plan like a marathon race: you must complete all twenty-six miles. If you don't cross the finish line, it doesn't matter if you ran only ten or all but the last ten feet, you still didn't finish—you didn't run a marathon. A 10K run is still a major accomplishment, but it isn't a marathon. And when you are running a marathon, the judges don't hand out 10K medals to the ones who don't finish.

So, treat your life plan like *iaijutsu*—don't accept anything less than winning. In this way you will be sure you achieve your goals.

This also means you must plan thoughtfully. Set realistic goals, and know what you *really* want to accomplish. Also, set only those goals that you are willing to sacrifice everything that isn't one of your goals to achieve. If you are really willing to settle for completing a 10K run instead of a marathon, then make a 10K run your life goal. Don't have "marathon" in your plan and think it will be alright to fall back to a 10K. It won't be. At your very core, you will think of yourself as a failure if you do not accomplish what you set out to do. Conversely, if a "marathon" is really what you have your heart set on achieving, then make it your goal, and then make a desperate effort to finish the race!

21. Never lose your "Beginner's Spirit." (*Shoshin o wasurubekarazaru koto*)

This admonition is much deeper than it at first seems. On the surface it means to maintain the freshness and excitement that you bring to any new endeavor as a beginner. Don't lose your eagerness to improve and learn and experience. And don't lose a beginner's humility and openness to instruction. But it also means to never lose touch with the basics in any area of life.

It is so easy to find ourselves caught up in the complexities of modern living that we lose track of the basics—those elements that bring true meaning and joy to life—love and friendship, an appreciation of nature, and the simple things of life itself.

In times of stress, difficulty, and setbacks, keeping your "Beginner's Spirit" means to go back to the fundamentals to find the solutions to your problems. The answers are seldom found in the complexities. Our hardships and failures are usually the result of losing touch with the basic principles of life, not the intricacies and minor details.

When adversities arise, you can actually use these twenty-one precepts as a diagnostic tool to find the area of life in which you may have gotten off track. Just start at the top and start asking yourself the questions: Do I truly know myself? Have I followed through on all my commitments? Have I been disre-

spectful to someone? As you work your way down the list, if you are honest
with yourself, you will probably find the cause of your difficulties.

Life's Laboratory

The precepts of *Samurai no Kokoro-e* apply as aptly to life in general as to *iai-jutsu* specifically, from knowing yourself to keeping your "Beginner's Spirit."
One of the major benefits of *iaijutsu* training, then, is the opportunity to use
the *dōjō* as a laboratory in which to experiment with, test, and perfect these
principles under controlled circumstances. Once refined, you can then apply
them in your own life.

Every day we can improve our character and experience the value of these
concepts in the microcosm of the *dōjō*. We can learn by trial and error under
the caring, corrective eye of our *sensei* and in the company of understanding
and compassionate fellow students who share our struggle with the same
lessons—before attempting to apply them in the broader world of daily life.

Rise Above the Ordinary

Animals live only day-by-day or even hour-by-hour, driven by instinct and reaction to their environment, and satisfied with whatever outcome befalls them.
Only humans have freedom of choice, the ability to set goals, to establish principles and ideals by which to live, and to strive for an improved life *despite* the
obstacles and circumstances of their environment. It is this very ability which
creates stress, worry, fear, and uncertainty, but it is also this ability which
allows us to persevere and overcome the trials of life and experience true victory and joy.

Those who have neither hope nor ideals to live by are living only on the
level of brute animals. Your first step in rising above a primitive existence is
to establish strong convictions which will form the basis for an enriched and
rewarding life and give you the emotional stamina to endure its hardships and
trials.

A person of high ideals and character appreciates the laws of nature and
the fundamental laws and mores of his or her society. Even if you disagree
with how some of these laws are enforced or applied, such principles give you
a foundation for exercising sound judgment, even in complex and difficult

circumstances. If you really know yourself and have compassion for yourself (as well as others), then every action or decision you make will polish your character—even those which turn out adversely—because you will accept responsibility and continue to strive for improvement.

It is this strength of character and commitment to continual improvement that will set you apart from the ordinary and mundane, and allow you to remain unaffected by your environment and circumstances. With a spirit of purpose and a dedication to continual self-improvement, you will learn to benefit almost equally from adversity as from success. When you can do this you will no longer find your emotions rising and falling with your changing fortunes. You will know and experience *heijōshin*.

Don't Be a Circus Elephant

Nearly all of us have seen a circus live, or at least watched one on television. Although the trapeze and high-wire acts are more daring and the acrobats more amazing, there is a magnificent, quiet power to the performance of the circus elephants. It is remarkable that they can raise and balance their enormous weight in a handstand. And for all their size and strength, they are so gentle and obedient with their handlers.

But one of the most interesting aspects of elephant behavior occurs when their performance is over. If you walk outside the Big Top when their act is finished, you will see the trainers tether the elephants by slender chains to foot-long stakes driven into the ground. What is amazing about this is that, with almost no effort at all, these mighty creatures could snap those inadequate shackles or uproot them from the ground, yet they remain leashed in place as if helpless. Why?

It is a result of conditioning. When the elephants were babies, they were kept tethered with heavy-gauge chains lashed to stout, immovable posts. Their attempts to pull free only chafed their ankles raw. After so many weeks and months of this, the baby elephants learned to avoid the pain by not tugging at their shackles. Once they were conditioned in this fashion, only a slender chain was necessary to keep them from trying to roam about.

People are conditioned in the same way by their experiences in life. We all develop ways in which we are physically or emotionally restrained by the pain or humiliation of previous mishaps. Sometimes the result is obvious, like the wallflower who is afraid to ask a girl to dance because the last one turned him down. But many of our conditioned behavior patterns are invisible to casual observation, such as the ways in which many of us mask parts of our identity with humor or bravado or deft conversation.

To perfect our character, to fulfill our purpose in life, to live up to our fullest potential, we must not allow ourselves to be held back by imaginary restraints. We must always be willing to *try*. And be willing to try again! We cannot allow a previous setback, failure, or humiliation condition us not to try again. How many wallflowers have missed out on a "Yes" from the girl of their dreams only because they first got a "No" from another, and were not willing to risk another minor humiliation?

To become all that you are capable of being, you have to be willing to risk all that you already are.

SAIGO NO HITO KOTO
A Closing Thought

Yu wa yasuku, okonai wa muzukashii.
Okonai wa yasuku, satoru koto muzukashii.

"Talk is easy; *action* is difficult. But, action is
easy; *true understanding* is difficult!"

The meaning of this proverb is fairly obvious. But, like all of *iaijutsu* philosophy, it has deeper and more subtle shadings of meaning the more it is contemplated.

At the obvious level, it tells you to get busy *right now* with your *iaijutsu* training. Thinking or talking about it are worthless unless you do something about it. So begin and persist in your training. Take action!

As you do so, the truth of the second half of the saying will become apparent. Compared to motivating yourself to action, the herculean task of acquiring true understanding of *iaijutsu* will prove to be a life-long endeavor.

If you are diligent in your training and attempt to practice *iaijutsu* philosophy in daily life, you will soon discover a subtler truth: that knowing *iaijutsu* philosophy and being able to explain it ("talk") is simple compared to applying it consistently in everyday life. Likewise, as you begin to apply *iaijutsu* philosophy on a daily basis, you will find that a true understanding of its limitless depth and applicability is a monumental but worthy undertaking.

Your journey will be fraught with difficulty, frustrations, adversities and setbacks—bruises, blisters, aches, and painful nicks on the body as well as the soul—but liberally seasoned with incomparable joys and triumphs. It is a journey of self-discovery, self-enrichment, and the discovery and enrichment of others.

Come join us on this journey of victorious living!

無双直伝英信流居合術

国際日本古武道直心会

Jikishin-Kai Locations

For those readers who wish to contact the Nippon Kobudō Jikishin-Kai USA or the Nippon Kobudō Jikishin-Kai International, we have included a list of the headquarters' addresses, plus the addresses of principle *dōjō* who are members of the Jikishin-Kai.

Hombu Dōjō
Nippon Kobudō Jikishin-Kai
Yasaka Jinja 11–13
Yasaka-cho, Neyagawa-shi
Ōsaka 572 JAPAN
(Mr. Takeyuki Miura, *Hanshi*)
TEL: (0720) 21–2656

U.S.A. Headquarters
Nippon Kobudō Jikishin-Kai USA
2618 Meadowlark Lane
Escondido, CA 92027 USA
(Mr. Masayuki Shimabukuro, *Kyōshi*)
TEL: (619) 743–3056
FAX: (619) 743–8865

San Diego Hombu Dōjō
Japan Karate Institute
5537 Clairemont Mesa Blvd.
San Diego, CA 92117
TEL: (619) 560–4517

Rancho San Diego Branch
Pacific Martial Arts Foundation
2940 Jamacha Road, Suite I
El Cajon, CA 92019
(Mr. Mike Conniry)
TEL: (619) 660–5272

El Cajon Branch
Pacific Martial Arts Foundation
2253 Fletcher Parkway
El Cajon, CA 92020
(Mr. Mike Conniry)
TEL: (619) 465–6770

Chula Vista Branch
Traditional Karate Center
23-A Naples Street
Chula Vista, CA 91911
(Mr. Julio Martinez)
TEL: (619) 426–2276

Spring Valley Branch
Seitō Karate-dō Ryūei-ryū
8365 Paradise Valley Road
Spring Valley, CA 91978
(Mr. Julio Martinez)
TEL: (619) 267–4037
FAX: (619) 267–0137

University of California, San Diego
UCSD Sports Facilities, 0074
9500 Gilman Drive
La Jolla, CA 92093–0074
(Mr. Alfonso Gomez)
TEL: (619) 534–8906 or (619) 581–3548

San Diego Branch Dōjō
Japan Karate Institute
5537 Clairemont Mesa Boulevard
San Diego, CA 92117
(Masayuki Shimabukuro, *Kyōshi*)
TEL: (619) 560–4517
FAX: (619) 743–8865

Azusa Branch Dōjō
Okinawa Gōjū-Ryū Karate-dō
310 North Citrus
Azusa, CA 91702
(Mr. Anthony Marquez, Sr.)
TEL: (818) 969–4242

Westminister Branch Dōjō
Shukokai International
15623 Brookhurst Avenue
Westminister, CA 92383
(Mr. Kunio Miyake)
TEL: (714) 775–7171

Nevada Hombu Dōjō
Las Vegas Shōtō-kan
2929 W. Sahara Avenue
Las Vegas, NV 89102
(Mr. Rey Braganza)
TEL: (702) 873–0891
FAX: (702) 362–5888

Colorado Hombu Dōjō
Seishin-Kan Dōjō
13918 E. Mississippi Avenue, #280
Aurora, CO 80012
TEL: (303) 693–8238 or (800) 995–7967

International Headquarters
Nippon Kobudō Jikishin-Kai
International
2618 Meadowlark Lane
Escondido, CA 92027 USA
(Mr. Masayuki Shimabukuro, *Kyōshi*)
TEL: (619) 743–3056
FAX: (619) 743–8865

Mexico Hombu Dōjō
Centro de Karate Tradicional
Avenue Universidado y Tecnologico
Centro Comercial Local 20-C
Tijuana, Baja California, Mexico
(Mr. Juan Ramiro Diaz Pelayo)
TEL: 82–18-03
(526) 682–1803 (from USA)

Mazatlan Branch Dōjō
Centro de Karate Tradicional
Papagayo 702-B
Mazatlan, Sinaloa, Mexico
(Mr. Rosalio Rios)

Ensenada Branch Dōjō
Association "Karate Shoto Kan"
Clzda. de las Aguilas 2345
Ensenada, Baja California, Mexico
(Mr. Alberto Ayala A.)
TEL: 6–85-10

Venezuela Hombu Dōjō
Qentro Comercial
Santa Rosa de Lima Local PS-1
Caracas, Venezuela
(Mr. Manuel Pazos)
TEL: (02) 92–69-15

武士の心得

SAMURAI NO KOKORŌE

Precepts of the Samurai

Since the *Samurai no Kokoro-e* is a solid foundation for developing *samurai* spirit and applying *iaijutsu* principles to everyday life, we have prepared this quick reference sheet of these basic principles which can be copied, posted, and easily reviewed on a daily basis.

1. **Know yourself.** (*Jikō o shiru koto*)

2. **Always follow through on commitments.** (*Jibun no kimeta koto wa saigo made jikkō suru koto*)

3. **Respect everyone.** (*Ikanaru hito demo sonke suru koto*)

4. **Hold strong convictions that cannot be altered by your circumstances.** (*Kankyō ni sayu sarenai tsuyoi shinnen o motsu koto*)

5. **Don't make an enemy of yourself.** (*Mizu kara teki o tsukuranai koto*)

6. **Live without regrets.** (*Koto ni oite kōkaisezu*)

7. **Be certain to make a good first impression.** (*Hito to no deai o taisetsu ni suru koto*)

8. **Don't cling to the past.** (*Miren o motanai koto*)

9. **Never break a promise.** (*Yakusoku o yaburanai koto*)

10. **Don't depend on other people.** (*Hito ni tayoranai koto*)

11. **Don't speak ill of others.** (*Hito o onshitsu shinai koto*)

12. **Don't be afraid of anything.** (*Ikanaku koto ni oite mo osorenai koto*)

13. **Respect the opinions of others.** (*Hito no iken o soncho suru koto*)

14. **Have compassion and understanding for everyone.** (*Hito ni taishite omoiyari o motsu koto*)

15. **Don't be impetuous.** (*Karuhazumi ni koto o okosanai koto*)

16. **Even little things must be attended to.** (*Chiisa na koto demo taisetsu ni suru koto*)

17. **Never forget to be appreciative.** (*Kansha no kimochi o wasurenai koto*)

18. **Be first to seize the opportunity.** (*Hito yori sossenshi kōdō suru koto*)

19. **Make a *desperate* effort.** (*Isshō kenmei monogoto o suru koto*)

20. **Have a plan for your life.** (*Jinsei no mokuhyō o sadameru koto*)

21. **Never lose your "Beginner's Spirit".** (*Shoshin o wasurubekarazaru koto*)

SAIGO NO HITO KOTO

A Closing Thought

Yu wa yasuku, okonai wa muzukashii. Okonai wa yasuku, satoru koto muzukashii.

"Talk is easy; *action* is difficult. But, action is easy; *true understanding* is difficult!"

筆者紹介

HISSHA SHŌKAI

About the Authors

Shimabukuro Masayuki *Shihan*

Masayuki Shimabukuro was born in March, 1948 in Ōsaka, Japan. His interest in martial arts began to flower as a teenager, when he studied *jūdō, karate-dō,* Okinawan *kobudō* weapons and other traditional Japanese martial arts. He achieved *dan* ranking in several of these arts before focusing his attention predominantly on *iaijutsu,* the art of *samurai* swordsmanship in face-to-face combat.

Since relocating to the United States in 1976, Shimabukuro *Shihan* has taught martial arts at his own *dōjō,* as well as conducting numerous demonstrations, seminars, and television appearances. In addition to his stature as a leading authority on *samurai* swordsmanship, he is a highly accomplished and well respected *karate-ka,* and is president of the International Shitō-Ryū Karate-dō Jikishin-Kai.

Shimabukuro *Shihan* is presently 7th *dan* in *Musō Jikiden Eishin-Ryū Iaijutsu,* and holds the coveted title of *Kyōshi* ("Warrior Instructor"). As chairman of the Nippon Kobudō Jikishin-Kai USA and the Nippon Kobudō Jikishin-Kai International, he is responsible for disseminating *Eishin-Ryū Iaijutsu* and maintaining its high standards of instruction in all countries outside of Japan. His duties regularly take him throughout North, Central, and South America performing *iaijutsu* demonstrations and seminars, certifying *dōjō,* and training *iaijutsu* instructors.

Leonard J. Pellman *Sensei*

Leonard Pellman was introduced to martial arts at the age of fourteen when, in 1966, his parents enrolled him in a *jūdō* school in San Diego, California. His fascination with *Iaijutsu* began in 1973, when he returned to Japan to visit the family with whom he had stayed as an exchange student five years earlier. At the wedding of his exchange student "sister" in Toyohashi, Japan, her uncle, a 5th *dan* at the time, performed an *iaidō* demonstration which kept Mr. Pellman spellbound with its elegance, artistry, and intense focus and precision. Despite his interest, he was unable to find a qualified *iaijutsu* instructor until he was introduced to Shimabukuro *Shihan* in 1991.

As a member of the Board of Directors of the Nippon Kobudō Jikishin-Kai USA, Mr. Pellman is currently a *yudansha* student under Shimabukuro *Shihan,* and heads the Colorado *Hombu Dōjō* in Aurura, Colorado.

国際日本古武道直心会

Instruction Videos Now Available!

Panther Video, the world's largest producer of martial arts instructional videos, now has available a seven-part series on *Musō Jikiden Eishin-Ryū Iaijutsu* featuring Shimabukuro *Shihan* and Pellman *Sensei*. These videos demonstrate each of the *waza, katachi,* and *seitei kata* described in this book, and are an excellent training supplement to this text.

To order these videos, contact the producer at:

Panther Video
1010 Calle Negocio
San Clemente, CA 92673
(800) 332–4442

Purchasers of this textbook are entitled to a discount on the video series by ordering directly from the Nippon Kobudō Jikisin-Kai USA. To order use a photocopy of the order form on the following page, or contact:

Nippon Kobudō Jikishin-Kai USA
7420 Clairemont Mesa Blvd. #103–303
San Diego, CA 92111
(800) 995–7967
FAX: (619) 743-8865

Order Form

ITEM#	DESCRIPTION	PRICE	QUANTITY	AMOUNT
SS-1	Volume 1 (*Shoden Waza*)	$29.95		$
SS-2	Volume 2 (*Chūden Waza*)	$29.95		$
SS-3	Volume 3 (*Suwari Waza*)	$29.95		$
SS-4	Volume 4 (*Tachi Waza*)	$29.95		$
SS-5	Volume 5 (*Katachi*)	$29.95		$
SS-6	Volume 6 (*Seitei Kata*)	$29.95		$
SS-7	Volume 7 (Interview)	$29.95		$
SS-SP7	7-Volume Set (Complete)	$185.00		$
NKJM	Jikishin-Kai Membership	$25.00		$
NKJP	Jikishin-Kai Patch	$7.00		$
			SUB-TOTAL:	$
SHIP TO:			**SALES TAX:**	$
_____			**SHIPPING:**	$
_____			**TOTAL:**	$
_____				

Make checks payable to:
Nippon Kobudō Jikishin-Kai USA
7420 Clairemont Mesa Blvd. #103–303
San Diego, CA 92111